54

Critical Essays on Sinclair Lewis

Critical Essays on Sinclair Lewis

Martin Bucco

G. K. Hall & Co. • **Boston, Massachusetts**

Library of Congress Cataloging-in-Publication Data

Main entry under title:
Critical essays on Sinclair Lewis.

  (Critical essays on American literature)
  Includes index.
  1. Lewis, Sinclair, 1885–1951—Criticism and
interpretation—Addresses, essays, lectures.
I. Bucco, Martin. II. Series.
PS3523.E94Z564 1986   813′.52   85–17553
ISBN 0–8161–8698–7

This publication is printed on permanent/durable acid-free paper
MANUFACTURED IN THE UNITED STATES OF AMERICA

CRITICAL ESSAYS ON AMERICAN LITERATURE

This series seeks to anthologize the most important criticism on a wide variety of topics and writers in American literature. Our readers will find in various volumes not only a generous selection of reprinted articles and reviews but original essays, bibliographies, manuscript sections, and other materials brought to public attention for the first time. This volume contains forty-one essays and reviews on the life and works of Sinclair Lewis. There are reprinted selections by many of the leading commentators on American letters, including H. L. Mencken, Henry Seidel Canby, Bernard DeVoto, Howard Mumford Jones, Edmund Wilson, Malcolm Cowley, John W. Aldridge, Mark Schorer, Sheldon Grebstein, Martin Light, and Warren Beck. In addition to an extensive introduction by Martin Bucco, which surveys Lewis's career and the history of scholarly comment on his works, there are original essays by Robert E. Fleming and James Lundquist. We are confident that this volume will make a permanent and significant contribution to American literary study.

Northeastern University   James Nagel, GENERAL EDITOR

For Tam and Jim

CONTENTS

ESSAYS

INTRODUCTION

"He was one of the worst writers in modern American literature, but without his writing one cannot imagine American literature." Thus the artistically conscious biographer, Mark Schorer, near the end of his mammoth *Sinclair Lewis: An American Life* (1961),[1] makes explicit his assessment of America's first winner of the Nobel Prize in Literature (1930). Like Schorer, earlier critics have seen in Sinclair Lewis's career his slow climb out of commercial romanticism, his phenomenal success in the 1920s, his decline in the 1930s, his fall into the mechanical and slipshod in the 1940s, and his pathetic end in Rome in 1951. Even during Lewis's lifetime, critics agreed that he had achieved his best work during the 1920s; still, the Marxists found nothing in his erraticism, the Freudians nothing in his psychology, and the New Critics nothing in his form.

Though the reader cannot help but admire the prodigious research and stunning organization of Mark Schorer's biography (and I doubt if any forseeable biography of Lewis will be as exhaustive or as stylishly written), more than a few recent critics have concluded that Schorer's Flaubertian detachment ill suits his subject, that the biographer patronizes Lewis the writer and caricatures Lewis the man. To Lewis the writer they would apply standards of satire, not sensibility; on Lewis the suffering man, they would confer charity, not ridicule. But like Schorer, most contemporary critics acknowledge Lewis's ambivalence, his confusion and misdirection. They acknowledge the clash between Lewis the social critic and Lewis the dreamy romantic, between Lewis the novelist and Lewis the journalist, between Lewis the artist and Lewis the entertainer. To some, he remains a keen writer of surfaces, to others a supreme fabulist.

This sixth and largest collection of criticism on Sinclair Lewis marks the centennial of the author's birth in Sauk Centre, Minnesota, on 7 February 1885. Though Harry Sinclair Lewis grew up respecting his family's medical tradition, he led a journalistic and literary boyhood. He was as ambivalent about his hometown as he was about Yale, where

1

he wrote romantic poetry and prose for literary magazines and reportage for local newspapers. An enemy of dullness, a free spirit, a youth in quest of experience, he twice traveled to England on a cattle boat. Again leaving Yale for a time, he worked as a janitor at Helicon Hall, Upton Sinclair's socialistic community in Englewood, New Jersey. He also lived in New York, editing and free-lancing. After voyaging to Panama in steerage, the quixote returned to Yale, receiving his degree in 1908. Roaming the country, he held a variety of editing and reporting jobs, free-lanced, and even sold plots to Jack London. Back in New York City, Lewis worked as a reader, editor, advertising manager, and reviewer. His first book, *Hike and the Aeroplane* (1912), by "Tom Graham," was a juvenile for his employer, Frederick A. Stokes Company. His early novels, like his many short stories, were uneven, conventional, and unoriginal.

I

Still, reviewers welcomed the new writer, who in *Our Mr. Wrenn: The Romantic Adventures of a Gentle Man* (1914) tells of a wanderlusting clerk who shuffles off his drab life by voyaging to England. Commenting on its mixture of romance and realism and on its similarity to Wells and Dickens, most reviewers found Lewis's gentle satire charming and his first labor of love promising, the *New York Times* indicating that "the rather whimsical little story is well off the usual line of fiction" in conception and character.[2] Still, other periodicals noted the novel's shaky form. "A respectful consideration of the claims of plot and construction," pointed out the *Boston Transcript*, "might be suggested as not out of place...."[3] Ironic (in light of Lewis's later depiction of George F. Babbitt) is the *Review of Reviews* recommendation that in this story "the tired business man will find just the right antidote for weariness."[4]

Although Lewis's second novel, *The Trail of the Hawk: A Comedy of the Seriousness of Life* (1915), lacked the humor of his first, reviewers again noted the romance of things-as-they-are, adventure, and young love. The *Wisconsin Library Bulletin* advised that this story of a small-town Minnesota youth who becomes "Hawk" Ericson, world-famous aviator, was not for "the young person," but a story which "men will like."[5] A buoyant Frederic Taber Cooper exclaimed in the *Bookman* that the novel gives the inexperienced "a kindred thrill of breathless flight, of danger that is a fearful joy, and of a confident omnipotence that is human."[6] Reviewers equated the young hero's exuberance with the pioneering spirit. A few thought the tale overwritten, but for the *New York Times Review of Books* there were "no heroics in the book, no highbrowism, no affectation; it's as sincere as sunlight and fresh air."[7]

Lewis showed marked literary power in *The Job* (1917), a realistic story of New York City. Reviewers praised his characterization of Una Golden, a stenographer who, after a disastrous marriage, blossoms into a successful businesswoman. They appreciated Lewis's accurate rendering of the everyday world of work, but concluded that the windy didacticism of this interesting "feminist document marred novelistic form. "The convenient method of emphasising a woman's strength," H. W. Boynton remarked in the *Bookman*, "is to surround her with feeble men."[8] Francis Hackett, writing in *New Republic*, hoped that young novelists would imitate Lewis's single "pilgrim afoot" in *The Job* rather than Frank Norris's manifold "frenzied finance" in *The Pit*. Though Hackett ranked *The Job* an important novel and extolled the author's "sympathetic insight" into even his minor characters, he took exception to the genial-swine caricature of Una's husband, the staccato prose, and the romantic ending.[9]

If a romantic ending vitiated the esteemed realism in *The Job*, Lewis's flagrant sentimentality undermined the whole of *The Innocents: A Story for Lovers* (1917), originally a syrupy *Woman's Home Companion* serial. Reviewers confessed surprise that the young realist's confection was so out of tune with the passionate seriousness of *The Trail of the Hawk* and *The Job*. Even so, a disconcerting number professed delight in the bathetic shenanigans of Father and Mother Appleby, an old Dickensian couple, cheery and cooing, who take to the open road for sweet adventure's sake. While the deft *Nation* reviewer went so far as to advance the questionable notion that *The Innocents* was the handiwork of a realist-turned-parodist,[10] the irritated *Dial* reviewer, saddened by traces of Lewis's "better self" walking down the primrose path of commercial romanticism, rejected outright "the facile smartness of phrase, the essential flimsiness."[11]

After this potboiler, Lewis's upgraded love-and-adventure story, *Free Air* (1919), surprised few reviewers. *Booklist* found Lewis's expanded *Saturday Evening Post* serial disappointing,[12] but other periodicals reported that his automotive odyssey about a smitten western garage mechanic who convoys a comely eastern socialite and her invalid father across the country was entertaining. They enjoyed Lewis's carefree defense of individualism, his affable humor, and his firsthand sketches of western scenes and characters. Mindful of the novel's banality, the *New Republic* reviewer nevertheless declared that the author writes "in a spirit of unaffected buoyant joyfulness which is certain to infect the reader sooner or later."[13]

Later—but not always with buoyant joyfulness—*Main Street: The*

Story of Carol Kennicott (1920) infected multitudes. Nearly 300,000 copies sold the first year, another 100,000 copies before cheaper editions appeared, infecting millions of readers with Sinclair Lewis's vision of "The Village Virus": the smug, intolerant, dull conformity of the American small town. Though many condemned its lumpy plot, flat characters, coarse composition, and excessive length, most reviewers found *Main Street* absorbing and significant as the sociology of small-town life. Where yea-sayers saw Carol's cultural battle with Gopher Prairie as balanced, whole, and hallowed, nay-sayers saw it as unfair, incomplete, and profane. *Main Street*, Francis Hackett announced in *New Republic*, was Lewis's best novel.[14] Ludwig Lewisohn in *Nation* compared the author to Sherwood Anderson and Theodore Dreiser.[15] Stanton Coblentz in the *Bookman* compared him to Jane Austen and George Eliot.[16] Genuinely amused, powerful H. L. Mencken of *Smart Set* picturesquely welcomed a blanch-faced Lewis bursting out of the literary hulks, "his eyes alight with high purpose." Mencken relished particularly Lewis's vivid dialogue, the ironic struggle between Will and Carol Kennicott, and the authentic Americanism of Lewis's characters. Most of all, Mencken eulogized *Main Street*'s "packed and brilliant detail."[17]

With *Babbitt* (1922) Lewis soared into further celebrity and notoriety. Reviews in business and club magazines naturally remonstrated against Lewis's best-selling raillery of a "standardized" American businessman discontented amid zippy fellow Rotarians, Realtors, and Boosters. But most *literary* reviews judged *Babbitt*'s sparkling focus an advance over the panoramic rawness of *Main Street*. Gleefully, Mencken revealed in *Smart Set* that *Main Street* had been no accident and that *Babbitt*—"at least twice as good"—was more coherent, more imaginative, more realistic. Himself an old professor of Babbittry, of *Boobus Americanus*, Mencken declared that George F. Babbitt "simply drips with human juices."[18] May Sinclair affirmed in *New York Times Book Review* that Lewis "has done his work with remorseless and unfaltering skill," that "you watch Babbitt with a continuous thrill of pleasurable excitement," and that in him "everybody will recognize somebody else."[19] In *Nation*, Ludwig Lewisohn cited many instances of Lewis's power to mold and list his "vast mass of observation"—for example, Babbitt's address before the Zenith Real Estate Board—"made eternal and perfect for our delectation and the terror and laughter of posterity."[20] Burton Rascoe praised *Babbitt* in the *New York Tribune* as a major contribution to social history and as "one of the finest social satires in the English language."[21] In *Appeal to Reason*, Upton Sinclair, wondering if Lewis's businessmen were, after all, only caricatures, rhetorically asked if it were possible to caricature commercial America![22] For Robert Littell of *New Republic*, *Babbitt*'s popularity resulted not from Lewis's presentation of the "whole" of American life, but from his expert one-sided attack on "what is hideously true of the worst things in America."[23] This preoccupation with surface ugliness, in Sherwood Anderson's opinion, prevented Lewis from seeing underlying beauty;[24] but Rebecca West stated in *New Statesman* that the true satirist hated the disappointing world out of love for it. ". . . One must write in denunciation of ugliness . . . yet keep this, as all written things, within the realm of beauty." Lewis, she avowed, had been equal to the miracle of satire.[25]

Even more than they cheered *Babbitt*, reviewers almost everywhere acclaimed *Arrowsmith* (1925), Lewis's popular exposé of the medical profession, first serialized in *Designer and the Woman's Magazine*. Some physicians spurned Lewis's atypical hero and medical knowledge; some reviewers found the story tedious and graceless. Most reviewers, however, commended the novel's positive and idealistic scientist-hero, Martin Arrowsmith (along with the characterization of his wife, Leora, and his mentor, Max Gottlieb), its sustained drama, and (thanks to Dr. Paul H. de Kruif) its bacteriological detail. Immensely satisfied with *Arrowsmith*'s truth-seeking hero, rich material, and succinct style, critic Stuart F. Sherman granted in the *New York Herald Tribune* that Lewis, though "disgracefully popular," nevertheless belongs "inside literature" and that *Arrowsmith* marks "a new flight for distance and altitude."[26] Admiring the book's penetration and justice, Robert Morss Lovett commented in *Dial* that it lacked the regional unity of Gopher Prairie and Zenith. Returning to the "naturalistic" formula of *Main Street* rather than to the "impressionistic" method of *Babbitt*, Lewis found under each stone "human nature in reptilian form." Lovett explains that the "air of unreality" hanging over the plague phenomenon is "in the interest of the reality of a public cause."[27] In *American Mercury*, Mencken prized Lewis's didacticism, his "moments of voluptuous lingering" without any "uncertainty of design," and his portrait of the ubiquitous quack Pickerbaugh.[28] In England, the *Times Literary Supplement* hailed the book's "stirring epic quality" and its "modern scientific consciousness,"[29] and though Edwin Muir in *Nation and Athenaeum* thought its satire on sham medicine effective, he found its treatment of science as a social problem "not convincing."[30] To Joseph Wood Krutch in *Nation*, however, Lewis's indictment of barbarous America was "more convincing" because it was "less absolute," and even his near-genius hero effectually "not quite what he might have been."[31] In *Saturday Review of Literature*, Henry Seidel Canby, extolling Leora's characterization, saw *Arrowsmith* as harsh, well-written, and intensely interesting—"an invaluable contribution to our knowledge of ourselves and our times."[32] T. K. Whipple, in his brilliant *New Republic* essay-review, found Lewis an effective critic of our "national gallery of frauds and fakes" and a recorder of "minute detail," but interesting chiefly as a "mangled artist"—a "product" of the practical society pictured and satirized. "Years of malicious scrutiny must have gone to the making of his last three volumes." The popularity of Lewis's romanticism, philistinism, and vulgarity makes him a powerful shocktrooper. "Lewis is the most successful critic of American society because he is himself the best proof that his charges are just."[33]

Grant Overton, for one, incautiously asserted in the *Bookman* that *Arrowsmith* should convince anyone of Sinclair Lewis's commitment to serious literature.[34] With much ado, Lewis declined the Pulitzer Prize (ostensibly for promoting novels depicting "the wholesome atmosphere of American life") and followed up the public fanfare with *Mantrap* (1926), about an urbanite's claptrap adventures in the Canadian wilds. Kind reviewers ranked it well below *Main Street*, *Babbitt*, and *Arrowsmith*, but assured readers that Lewis's "holiday" potboiler, a *Collier's* serial, was as entertaining as *The Innocents* and *Free Air*. Less kind, more precise, Edwin Muir in *Nation and Athenaeum* not only deplored *Mantrap*'s sentimentality, but found "the construction slovenly, the dialogue flaccid, and the style weakly loquacious."[35] In Lewis's imaginative world, declared the *Independent*, "brittle, clean-cut figures execute fantastic gestures like marionettes, independent of their own souls."[36]

Unlike the appearance of *Mantrap*, the advent of *Elmer Gantry* (1927) caused a howl. If clergymen and churchgoers saw Lewis's tractarian attack on Fundamentalism as cynical, coarse, and monotonous—even blasphemous, obscene, and monstrous—so did most reviewers. A disappointed Rebecca West, for example, took Lewis to task in the *New York Herald Tribune Books* for loathsome usage, lethargic plotting, and, most of all, for failing to understand the condemned religion by wasting his genius on petty impieties.[37] In the *Bookman* Charles W. Ferguson noted: "To say that the man has not fairly represented the ministry is to be unfair to him—obviously he never intended to."[38] An angry Elmer Davis in the *New York Times Book Review* pointed to Lewis as preaching the gospel according to the prophet Mencken,[39] who in *American Mercury* delighted in the "gaudy and glorious" crusading rogue, Elmer Gantry; Mencken kudized the book's beautiful design, the shrewd observations, the gargantuan humor, and the fuguelike movement—"as American as goose-stepping or the mean admiration of mean things."[40] Krutch's more balanced *Nation* review linked the grotesque *Elmer Gantry* to *Main Street* and *Babbitt*—a companion volume typically Lewisian in its amazing documentation, powerful mimicry, and inexplicable gusto.[41]

Lewis followed up this major effort with a minor one—*The Man Who Knew Coolidge* (1928)—a monologic tour de force from the vociferous soul of Lowell Schmaltz, Constructive and Nordic Citizen. Reviewers divided generally between those who magnified the six vocalizations as valuable and funny and those who belittled them as facile and wearisome. The cause of critical hostility—so Burton Rascoe

claimed in the *Bookman*—was Lewis's phenomenal success.[42] L. P. Hartley in *Saturday Review* (London) esteemed Lewis's controlled venom.[43]
Mencken in *American Mercury* endorsed his accurate portraiture.[44] In
New Republic, however, Malcolm Cowley characterized the 250-page
declamation as interminable and shopworn.[45] For Dorothy Parker of
the *New Yorker*, the whole caricature was "heavy-handed, clumsy, and
dishonest."[46] In his lengthy discussion in the *Saturday Review of Literature*, Henry Seidel Canby compared the author to Dickens and Twain,
wishing, finally, that Lewis had their charity toward the sow's ears of
machine-driven humanity.[47]

But in *Dodsworth*, Lewis's sympathetic novel about an admirable
but unhappily married businessman abroad, Canby discerned "the gifts
of a great social historian."[48] Hesitant to call *Dodsworth* Lewis's best
book, reviewers found it highly readable. The novel added little to the
international theme, Carl Van Doren indicated in *Nation*, but it stood
out from the "comic documents."[49] Louis Kronenberger recommended it
in the *New York Times Book Review* as a fine novel.[50] Mary Ross in
Survey considered Sam Dodsworth the author's best character.[51] Spleen-
lovers appreciated the author's rendering of delicate relationships less
than the marital strife between the Dodsworths, the likable Sam and
the detestable Fran. In *Outlook and Independent*, Frances Lamont
Robbins commented: "The Sams of America are Samsons, easily shorn
of their strength by the shears which the Frans, their brummagem
Delilahs, wield."[52] Mencken in *American Mercury* relished Lewis's acid
wit, but rejected the Sam-Fran marriage as improbable.[53] The *New
Yorker*'s Dorothy Parker accepted the union, but not the savor of travel-
ogue.[54] While English novelist Ford Maddox Ford in the *Bookman*
hymned the praises of the American protagonist thinking and feeling
his poetic way through European culture,[55] English novelist E. M.
Forster in *Life and Letters* agreed with Parker about the "spiritless
general catalog." Although Lewis's early snapshots of America had
lodged "a piece of a continent in our imagination," wrote Forster, the
method no longer worked, for Lewis's youthful "spontaneity" as a
literary photographer has flown. "If this view of his development is
correct," Forster added, "the later stages of it are bound to be disappointing."[56]

After the hullabaloo of Lewis's Nobel Prize in 1930—awarded primarily for *Babbitt*—and the publication in 1933 of *Ann Vickers*, his
ragged muckraking tale of a prison-reforming feminist, more reviewers
seemed to adopt Forster's insight. Some even claimed to detect the
commencement of Lewis's decline earlier—for example, Fred Lewis
Pattee after *Babbitt*[57] and Ludwig Lewisohn after *Arrowsmith*.[58] Negative and mixed reviews pointed time and again to what Herschel Brickell
referred to in *North American Review* as "undigested lumps."[59] For Mal-

colm Cowley of *New Republic*, the popular *Ann Vickers* was a fragmented failure.[60] Michael Williams in *Commonweal* saw the central character as close to the heroines of Lewis's popular romances—the sentimentalist as a shallow and amoral feminist.[61] "Persons unused to horrid and filthy things," warned *Catholic World*, "had therefore better stay at a safe distance from this book."[62] Even the earlier asceptic serial version had induced many readers to cancel their subscriptions to *Redbook*. Bernard DeVoto proclaimed in *Saturday Review of Literature* that Carl Van Doren had overrated Lewis, especially Lewis's "fidelity" to speech.[63] Even Lewis's partisans had reservations. Mencken in *American Mercury*, for example, called it "partly very good, but mainly bad," for Lewis did not satirize Ann as often as she deserved.[64] Still, Burton Rascoe celebrated the novel's beauty, terror, and truth in the *New York Herald Tribune Books*[65] and J. Donald Adams of the *New York Times Book Review* pronounced it one of Lewis's best novels.[66]

The following year Adams confessed in the *New York Times Book Review* that he had overrated *Ann Vickers*—only to compound his blunder by ranking *Work of Art* (1934) with *Babbitt*, *Arrowsmith*, and *Dodsworth*.[67] Other reviewers, even those who could appreciate Lewis's sentimental humor, skillful reportage, and hopeful ending, saw this tale of hotel-keeping as a "lesser" work. The more perceptive remarked on the wooden plot, thin characters, heavy-handed satire, and endless slang. From one Marxist perspective, V. F. Calverton in *Modern Monthly* lamented that Lewis no longer composed satire in the service of reform;[68] from another, Granville Hicks in *New Masses* looked forward to Lewis's long-planned labor novel.[69] In *New Republic*, T. S. Matthews asserted that *Work of Art* proved Matthews's own early contention that Lewis's reputation as a great satirist was a great joke.[70]

The next year, 1935, reviewers faced three Sinclair Lewis books: a story collection, a play, and a novel. Some reviewers found *The Selected Short Stories*—a hastily-assembled and uneven collection of thirteen Lewis potboilers—"entertaining." Others found it "banal." Peter Monro Jack of the *New York Times Book Review* found the poor-selling volume "baroque."[71] Howard Mumford Jones in *Saturday Review of Literature* was taken, as usual, with Lewis's "infectious zest."[72] In spite of "Young Man Axelbrod" and "The Willow Walk," Fadiman of the *New Yorker* frowned upon the lot as a waste both of the reader's and the author's time.[73] Reviewers for the *Herald Tribune*,[74] *Times*,[75] and *Theatre Arts Monthly*[76] found more pleasure in reading Sinclair Lewis's drama about the Civil War in Kansas, *Jayhawker: A Play in Three Acts* (written with Lloyd Lewis), than in seeing the weak second and third acts of the Broadway production. Most reviewers deemed the futuristic narrative, *It Can't Happen Here* (1935), wretched art but salutary propaganda. R. P. Blackmur begins his review in *Nation* by noting that "there is hardly a rule for the good conduct of novels that it does 'not break."[77] Brickell, among others, pointed out in *North American Review* that Lewis had drawn on European Fascism for his plot and on the biography of Huey Long for his archvillain.[78] To reviewers like Elmer Davis of *Saturday Review of Literature*, Lewis's timely nightmare seemed terrifyingly possible.[79] To reviewers like Robert Morss Lovett and Robert Cantwell of *New Republic*, Lewis's oversimplified ironheel takeover (in spite of his feverish research) revealed his ignorance of Fascism.[80] Granville Hicks congratulated Lewis in *New Masses* for discovering and diving into "the great issues of his day," but regretted Lewis's failure to exhibit the full range of "capitalist terror" and liberal courage.[81] Feeling certain that *It Can't Happen Here* would waste no one's time—was, in fact, everyone's "duty" to read—an exuberant Clifton Fadiman glorified Lewis's effort as not only his most important book, "but one of the most important books ever produced in this country."[82]

But practically all reviewers turned thumbs down on Lewis's flip-flop satire, *The Prodigal Parents* (1938), which pokes fun at the preposterous radical offspring of the Babbitt-like hero, Fred Cornplow. As ever, a few reviewers found Lewis's about-face novel amusing. A few took his comic-strip characters seriously—a corrective to the politics of *It Can't Happen Here*. Alluding to the popularity of that anti-Fascist novel among radical critics, *Time* judged *The Prodigal Parents* "inconsequential," a work that "makes it reasonably certain" that left-wingers will throw Sinclair Lewis no party this time.[83] Indeed, left-wing reviewers expressed disgust. Once more Calverton asserted in *Modern Monthly* that Lewis has lost touch with social realities.[84] Hicks in *New Masses* viewed the Red-baiting *Prodigal Parents* as Lewis's worst book.[85] Cowley in *New Republic* called it "stupid."[86] In *Nation*, Louis Kronenberger thought it "fatally illiberal," a product of "philistinism," the quality in a writer that is "the sin against the Holy Ghost."[87] His time once more wasted, Fadiman in the *New Yorker* classed it with such diversions as *Mantrap* and *Work of Art*.[88] Even Adams in the *New York Times Book Review* pronounced it a flat failure.[89]

An unexpected number of reviewers seemed to like the warmth and verve of *Bethel Merriday* (1940), a mellow (even maudlin) story of a girl who makes good in the theater. Although lacking Lewis's customary "bite," the novel holds his usual freight of essentially accurate, often dull, factual information—in this case lore about one of his favorite institutions. That Lewis's world of greasepaint and footlights was held together by a feeble plot, stock characters, and shallow notions escaped few reviewers. Harry Lorin Binsse in *Commonweal* found the book "pleasant,"[90] but most continued to expect something better. Edgar Johnson announced in *New Republic* that the Nobel Prize winner was gone, the *Saturday Evening Post* writer back.[91] Though Lionel Trilling defended the venerable "improvisatorial" style in *Kenyon Review*, he saw this later novel as "another and redundant episode," as "an indulgence of Mr. Lewis's dream life," as the upshot of a mistaken sense of power caused, in part, by the absence in American economics of "any real conception of literature as a profession."[92] Fadiman, still smarting over *Prodigal Parents*, nevertheless recommended *Bethel Merriday* in the *New Yorker* as first-rate light reading, "not so much the story of a stage-struck young girl as the story of a stage-struck middle-aged novelist who uses the young girl as a ventriloquist's dummy."[93]

Like *Bethel Merriday*, Lewis's next novel, *Gideon Planish* (1943), his satiric exposé of philanthropic fundraising, received mixed reactions. No one considered it top-notch. Those reviewers who felt that Lewis's attack on organized virtue redeemed his bewhiskered techniques confessed that his satire was unwieldy. Some claimed that Lewis's humor saved the novel, others (like Howard Mumford Jones in *Saturday Review of Literature*) that Lewis's dated slang contributed to its failure.[94] Diana Trilling of *Nation* found *Gideon Planish* dull and sloppy, Gideon himself dead.[95] Still, some reviewers looked upon Peony Planish as Lewis's best female character since Leora Arrowsmith. Fadiman in the *New Yorker*[96] and Geismar in *American Mercury*[97] appreciated Lewis's iconoclasm. Most reviewers agreed that Lewis ran fast—but the world ran faster.

Reviewers judged *Cass Timberlane: A Novel of Husbands and Wives* (1945) from fair to good, better than most recent Lewis novels, but far from his best. Featuring Lewis on its cover, *Time* ranked *Cass Timberlane*—600,000 sold in 1945—with *Ann Vickers* and *Dodsworth*.[98] Reviewers nostalgically compared and contrasted the Minnesota settings in *Cass Timberlane* and *Main Street*. As ever, some reviewers insisted that the novel was closer to satire than to realism, some that it was closer to caricature than to satire. The novel, serialized first in *Cosmopolitan*, attracted women reviewers: Mary M. Colum labeled it "brilliant" in *Saturday Review*;[99] for *New Republic*'s Marjorie Farber it displayed the worst ingredients of women's magazine fiction;[100] disappointed, Diana Trilling concluded in *Nation* that Judge Timberlane's infatuation with the birdlike Jenny was incredible[101]. Though Edward Weeks of *Atlantic Monthly* enjoyed the novel, he saw no advance in style and characterization.[102] As Philip Wylie expressed it in *American Mercury*, the novel "displays reel after reel of new film in the old technique."[103] Edmund Wilson, who appreciated the flawed effort—particularly the interspersed sketches of marred marriages—credited Lewis in the *New Yorker* for persisting, for creating (like his title character) "interest and values."[104]

The fanfare surrounding *Kingsblood Royal* (1947) induced *Life* to theorize about the dilemma of critics who encounter poor literary form with content for social good.[105] In reviewing Lewis's novel about a "white" man who switches to the "Negro" world after accidentally discovering "colored" blood in his family, most critics drew attention to the poor art (puppet characters, improbable motivation, melodramatic plot, farcical dialogue, sarcastic tone) and the social good (attack on racism, timeliness, slashing honesty, propaganda value). Writing in *Yale Review*, Orville Prescott, for one, tried to respect the book's propaganda value,[106] but Charles Poore, in the *New York Times Book Review*, pronounced even Lewis's propaganda bluntly ineffective.[107] *New Republic*,[108] *Nation*, [109] and *Ebony* [110] reviewed the book positively. Cowley concluded in the *New Yorker* that the "problem" novel has to be judged by the same standards as all novels. George Babbitt, he added, will be remembered longer than Neil Kingsblood.[111] In *Survey*, Harry Hanson called the novel "class B Lewis," comparing it to the "synthetic" plot of Laura Z. Hobson's novel on anti-Semitism, *Gentleman's Agreement*,[112] an observation closer to the mark than Robert Henderson's proclamation in *Library Journal* that *Kingsblood Royal* was Sinclair Lewis's "greatest book."[113]

"Loose-jointed," "facetious," "padded," "awkward" are a few of the tags reviewers pinned on *The God-Seeker* (1949), Lewis's historical satire on the hypocrisies of missionaries, traders, and government agents bent on converting the Minnesota Indians. Reviewers noted that Lewis's sympathy for the religion of his hero, Aaron Gadd, accented the positive, affirmed the American Dream, and made *The God-Seeker* a "cleaner" book than *Elmer Gantry*. Some liked the local historical detail, but most found it dull. John Woodburn, who complained in *New Republic* about the badness of Lewis's last six books, compared *The God-Seeker* to the historical shockers of Frank Yerby.[114] Liking its "bounce and energy," Howard Mumford Jones in *Saturday Review* judged *The God-Seeker* better than *Kingsblood Royal*.[115] But *Newsweek* expressed the prevailing opinion that Lewis, "somewhat on the downgrade these recent years, seems at last to have hit bottom. . . ."[116]

At best, reviewers read the posthumous *World So Wide* (1951) as the valedictory of a once-gifted writer. The *Times Literary Supplement*, for one, regretted its publication.[117] This story about another of Lewis's American innocents abroad loomed, Cowley wrote in the *New York Times Book Review*, as a "pale reflection" of *Dodsworth*.[118] C. J. Rolo spoke of it in *Atlantic Monthly* as "egregiously ingenuous."[119] Despite the magic of the name "Sinclair Lewis," reviewers felt no compunction in pointing out the paper-thin characters, clanging prose, soap-opera action, inconsistent point of view, superficial detail, and hoary slang. Harold C. Gardiner declared in *America* that Lewis never really knew the United States, "save in a caricature of his own making."[120] While conservatives chose to see Lewis as the prodigal son reconciled with America at last, liberals liked to see him as the eternal critic ambivalent to the bitter end. C. Hartley Grattan in *New Republic* blamed Lewis's interpreters for trying to make a "major critic of American life" out of a mere story-teller,[121] while Serge Hughes, unhappy with Lewis as a mere storyteller, asserted in *Commonweal* that the novelist's treatment of moral issues far surpassed his solutions.[122] Most reviewers who reported Lewis's "falling off" during the past two decades reminded readers of his great accomplishments during the 1920s. *Main Street, Babbitt, Arrowsmith, Elmer Gantry*, and *Dodsworth* would survive—if not widely read, at least remembered for their historical interest.

Reviewers found Sinclair Lewis's pungent letters in *From Main Street to Stockholm* (1952) amusing and revealing. They discovered in Lewis's correspondence to his publishers (Harcourt Brace [1919–1930]) the retaliatory author pursuing the Pulitzer Prize in order to reject it and grooming himself for the Nobel Prize in order to accept it. Weeks, in *Atlantic*, described the letters, collected by Harrison Smith, as "compelling."[123] *Newsweek* read them as "a blow by blow description" of Lewis's career.[124] In the *New York Herald Tribune* Ramon Guthrie interpreted them as expressions of a complex man, generous and irritable.[125] The *New Yorker* depicted them as revealing an "odd mixture of vanity, irascibility, sentimentality, childishness, and talent."[126] Geismar, in *Saturday Review*, glimpsed the artist obsessed with publicity.[127] Fascinated by the letters, Perry Miller saw in them an "astonishing revelation" of the problem in America of the artist torn between money and art.[128]

After Lewis's death, his executors, Harry E. Maule and Melville H. Cane, inventoried his nonfiction and gathered the "cream" of his articles, columns, reviews, and outlines in *The Man From Main Street* (1953), a kind of companion volume to *From Main Street to Stockholm*. The *New Yorker* declared the essays "never dull,"[129] though they appeared dull at times to *Reporter*'s Daniel Aaron, for whom they recalled Lewis's democratic attitudes, respect for truth, and hatred of hypocrisy.[130] As for attacking problems, the *Times Literary Supplement* thought Lewis's nonfiction less effective than his fiction,[131] though Guthrie wished, in the *Tribune*, that Lewis had written more nonfiction.[132] For John W. Aldridge of the *New York Times Book Review*, the essays, surprisingly good, helped explain Lewis's popularity and failure as a novelist, "a first-rate practical mind coupled with an arrested and largely third-rate creative sensibility."[133] Reviews of two later posthumous publications—*I'm a Stranger Here Myself and Other Stories* (1962), edited by Mark Schorer, and the screenplay *Storm in the West* (1963), written with Dore Schary—were negligible. The latter, an allegory of Nazism set in the Old West, prompted John Fuller to remark in *New Statesman*: "It's so bad it's not even funny."[134]

II

Although Sinclair Lewis's popular novels attracted contemporary reviewers and essayists, most serious critics ignored his work. Early critical biographies—actually promotional pamphlets—include Stuart Pratt Sherman's adulatory *The Significance of Sinclair Lewis* (1922)[135] and the eulogistic *Sinclair Lewis* (1925) by Oliver Harrison [Harrison Smith], Harcourt, Brace editor and Lewis's friend.[136] Independently approbatory, however, are Vernon Parrington's flashy *Sinclair Lewis: Our Own Diogenes* (1927)[137] and Hans Kriesi's glowing *Sinclair Lewis* (1928).[138] Lewis's next publisher, Doubleday, issued *Sinclair Lewis: A Biographical Sketch* (1933), the first part honeyed prose by Carl Van Doren, the second part bibliography by Harvey Taylor.[139]

Essays on Lewis during the 1920s by James Branch Cabell,[140] Paul de Kruif,[141] Waldo Frank,[142] Virginia Woolf,[143] Percy H. Boynton,[144] Walter Lippmann,[145] Edith Wharton,[146] and Regis Michaud[147] retain interest. Erik Axel Karlfeldt's "Why Sinclair Lewis Got the Nobel Prize" (1930) has been reprinted several times.[148] During the 1930s literary scholars and critics like Fred Lewis Pattee,[149] Russell Blankenship,[150] V. F. Calverton,[151] Henry Seidel Canby,[152] Christian Gauss,[153] Howard Mumford Jones,[154] Lewis Mumford,[155] William Lyon Phelps,[156] Constance Rourke,[157] Joseph Warren Beach,[158] Ludwig Lewisohn,[159] Granville Hicks,[160] Harry Hartwick,[161] Robert Cantwell[162] reviewed Lewis's achievement and endeavored to locate his place in American literature. In the 1940s Lewis came under the scrutiny of Alfred Kazin,[163] Bernard DeVoto,[164] John T. Flanagan,[165] and Maxwell Geismar.[166] Warren Beck in 1948 stirred up discussion with his essay "How Good Is Sinclair Lewis?"[167]

Following Lewis's death, scholars argued about his place in American literature while writers whom he influenced paid him tribute.[168] In the early 1960s Mark Schorer's giant biography stimulated interest in Lewis, as did the by-products of Schorer's enterprise—essays, a critical collection, introductions and afterwords to several paperback reprints.[169] In summary, besides other critical essays and other biographies at the time, there followed a number of critical books, checklists, and critical collections. In 1969 James Lundquist began editing the *Sinclair Lewis Newsletter* at St. Cloud State University, not far from Sauk Centre.[170] Essays on Lewis continued to appear in literary journals from time to time.

Robert E. Fleming's indispensable *Sinclair Lewis: A Reference Guide* (1980), a 240-page secondary bibliography edited with the help of Esther Fleming, chronologically annotates writings, mainly American and English, about Lewis from 1914 to 1978—important reviews, newspaper and magazine articles, interviews, parodies, biographies, journal essays, book chapters, dissertations, and critical volumes, as well as American and foreign bibliographies.[171] Among several handy selective bibliographies in pamphlet form are *The Merrill Checklist of Sinclair Lewis* (1970), edited by James Lundquist, and *The American Novel: Sinclair Lewis to the Present* (1970), edited by Blake Nevius.[172] *American Literary Manuscripts* (1978), edited by J. Albert Robbins et al., lists holdings of Sinclair Lewis papers.[173] "A Descriptive Catalogue of Sinclair Lewis Novels" (1976), by James S. Measell, appears in the *Sinclair Lewis Newsletter*.[174] Appended to Schorer's biography is a near-reliable checklist of more than 400 items by Lewis—fiction, nonfiction, and poetry.

Praised almost without qualification at first, Schorer's giant biography seemed to critics like Irving Howe and Steven Marcus to lack the vital connection between Lewis's life and Lewis's work. They felt that in spite of Schorer's own Midwest village background and his exclusive access to Lewis's manuscripts, diaries, letters, and other personal papers (now at Yale University); his consultations with hundreds of persons; and his reading of scores of personality sketches, anecdotes, literary portraits, capsule biographies, book-length biographies, memoirs, background histories, and articles on such matters as Sinclair Lewis as a mimic, a teacher, a lecturer, an actor, a clown, a lover, a husband, a father, an alcoholic, a traveler, a worker, a friend, and a foe (see Fleming's *Guide*), the biographer failed to grasp Lewis's inner life, the real nature of his art, his essential kindness and sense of justice. In "Mark Schorer's *Sinclair Lewis*" (1971), Jack L. Davis takes Schorer to task for "numerous biases and discrepancies," charging that, to exorcise his own private demon, Schorer obsessively focused on Lewis's idiosyncrasies and darker side, finding the theme for his whole biography in the fact that Lewis had died in Rome of "paralysis of the heart." Davis further suggests in his study of Schorer on Lewis that not until the formalist critic came to write his short essay, "Sinclair Lewis: *Babbitt*" (1969), did he come to terms with Lewis's integrated vision.[175]

Using biography and scholarship to illuminate Lewis's work, Sheldon Grebstein, in *Sinclair Lewis* (1962), his compact Twayne volume completed before but published soon after Schorer's biography, argues against lumping together Lewis's good and bad books: "He was at his best in denunciation, and at his best he created an image of twentieth-century American society which continues to haunt us in its essential truth."[176] In *The Art of Sinclair Lewis* (1967)—its title a bit misleading— D. J. Dooley defends Lewis as an "objective" writer who should be judged by "objective" standards. Dooley sees Lewis's behavior and achievement as the result of an anguished inner life, one which kept faith, however, in the American Dream: "The ambiguities in his novels, therefore, have a connection with the conception of liberty."[177] Besides introducing the reader to Lewis's works, James Lundquist's little *Guide to Sinclair Lewis* (1970) suggests new approaches to the major novels and reassesses Lewis's importance to American literature. Lundquist maintains that *Ann Vickers, It Can't Happen Here, Cass Timberlane,* and *Kingsblood Royal* survive Lewis's work of the 1930s and 1940s because they identify repressive organizations.[178] Richard O'Connor's *Sinclair Lewis* (1971) surveys the life and career of the writer on the junior high school level.[179] In his sympathetic *Sinclair Lewis* (1973), James Lundquist asserts that "the melodrama of Sinclair Lewis's life has been greatly exaggerated." Without melodrama, then, he once more takes up the life and work, finding in *Main Street* and *Babbitt,* for example, a contrast between the dominant everyday world and the nightmarish quality that commonplace world sets in motion. "The easiest way to understand Lewis's artistry," says Lundquist, "is to think of him simply as a master of the popular novel."[180] Like Grebstein, Schorer, Lundquist, and others, Martin Light sees in Lewis the not uncommon conflict of the 1900s between romance and realism. In his more specialized study, *The Quixotic Vision of Sinclair Lewis* (1975), Light persuasively analyzes this conflict in Lewis's apprenticeship novels, major work, and later fiction as an expression of quixotism—an affliction that begins under the influence of reading romantic literature and continues as the inspired reader ventures forth into a world he both finds and makes. The accompanying impulse to reject romanticism results both in realism and in comic exaggeration. Light concludes that even as Lewis fought romanticism, medievalism, and chivalry, he succumbed to them.[181]

Sinclair Lewis has not lacked for critical collections about him and his work. The first collection, *Sinclair Lewis: A Collection of Critical Essays* (1962), edited by Mark Schorer, contains a mix of twenty-four reviews and essays, twenty-two written during Lewis's lifetime by eighteen prominent writers and critics.[182] In 1968 Robert J. Griffin edited the more focused companion volume, *Twentieth Century Interpretations of Arrowsmith.*[183] The next year, the *New York Times Book Review Critiques of Sinclair Lewis's Works* (1969) reproduced twenty-four of its reviews and articles in a forty-one page portfolio. Martin Light compiled the fourth collection, *The Merrill Studies in Babbitt* (1971), beginning with Lewis's letters on *Babbitt* to his publishers, as well as his unpublished introduction to the novel, and following with alternating selections of positive and negative criticism of the novel.[184] The time seems ripe for some publisher to contract for similar collections on *Main Street,*[185] *Elmer Gantry,*[186] and *Dodsworth.*[187] *Sinclair Lewis at 100* (1985), edited by Michael Connaughton, contains papers presented at the Sinclair Lewis Centennial Conference in St. Cloud, Minnesota, 7–9 February 1985.

With book reviews ranging from 1914 to 1953 and critical essays spanning the late 1940s to the present, this collection displays a diversity of attitudes toward Sinclair Lewis and an array of insights into his writings, thus enabling the reader to see the man and his work from a variety of perspectives. In "A Long Way to Gopher Prairie: Sinclair Lewis's Apprenticeship" (1947), John T. Flanagan finds in the early novels realistic touches, satiric flashes, embryonic characters, and parenthetical exposition, the signs that point to Lewis's evolution into a mature realist saturated with knowledge of American life. But questioning Lewis's "vaunted realism," Warren Beck in "How Good Is Sinclair Lewis?" uses *Kingsblood Royal* as a springboard back to the major work of the 1920s and concludes that the reputation of "this novelist stranger than any of his fictions" is extravagantly inflated. Aware of Lewis's limitations, George J. Becker in "Apostle to the Philistines" (1952) argues that because Lewis as a social novelist attacked various forms of tyranny, he is a significant figure in America's coming of age, not so much for the profundity as for the amplitude of his evaluation. Mark Schorer contends in "Sinclair Lewis and the Method of Half-Truths" (1956), however, that Lewis's "proliferation of detail," though forcible, lacks genuine largeness, that his perspective on American standardization and convention is "extremely narrow and intellectually feeble," that, as in *Elmer Gantry*, his partial world is "dominated by monstrous parodies of human nature." That Lewis's fiction, however monstrous or parodic, lost power after 1930 is clear, and Sheldon Grebstein in "Sinclair Lewis's Unwritten Novel" (1959) investigates as an important factor in the writer's decline the massive labor novel that, since the early 1920s, he had tried again and again to write but failed. Unable to create his rebellious labor hero, Lewis created instead his rebellious medical hero, the story of *Arrowsmith*'s genesis, development, strengths, weaknesses, and reputation discussed by D. S. Dooley in Chapter 4, "Aspiration and Enslavement," of his *Art of Sinclair Lewis* (1967). As Lyon N. Richardson earlier had compared the serial and book versions of *Arrowsmith*, so Martin Bucco compares the serial and book versions of *The Innocents, Free Air, Mantrap, Ann Vickers, Cass Timberlane*, and *World So Wide* in "The Serialized Novels of Sinclair Lewis" (1969), thereby making more visible the writer's split sensibility. Also aware of the ambivalence in Lewis's work, James C. Austin in "Sinclair Lewis and Western Humor" (1970) shows how Lewis absorbed native American humor, particularly the two-sided humor of pride and complaint in the Northern states west of Ohio. Directing his analysis less to folk art than to popular art, Robert L. Coard in "*Dodsworth* and the Question of Art" (1971) sees as Lewis's strengths the characteristics of the popular novelist of his time—controversial topics, contemporary settings, observed details, simple plots, bold contrasts, and flashy sentences. In "The Quixotic Motifs of *Main Street*" (1973), Martin Light studies Carol Kennicott in term of her "literary" imagination, her crusade to redress wrongs, and her need to romanticize reality. By viewing seven Lewis novels in their historical chronology—*The God-Seeker* (1830–1856), *Main Street* (1907–1920), *Babbitt* (1920–1922), *Arrowsmith* (1897–1923), *Elmer Gantry* (1902–1926), *Dodsworth* (1903–1928), *Kingsblood Royal* (1944–46)—James Lea in "Sinclair Lewis and the Implied America" (1973) maintains that as a social satirist with a historical perspective Sinclair Lewis wrote out of the conviction that not only could there be a better America, but that there *had been* a better America—an America with a potential for freedom and happiness betrayed by the twentieth-century. Employing an American Studies approach, Stephen S. Conroy, like Coard and other recent Lewis critics, makes a case in "Popular Artists and Elite Standards" (1974) for Lewis, in his search for the adulation of the mass audience and financial success, as a type of the versatile popular-culture artist. But David G. Pugh wonders in "Baedekers, Babbittry, and Baudelaire" (1975) if Lewis's popular figures (e.g., George F. Babbitt) are still potent objective correlatives in today's world of flow charts and sociograms, if young readers can respond adequately to the detailed "updateness" of Babbitt's world, if they can translate that world into ours. Though hurriedly written, *Kingsblood Royal* troubled the nation's conscience in the 1940s; in "*Kingsblood Royal* and the Black 'Passing' Novel" (1986) Robert E. Fleming places Lewis's novel of a black person passing for white in the context of earlier novels with the same theme, and he demonstrates Lewis's particular indebtedness to James Weldon Johnson's *The Autobiography of an Ex-Coloured Man* (1912). Finally, to account for Lewis's phobic flights from his native ground, for his reluctance to write accurate subjective autobiography, and for *Main Street*'s strange inclusions and stranger exclusions, James Lundquist in "The Sauk Centre Sinclair Lewis Didn't Write About" (1986) examines local newspapers of the 1890s, forcing the reader to confront young Harry Lewis's "unacknowledged background of horror," his gruesome village and rural surroundings of "bizarre brutality." Thus a hundred years after Sinclair Lewis's birth, a surprising number of scholars and critics continue to delve into and speculate on the life and writings of this strangely compelling figure in American literature.[188]

For making smoother the editorial way, my thanks go to Susan Buffett, Stephen S. Conroy, Robert E. Fleming, Warren French, Jill Frisch, Albert F. Gugenheimer, Ann Geismar, Averil Kadis, James Lundquist, Thomas J. Lyon, James Nagel, Edward S. Skillin, Edith Smith, Emily Taylor, Rosemary Whitaker, Robley Wilson, Jr., and, as always, my wife, Edith.

Colorado State University   MARTIN BUCCO

Notes

1. Mark Schorer, *Sinclair Lewis: An American Life* (New York, Toronto, and London: McGraw-Hill, 1961), 313.

2. *New York Times Review of Books*, 1 March 1914, 100.

3. *Boston Transcript*, 29 April 1914, 24.

4. *Review of Reviews* 49 (May 1914):628.

5. *Wisconsin Library Bulletin* 11 (December 1915):371.

6. Frederic Taylor Cooper, review of *Trail of the Hawk, Bookman* 42 (October 1915):214.

7. *New York Times Review of Books*, 10 October 1915, 362.

8. H. W. Boynton, "Some Sories of the Month," *Bookman* 45 (May 1917): 316–17.

9. Francis Hackett, "A Stenographer," *New Republic* 10 (24 March 1917): 234–35.

10. "True Sentiment and False," *Nation* 105 (15 November 1917):540.

11. "Notes on New Fiction," *Dial* 63 (22 November 1917):531.

12. Review of *Free Air, Booklist* 16 (December 1919):94.

13. Review of *Free Air, New Republic* 21 (28 January 1920):275.

14. Francis Hackett, "God's Country," *New Republic* 25 (1 December 1920): 20–21.

15. Ludwig Lewisohn, "The Epic of Dullness," *Nation* 111 (10 November 1920):536–37.

16. Stanton Coblentz, "Main Street," *Bookman* 52 (January 1921):[457–58].

17. H. L. Mencken, "Consolation," *Smart Set* 64 (January 1921):138–44.

18. H. L. Mencken, "Portrait of an American Citizen," *Smart Set* 69 (October 1922):138–40.

19. May Sinclair, "The Man from Main Street," *New York Times Book Review*, 24 September 1922, 1, 11.

20. Ludwig Lewisohn, review of *Babbitt, Nation* 115 (20 September 1922): 284–85.

21. Burton Rascoe, *New York Tribune*, 17 September 1922, sec. 5, 8.

22. Upton Sinclair, "Standardized America," *Appeal to Reason*, 23 September 1922, 1.

23. Robert Littell, "Babbitt," *New Republic* 32 (4 October 1922):152.

24. Sherwood Anderson, "Four American Impressions," *New Republic* 32 (11 October 1922):171–73.

25. Rebecca West, "Notes on Novels: *Babbitt*," *New Statesman* 23 (21 October 1922):78, 80.

26. Stuart F. Sherman, "A Way Out: Sinclair Lewis Discovers a Hero," *New York Herald Tribune Books*, 8 March 1925, 1–2.

27. Robert Morss Lovett, "An Interpreter of American Life," *Dial* 78 (June 1925):[515]–18.

28. H. L. Mencken, review of *Arrowsmith, American Mercury* 4 (April 1925): 507–9.

29. "Martin Arrowsmith," *Times Literary Supplement* 24 (5 March 1925):153.

30. Edwin Muir, review of *Martin Arrowsmith*, *Nation and Athenaeum* 36 (14 March 1925):818.

31. Joseph Wood Krutch, "A Genius on Main Street," *Nation* 120 (1 April 1925):359–60.

32. Henry Seidel Canby, "Fighting Success," *Saturday Review of Literature* 1 (7 March 1925):575.

33. T. K. Whipple, "Sinclair Lewis," *New Republic* 42 (15 April 1925): pt. 2, 3–5.

34. Grant Overton, "The Salvation of Sinclair Lewis," *Bookman* 61 (April 1925): 179–85.

35. Edwin Muir, "Fiction," *Nation and Athenaeum* 39 (31 July 1926):506.

36. D. J., review of *Mantrap*, *Independent* 116 (19 June 1926):721.

37. Rebecca West, "Sinclair Lewis Introduces Elmer Gantry," *New York Herald Tribune Books*, 13 March 1927, 1.

38. Charles W. Ferguson, "Sinclair Lewis and Blasphemy," *Bookman* 65 (March 1927):216–18.

39. Elmer Davis, "Mr. Lewis Attacks the Clergy," *New York Times Book Review*, 13 March 1927, 1, 22.

40. H. L. Mencken, "Man of God: American Style," *American Mercury* 10 (April 1927):506–8.

41. Joseph Wood Krutch, "Mr. Babbitt's Spiritual Guide," *Nation* 124 (16 March 1927):291–92.

42. Burton Rascoe, "Bad Girls and Babbitts," *Bookman* 67 (May 1928):306–7.

43. L. P. Hartley, "New Fiction," *Saturday Review* 145 (9 June 1928):738.

44. H. L. Mencken, "Babbitt Redivivus," *American Mercury* 14 (June 1928): 253–54.

45. Malcolm Cowley, "Babbilogues," *New Republic* 54 (25 April 1928):302.

46. Dorothy Parker, "Mr. Lewis Lays It on with a Trowel," *New Yorker* 4 (7 April 1928), 106–7.

47. Henry Seidel Canby, "Schmaltz, Babbitt & Co.," *Saturday Review of Literature* (24 March 1928):[697]–98.

48. Henry Seidel Canby, "Sex War," *Saturday Review of Literature* 5 (30 March 1929):821–22.

49. Carl Van Doren, "Zenith Meets Europe," *Nation* 128 (3 April 1929):400–1.

50. Louis Kronenberger, "Sinclair Lewis Parts Company with Mr. Babbitt," *New York Times Book Review*, 17 March 1929, 2.

51. Mary Ross, "Travelog by Mr. Lewis," *Survey* 62 (1 May 1929):202–3.

52. Frances Lamont Robbins, "Samson Agonistes," *Outlook and Independent* 151 (20 March 1929):446–67.

53. H. L. Mencken, "Escape and Return," *American Mercury* 16 (April 1929): 506–8.

54. Dorothy Parker, "And Again, Mr. Lewis," *New Yorker* 5 (16 March 1929): 106–7.

55. Ford Madox Ford, review of *Dodsworth*, *Bookman* 69 (April 1929):191–92.

56. E. M. Forster, "A Camera Man," *Life and Letters* 2 (May 1929):336–43.

57. Fred Lewis Pattee, "Revolt from the Frontier," *The New American Literature: 1890–1930* (New York and London: Century, 1930), 338–45.

58. Ludwig Lewisohn, "The Naturalist," *Expression in America* (New York, London: Harper and Brothers, 1932), 492–513.

59. Herschel Brickell, "The Literary Landscape," *North American Review* 325 (April 1933):383.

60. Malcolm Cowley, "Tired Feminist," *New Republic* 74 (15 February 1933): 22–23.

61. Michael Williams, "Babbittry into Vickery," *Commonweal* 17 (22 March 1933):567–69.

62. J. McS, review of *Ann Vickers, Catholic World* 136 (February 1933):622–24.

63. Bernard DeVoto, "Sinclair Lewis," *Saturday Review of Literature* 9 (28 January 1933):[397]–98.

64. H. L. Mencken, "A Lady of Vision," *American Mercury* 28 (March 1933): 382–83.

65. Burton Rascoe, "The Old Sinclair Lewis with his Great Gifts," *New York Herald Tribune Books*, 29 January 1933, 1–2.

66. J. Donald Adams, "A New Novel by Sinclair Lewis," *New York Times Book Review*, 29 January 1933, 1.

67. J. Donald Adams, "A New Novel by Sinclair Lewis," *New York Times Book Review*, 28 January 1934, 1, 19.

68. V. F. Calverton, "Sinclair Lewis: The Last of the Literary Liberals," *Modern Monthly* 8 (March 1934):77–86.

69. Granville Hicks, review of *Work of Art, New Masses*, 30 January 1934, [25].

70. T. S. Matthews, "Including Sinclair Lewis," *New Republic* 77 (31 January 1934):343.

71. Peter Monro Jack, "Sinclair Lewis's First Collection of Short Stories," *New York Times Book Review*, 30 June 1935, 3, 17.

72. Howard Mumford Jones, "Mr. Lewis and the Primitive American," *Saturday Review of Literature* 12 (6 July 1935):7.

73. Clifton Fadiman, "Nobel Prizewinner," *New Yorker* 11 (13 July 1935):56–58.

74. Walter Prichard Eaton, "Clifford Odets and Others," *Herald Tribune*, 28 July 1935, 15.

75. Lewis Nichols, "The Recent Plays," *Times*, 28 July 1935, 17.

76. Edith J. R. Isaacs, "Without Benefit of Ingenue: Broadway in Review/*Jayhawker*," *Theatre Arts Monthly* 19 (January 1935):9–10.

77. R. P. Blackmur, "Utopia, or Uncle Tom's Cabin," *Nation* 141 (30 October 1935):516.

78. Herschel Brickell, review of *It Can't Happen Here, North American Review* 240 (December 1935):543–46.

79. Elmer Davis, "Ode to Liberty," *Saturday Review of Literature* 12 (19 October 1935):5.

80. Robert Morss Lovett and Robert Cantwell, "Mr. Lewis Says It Can," *New Republic* 85 (6 November 1935):366–67; review of *It Can't Happen Here, New Republic* 85 (11 December 1935):152.

81. Granville Hicks, "Sinclair Lewis—Anti-Fascist," *New Masses* 14 (29 October 1935):22–23.

82. Clifton Fadiman, "Books: Red Lewis," *New Yorker* 11 (26 October 1935): 83–84.

83. "Red Menace," *Time* 31 (24 January 1938):61–62.

84. V. F. Calverton, "The Prodigal Lewis," *Modern Monthly* 10 (February 1938):11–13, 16.

85. Granville Hicks, "Sinclair Lewis's Stink Bomb," *New Masses* 26 (25 January 1938):19–21.

86. Malcolm Cowley, "George F. Babbitt's Revenge," *New Republic* 93 (26 January 1938):342–43.

87. Louis Kronenberger, "The Prodigal Lewis," *Nation* 146 (22 January 1938): 101.

88. Clifton Fadiman, "Books: Sinclair Lewis Sets 'Em Up and Knocks 'Em Down," *New Yorker* 13 (22 January 1938):61.

89. J. Donald Adams, "A New Novel by Sinclair Lewis," *New York Times Book Review*, 23 January 1938, 1.

90. Harry Lorin Binssee, review of *Bethel Merriday, Commonweal* 31 (22 March 1940):477.

91. Edgar Johnson, "Sinclair Lewis's Understudy," *New Republic* 102 (25 March 1940):413.

92. Lionel Trilling, "Mr. Lewis Goes Soft," *Kenyon Review* 2 (Summer 1940): 64–67.

93. Clifton Fadiman, "Mr. Lewis and the Stage—Catalogue," *New Yorker* 16 (23 March 1940):71–72.

94. Howard Mumford Jones, "Sinclair Lewis and the Do-Gooders," *Saturday Review of Literature* 26 (24 April 1943):6.

95. Diana Trilling, "Fiction in Review," *Nation* 156 (8 May 1943):675–76.

96. Clifton Fadiman, "Return of Mr. Lewis," *New Yorker* 19 (24 April 1943): 76.

97. Maxwell Geismar, "Young Sinclair Lewis and Old Dos Passos," *American Mercury* 56 (May 1943):624–28.

98. "Laureate of the Booboisie," *Time* 46 (8 October 1945):100, 103–4, 106, 108.

99. Mary M. Colum, "Sinclair Lewis's New Thesis Novel," *Saturday Review* 28 (6 October 1945):8–9.

100. Marjorie Farber, "Recent Fiction," *New Republic* 113 (22 October 1945): 542.

101. Diana Trilling, "Of Husbands and Wives," *Nation* 161 (13 October 1945): 381–[382].

102. Edward Weeks, "The Peripatetic Reviewer," *Atlantic Monthly* 176 (October 1945):139, 141.

103. Philip Wylie, "Sinclair Lewis," *American Mercury* 61 (November 1945): 629–32.

104. Edmund Wilson, "Salute to an Old Landmark: Sinclair Lewis," *New Yorker* 21 (13 October 1945):98–104.

105. "White Man Turns Negro," *Life* 22 (9 June 1947):131–32, 134, 137.

106. Orville Prescott, "Outstanding Novels," *Yale Review* n.s. 37 (September 1947):189.

107. Charles Poore, "Trouble in Grand Republic, Minn.," *New York Times Book Review*, 25 May 1947, 1.

108. Bucklin Moon, "Big Red," *New Republic* 116 (26 May 1947):26–27.

109. Margaret Marshall, "Notes by the Way," *Nation* 164 (7 June 1947):[689].

110. Wayne Miller, "*Kingsblood Royal:* Sinclair Lewis Writes a Best Seller on Negroes," *Ebony* 2 (June 1947):9–13.

111. Malcolm Cowley, "Problem Novel," *New Yorker* 23 (24 May 1947):100–1.

112. Harry Hanson, "The Fiction Shelf," *Survey* 36 (August 1947):449–50.

113. Robert Henderson, review of *Kingsblood Royal, Library Journal* 72 (15 May 1947):809.

114. John Woodburn, "Lament for a Novelist," *New Republic* 120 (16 May 1949):16–17.

115. Howard Mumford Jones, "Mission in Minnesota," *Saturday Review* 32 (12 March 1949):11–12.

116. "Lewis's Latest," *Newsweek* 33 (14 March):87.

117. "Craft and Contrivance," *Times Literary Supplement* 50 (October 1951):625.

118. Malcolm Cowley, "The Last Flight from Main Street," *New York Times Book Review*, 25 March 1951, 1, 16.

119. C. J. Rolo, "Reader's Choice," *Atlantic Monthly* 187 (April 1951):75.

120. Harold C. Gardiner. "Sauk Centre Was Home Still," *America* 85 (7 April 1951):19–20.

121. C. Hartley Grattan, "Sinclair Lewis: The Work of a Lifetime," *New Republic* 124 (2 April 1951):19–20.

122. Serge Hughes, "From Main Street to the World So Wide," *Commonweal* 53 (6 April 1951):648–50.

123. Edward Weeks, "What Lewis Was Like," *Atlantic* 191 (April 1953):78, 80.

124. "The Lewis Letters," *Newsweek* 40 (24 November 1952):102–3.

125. Ramon Guthrie, "Restless, Lonely, Sensitive–'Red' Lewis' Letters Are a self-Portrait," *Herald Tribune* 29 (16 November 1952):1.

126. "Books: Briefly Noted," *New Yorker* 28 (24 January 1953):86, 88.

127. Maxwell Geismar, "Native Prizewinner," *Saturday Review* 36 (28 February 1953):17.

128. Perry Miller, "Portrait of Sinclair Lewis," *Nation* 175 (6 December 1952): 531–32.

129. "Books: Briefly Noted," *New Yorker* 28 (14 February 1953):116.

130. Daniel Aaron, "The Proud Prejudices of Sinclair Lewis," *Reporter* 9 (4 August 1953):37–39.

131. "Powders and Jams," *Times Literary Supplement* 53 (2 April 1954):212.

132. Ramon Guthrie, *Herald Tribune Book Review*, 15 February 1953, 3.

133. John W. Aldridge, "Mr. Lewis As Essayist," *New York Times Book Review*, 15 February 1953, 6, 23.

134. John Fuller, "Hick and Hop," *New Statesman* 68 (4 September 1964):327–28.

135. Stuart Pratt Sherman, *The Significance of Sinclair Lewis* (New York: Harcourt, Brace, 1922).

136. Oliver Harrison, *Sinclair Lewis* (New York: Harcourt, Brace, 1925).

137. Vernon Parrington, *Sinclair Lewis: Our Own Diogenes*, University of Washington Chapbooks, no. 5 (Seattle: University of Washington Book Stores, 1927).

138. Hans Kriesi, *Sinclair Lewis* (Frauenfeld and Leipzig: Von Huber, 1928).

139. Carl Van Doren and Harvey Taylor, *Sinclair Lewis: A Biographical Sketch* (Garden City, N.Y.: Doubleday, Doran, 1933).

140. James Branch Cabell, "The Way of Wizardry," in *Straws and Prayer Books* (New York: Robert M. McBride, 1924).

141. Paul de Kruif, "An Intimate Glimpse of a Great American Novel in the Making," *Designer and the Woman's Magazine* 60 (June 1924):64.

142. Waldo Frank, "Profiles: In America's Image," *New Yorker* 1 (18 July 1925): 10–11.

143. Virginia Woolf, "American Fiction," *SRL* 2 (1 August 1925):1–2.

144. Percy H. Boynton, "Sinclair Lewis," *EJ* 16 (April 1927):251–60.

145. Walter Lippman, "Sinclair Lewis," in *Men of Destiny* (New York: Macmillan, 1927), 71–92.

146. Edith Wharton, "The Great American Novel," *YR* 16 (July 1927):646–56.

147. Regis Michaud, "Sinclair Lewis and the Average Man," in *The American Novel To-Day* (Boston: Little, Brown, 1928), [128]–53.

148. Erik Axel Karlfeldt, "Why Sinclair Lewis Got the Nobel Prize" (New York: Harcourt, Brace, 1930).

149. Fred Lewis Pattee, "Revolt from the Frontier," in *The New American Literature: 1890–1930* (New York and London: Century, 1930), 338–45.

150. Russell Blankenship, "Sinclair Lewis," in *American Literature as an Expression of the National Mind* (New York: Henry Holt, 1931), 657–64.

151. V. F. Calverton, "Sinclair Lewis: The Last of the Literary Liberals," *Modern Monthly* 8 (March 1934):77–86.

152. Henry Seidel Canby, "Sinclair Lewis," *American-Scandinavian Review* 19 (February 1931):[72]–76. See also Canby's later discussion in *Literary History of the United States* (New York: Macmillan, 1948), 1223–28, 1377–88.

153. Christian Gauss, "Sinclair Lewis vs. His Education," *SEP* 204 (26 December 1931):20–21, 54–56.

154. Howard Mumford Jones, "Mr. Lewis's America," *VQR* 7 (7 July 1931): [427]–32.

155. Lewis Mumford, "The America of Sinclair Lewis," *CH* 33 (January 1931): 529–33.

156. William Lyon Phelps, "Men Now Famous," *Delineator* 117 (September 1930):17, 94.

157. Constance Rourke, "Round Up," in *American Humor* (New York: Harcourt, Brace and World, 1931), 283–86.

158. Joseph Warren Beach, *The Twentieth-Century Novel: Studies in Technique* (New York: Appleton-Century Crofts, 1932), 263–66.

159. Ludwig Lewisohn, "The Naturalist," in *Expression in America* (New York: Harper and Brothers, 1932), 492–513.

160. Granville Hicks, *The Great Tradition* (New York: Macmillan, 1933), 230–31, 234–36; "Sinclair Lewis and the Good Life," *EJ* 25 (April 1936):265–73.

161. Harry Hartwick, "The Village Virus," in *The Foreground of American Fiction* (New York: American Book Company, 1934), 250–81.

162. Robert Cantwell, "Sinclair Lewis," *New Republic* 88 (21 October 1936): 298–301.

163. Alfred Kazin, "The New Realism: Sherwood Anderson and Sinclair Lewis," in *On Native Grounds* (New York: Reynal and Hitchcock, 1943):217–26.

164. Bernard DeVoto, "Waste Land," in *The Literary Fallacy* (Boston: Little, Brown, 1944), 95–102. Lewis hotly responds in "Fools, Liars and Mr. DeVoto," *SRL*, 15 April 1944, 9–12.

165. John T. Flanagan, "A Long Way to Gopher Prairie: Sinclair Lewis's Apprenticeship," reprinted in this volume.

166. Maxwell Geismar, "Sinclair Lewis: The Cosmic Bourjoyce," in *The Last of the Provincials* (Boston: Houghton Mifflin, 1947), 69–150.

167. Warren Beck, "How Good is Sinclair Lewis?," reprinted in this volume.

168. See, for example, Frederick Hoffman, "The American Novel Between Wars," in *The Modern Novel in America: 1900–1950* (Chicago: Henry Regnery, 1951), 110–17; C. Carrol Hollis, "The American Novel Through Fifty Years: 5. Sinclair Lewis," *America* 85 (28 April 1951):99–102; Gerald W. Johnson, "Romance and Mr. Babbitt," *New Republic* 124 (29 January 1951):14–15; see below, George F. Becker, "Sinclair Lewis: Apostle to the Philistines," *American Scholar* 21 (Autumn 1951):423–32; Cesare Pavese, "Sinclair Lewis," in *La letteratura americana e altri saggi* (Torino: Giulio Einaudi, 1951), 5–32; Perry Miller, "The Incorruptible Sinclair Lewis," *Atlantic Monthly* 187 (April 1951):30–34; Barnaby Conrad, "Get to the Story!" *The Writer* 64 (June 1951):188–89; Edward Wagenknecht "Sinclair Lewis and the Babbitt Warren," in *Cavalcade of the American Novel* (New York: Henry Holt, 1952), 354–67, 543–45; Frederick F. Manfred, "Sinclair Lewis: A Portrait," *American Scholar* 23 (Spring 1954):162–84; James T. Farrell, "A Souvenir of Sinclair Lewis," *New Leader* 38 (14 November 1955):23–25. In her poignantly resentful *With Love from Gracie* (New York: Harcourt, Brace, 1955)—a nonfiction version of her roman à clef novel *Half a Loaf* (1931)—Grace Hegger Lewis pieces together letters and memories to show Lewis's calf-love in 1912, his marriage to her in 1914, his successful years at home and abroad, his early alcoholic behavioral excesses, and their separation in 1925. In the popular *Dorothy and Red* (Boston: Houghton Mifflin, 1963), Vincent Sheean examines in detail the Lewis-Thompson marriage, recalling his friendship with the pair and drawing heavily on the Dorothy Thompson Papers at Syracuse University.

169. "My Life and Nine-Year Captivity with Sinclair Lewis," *New York Times Book Review*, 20 August 1961, 7, 26; "Sinclair Lewis and the Nobel Prize," *Atlantic Monthly* 208 (October 1961): 83–88; "Sinclair Lewis as a Young Publisher," *Publishers Weekly* 180 (24 July 1961):36–39; "The Burdens of Biography," *Michigan Quarterly Review* 4 (Autumn 1962):249–58; *Sinclair Lewis*, University of Minnesota Pamphlets on American Writers, no. 27 (Minneapolis: University of Minnesota Press, 1963); "Sinclair Lewis: *Babbitt*," in *Landmarks of American Writing*, ed. Hennig Cohen (New York: Basic Books, 1969), 315–27; and "Sinclair Lewis," *American Writers: A Collection of Literary Biographies*, vol. 2 (New York: Charles Scribner's Sons, 1974), 439–60. *Sinclair Lewis: A Collection of Critical Essays*, Twentieth Century Views Series (Englewood Cliffs, N.J.: Prentice Hall, 1963), 1–9. Afterword to *Arrowsmith*, Signet Classic Edition (New York: New American Library, 1961), 431–38; afterword to *Babbitt*, Signet Classic Edition (New York: New American Library, 1961), 320–27; afterword to *Main Street*, Signet Classic Edition (New York: New American Library, 1961), 433–39; introduction to *It Can't Happen Here* (New York: Dell, 1961), 5–17; introduction to *Lewis at Zenith: A Three-Novel Omnibus* (New York: Harcourt, Brace and World, 1961), [vii]–xii; introduc-

tion to *Ann Vickers* (New York: Dell, 1962), 5–17; introduction to *I'm a Stranger Here Myself and Other Stories by Sinclair Lewis* (New York: Dell, 1962), [7]–16; afterword to *Elmer Gantry*, Signet Classic Edition (New York: New American Library, 1967), 419–30; and afterword to *Dodsworth*, Signet Classic Edition (New York: New American Library, 1972), 355–63.

170. *Sinclair Lewis Newsletter* 1 (Spring 1969); 2 (Spring 1970); 3 (1971); 4 (1972); 5–6 (1973–74); 7–8 (1975–76).

171. Robert E. Fleming, *Sinclair Lewis: A Reference Guide* (Boston: G. K. Hall & Co., 1980).

172. James Lundquist, ed., *The Merrill Checklist of Sinclair Lewis* (Columbus, Ohio: Charles E. Merrill 1970); Blake Nevius, ed., *The American Novel: Sinclair Lewis to the Present*, Goldentree Bibliographies in Language and Literature (New York: Appleton-Century-Crofts, 1970).

173. "Lewis, Sinclair," in *American Literary Manuscripts*, ed. J. Albert Robbins et. al. (Athens: University of Georgia Press, 1978).

174. James S. Measell, "A Descriptive Catalogue of Sinclair Lewis Novels," in *SLN* 7–8 (1975–1976):2–5.

175. Jack L. Davis, "Mark Schorer's *Sinclair Lewis*," *SLN* 3 (Spring 1971):3–9.

176. Sheldon Grebstein, *Sinclair Lewis*, Twayne's United States Authors Series (New York: Twayne Publishers, 1962).

177. D. J. Dooley, *The Art of Sinclair Lewis* (Lincoln: University of Nebraska Press, 1967).

178. James Lundquist, *The Merrill Guide to Sinclair Lewis* (Columbus, Ohio: Charles E. Merrill, 1970).

179. Richard O'Connor, *Sinclair Lewis*, American Writers Series (New York: McGraw-Hill, 1971).

180. James Lundquist, *Sinclair Lewis*, Modern Literature Monograph (New York: Frederick Ungar, 1973).

181. Martin Light, *The Quixotic Vision of Sinclair Lewis* (West Lafayette, Indiana: Purdue University Press, 1975).

182. H. L. Mencken, Rebecca West, Sherwood Anderson, Constance Rourke, Robert Morss Lovett, Joseph Wood Krutch, Vernon L. Parrington, T. K. Whipple, Walter Lippman, E. M. Forster, Ford Madox Ford, Lewis Mumford, R. P. Blackmur, Robert Cantwell, Alfred Kazin, Maxwell Geismar, Edmund Wilson, Malcolm Cowley, Mark Schorer, and Geoffrey Moore.

183. Stuart P. Sherman, T. K. Whipple, Lyon N. Richardson, Mark Schorer, Charles E. Rosenberg, William B. Ober, D. J. Dooley, Sheldon Grebstein, Erik Axel Karlfeldt, Carl Van Doren, T. R. Fyvel, H. L. Mencken, Robert Morss Lovett, Joseph Wood Krutch, Haven Emerson, Edwin Muir, Henry Seidel Canby, and Lucy L. Hazard.

184. May Sinclair, Ludwig Lewisohn, Robert Littell, H. L. Mencken, Upton Sinclair, Sheldon Grebstein, Frederick J. Hoffman, Daniel Brown, Philip Allan Friedman, T. K. Whipple, Anthony Channell Hilfer, Maxwell Geismar, Alfred Kazin, and Mark Schorer.

185. For example, in "Revolt from the Village: 1920," *Nation* 113 (12 October 1921):407–12, Carl Van Doren placed *Main Street* in an important tradition. Among several interesting defenses of the small town are Archibald Marshall's "Gopher Prairie" *North American Review* 215 (March 1922):[394]–402, and George E. O'Dell's "The American Mind and 'Main Street,'" *Standard* (8 July 1922):17–20.

Edith Wharton indicated in "The Great American Novel," *Yale Review* 16 (July 1927):646–56, that Lewis had created interest in the small town—perhaps too much interest—but that *Main Street* is not the Great American Novel. In "Social Distance in Fiction," *Sociology and Social Research* 14 (November–December 1929):[174]–80, Emory S. Bogardus focuses on Carol and Will, Carol and Bea, Carol and Gopher Prairie clubwomen, the older English and the new Scandinavian. Ernest Brace discusses the popularity and influence of the novel in "Cock, Robin & Co., Publishers," *Commonweal* 13 (10 December 1930):147–49.

In his introduction to *Main Street* (Cleveland and New York: World Publishing, 1946), 7–9, Carl Van Doren tells of the furor surrounding its publication. In his afterword to the Signet *Main Street* (New York: New American Library, 1961), 433–39, Mark Schorer says that Lewis presents an effective picture of American small-town life in rendering Carol from the beginning (1912) to the end (1920) of an era. In "*Main Street* by Sinclair Lewis," *Carleton Miscellany* 4 (Fall 1963): 95–101, Donald Schier complains about Lewis's wavering satire, external realism, boring husband, and flighty wife. G. Thomas Tanselle in "Sinclair Lewis and Floyd Dell: Two Views of the Midwest," *Twentieth Century Literature* 9 (January 1964): 175–84, compares the dreamy growing youth of *Moon Calf* with the rebellious stifled woman of *Main Street*.

186. For example, besides the many heated book reviews of the novel, one finds L. M. Birkhead defending Lewis in two essays in his pamphlet *Is "Elmer Gantry" True?* (Girard, Kans.: Haldeman-Julius, 1928). In "Schorer and Satire," *New Republic* 133 (28 November 1955):23, Norbert F. O'Donnell accuses the critic of misreading *Elmer Gantry* in his "The Monstrous Self-Deception of Elmer Gantry" (1955), expanded in "Sinclair Lewis and the Method of Half-Truths," *Society and Self in the Novel* (New York: Columbia University Press, 1956), 117–44. Horton Davis, in *A Mirror of the Ministry in Modern Novels* (New York: Oxford University Press, 1959), 23–40, compares the central figures in *Elmer Gantry* and *The God-Seeker*, seeing Elmer Gantry surrounded by a few good ministers and Aaron Gadd surrounded by many bad missionaries. In "The Sources of 'Elmer Gantry,'" *New Republic* 143 (8 August 1960):17–18, James Benedict Moore discusses Gantry's real-life counterparts. Charles W. Genthe compares the religious novels of Frederic and Lewis in "*The Damnation of Theron Ware* and *Elmer Gantry*," *Research Studies of Washington State University* 32 (December 1964):334–43. Bruce D. Lockerbie suggests a likely background for *Elmer Gantry* in "Sinclair Lewis and William Ridgway," *American Literature* 36 (March 1964):68–72. In his afterword to the Signet *Elmer Gantry* (New York: New American Library, 1967), 419–30, Mark Schorer discusses Lewis's research, the novel's currency, form, and characterization. Samuel J. Rogal in "The Hymns and Gospel-Songs in *Elmer Gantry*," *SLN* 4 (Spring 1972): 4–8, identifies twenty-four items and explains their function. In "'Vulgar Barnyard Illustrations' in *Elmer Gantry*," *SLN* 4 (Spring 1972):8–10, Robert L. Coard likens the art of Lewis's animal imagery to that of a caricaturist or newspaper cartoonist.

187. For example, in his foreword to *Dodsworth* (New York: Modern Library, 1947), v–vii, Clifton Fadiman insists that though Lewis's language is dated, the problems he treats are not. In "Sinclair Lewis, *Dodsworth*, and the Fallacy of Reputation," *Books Abroad* 34 (Autumn 1960):[349]–55, Martin R. Asmus sees as an important ingredient in Lewis's reputation his truth-seeking, exemplified well in *Dodsworth*. Ramon Guthrie, in "The Birth of a Myth, or How We Wrote 'Dodsworth,'" *Dartmouth College Library Bulletin* 3 (April–October 1960):50–54, disavows any credit for helping Lewis. To reveal Lewis's ambivalence toward the businessman, Michael Millgate in "Sinclair Lewis and the Obscure Hero," *Studi Americani* 8 (1962):[111]–27, contrasts the typical middleman, Babbitt, with the

creative businessman, Dodsworth. In "A Whartonian Woman in *Dodsworth*," *SNL* 1 (Spring 1969):5–6, Hilton Anderson identifies the American expatriot Edith Cortright with Edith Wharton and three of her characters. Because James D. Barry, in "*Dodsworth*: Sinclair Lewis's Novel of Character," *Ball State University Forum* 10 (Spring 1969):8–14, reads the book as a novel of character, of awakening, instead of a sociological tract, he ranks it Lewis's best. Agreeing that it is Lewis's best novel, Daniel Brown in "The Cosmopolitan Novel: James and Lewis," *SLN* 1 (Spring 1969):6–9, compares it with *The Ambassadors*, both books posing the problem of how to live in the tense context of opposing cultures. John S. Hill in "Sinclair Lewis, *Dodsworth*, and the Nobel Prize," *Husson Review* 3 (May 1970):105–11, speculates about the impact the deeper, less satirical, more mature book had on the decision to award Lewis the Nobel Prize. While some critics praised Lewis for his new maturity, Robert L. Coard in "*Dodsworth* and the Question of Art," *SLN* 3 (Spring 1971):16–18, regards Lewis's strengths, after all, as those of the popular novelist of his time. In his Signet afterword to *Dodsworth* (New York: New American Library, 1972), 355–63, Schorer ranks the novel well above Lewis's first novel, *Our Mr. Wrenn*, and his last, *World So Wide*, and discusses the strength and weakness of the unsophisticated American character in a European context. Though the type appears in later books by Lewis, Glen A. Love in "New Pioneering on the Prairies: Nature, Progress, and the Individual in the Novels of Sinclair Lewis," *American Quarterly* 25 (December 1973):[558]–77, sees Dodsworth as Lewis's fullest and finest "Western idealist" equipped to create a better American city.

188. Readers of papers at the Sinclair Lewis Centennial Conference, St. Cloud, Minnesota, 7–9 February 1985, included: David D. Anderson, Lydia Blanchard, Martin Bucco, Walter H. Clark, Robert Coard, David Crowe, Garvin Davenport, Wheeler Dixon, Robert E. Fleming, Roger Forseth, Barry M. Gross, James Jones, Anna B. Katona, Bea Knodel, Eleanor Lincoln, Glen A. Love, James Lundquist, Frederick Manfred, James Marshall, T. J. Matheson, Wayne Meyer, W. Gorden Milne, Clara Lee Moodie, Salley E. Parry, Judy Parham, Edward J. Piacentino, John Rylander, Elmer Suderman, and Stephen L. Tanner. See *Sinclair Lewis at 100*, ed. Michael Connaughton (St. Cloud: St. Cloud State University, 1985).

REVIEWS

[Review of *Our Mr. Wrenn*]   Anonymous*

This is a story about a thoroughly nice little man whom one of his friends describes as having "an embryonic imagination and a virgin soul." The author makes him, for a New Yorker, singularly unsophisticated. But his type is all the more interesting for being unusual. In story and in treatment the novel is wholly of our own day, but in spirit and feeling it makes evident the paternity of Dickens. Mr. Wrenn is "ours" to his business employers—an art-souvenir company, for which he is sales entry clerk at a salary of $19 per week. He lives in the third floor front hall bedroom of a cheap lodging house, eats at a dairy lunch and is a bachelor thirty years old. But in the evening he enters paradise, for he reads descriptions of far countries in steamship and railroad folders, revels in moving picture shows of harrowing scenes and wonderful scenery of the mountains and deserts and islands of strange lands, and tantalizes himself with hints of "foreign color" in shabby New York streets. Desire of the distance is strong in his heart and life is one long dream of that Some Day when he will pack his grip and go holiday making across oceans and continents.

And at last he has a multiplicity and variety of adventures and experiences and sensations, which all fit neatly into the drawing. They are what might be expected to happen to "our Mr. Wrenn." And they are not at all what might be expected to happen to any one else. The rather whimsical little story is well off the usual line of fiction in its conception and especially so in its leading character. The author is said to have based some of his hero's experiences upon happenings which befel[l] himself while voyaging across the Atlantic on a cattle boat and wandering about England in desultory fashion.

*Reprinted, with permission, from the *New York Times Review of Books*, 1 March 1914, 100. Copyright 1914 by the New York Times Company.

[**Review** of *The Trail of the Hawk*]   Frederic Taber Cooper*

The Trail of the Hawk, by Sinclair Lewis, is the chronicle of an inveterate Rolling Stone, who nevertheless succeeds in gathering a modicum of Moss, in the shape of the pure, unadulterated joy of living. Carl Ericson, a born rebel against conventions, finds himself from boyhood up at war with the combined forces of family, school and society, all three of which unite in trying to mould him into the average colourless human being. Consequently throughout his earlier years he is in perpetual disgrace, at home, at school and at college,—to which last-named institution his father sent him at the cost of many sacrifices, and from which he was ignominiously dismissed because he espoused the cause of a discredited socialistic professor. Thus it happens that we find Carl in early adolescence a friendless and penniless wanderer, undaunted and thrilling with a sense of freedom and the boundless opportunity of satisfying his unquenchable curiosity about life. Picture him a big, broad-shouldered young Norseman, although the third generation of American birth,—with a skin as white as a girl's, cheeks like a rosy apple, and a smile that invariably inspires confidence. Getting a job is the easiest matter imaginable; jobs simply fall into his hands. The only difficulty is to keep them, for his unconquerable *wanderlust* forever goads him onward, not to something higher and better, but simply to something different, something that will enrich the variety of his experiences of life. The first of the three parts into which this chronicle is divided, "The Adventure of Youth," frankly drags a little. It covers, to be sure, the formative years and helps to explain why Carl is what he is, and not otherwise. Yet the author has overrated the importance of much of its detail. In fact, if the reader starts the story at the opening of Part II, "The Adventure of Adventuring," he will find that he knows almost as much about the hero and understands him as well as he does after he reverts to those opening chapters and'fills in the gap. That second part, on the contrary, is an undiluted joy. It is improbable, to be sure, almost burlesque, yet so joyous, so spontaneous, so kaleidoscopic in its varied scene and shifting action, that one needs must accept it with indulgent credulity. Not since Charles Reade wrote *Jack-of-all-Trades* has any hero of fiction filled so rapidly and so successfully such a motley assortment of crafts and trades, or with anything approaching such efficiency. Packer in a department store, waiter in a third-class restaurant, mechanic in an automobile factory, chauffeur, professional tramp and candidate for the bread line, porter in a Bowery saloon, facing the problem of saving four dollars out of a weekly salary of eight, in order to gratify a new ambition, namely to see the Panama Canal,—such is a brief epitome

*Reprinted from the *Bookman* 42 (October 1915):214–15.

of one phase of our Rolling Stone's career, a phase that all unconsciously is shaping him for bigger things. At Colon Carl makes friends of the right sort; work in the mines, at generous wages, soon puts a substantial reserve fund in his pocket, and the following year finds him in California, a partner in a profitable automobile repair shop. Then the big news reaches him of the first successful flights of Curtis and the Wright Brothers, and Carl recognises by instinct that here is the outlet for his pent-up energies, the one career for which his whole undisciplined nature has been crying out. Much has been written about aviation, both from the technical and the popular standpoint; but it would be hard to find anywhere else in current fiction any description that would give to the inexperienced a kindred thrill of breathless flight, of danger that is a fearful joy, and of confident omnipotence that is superhuman. And then, when this unrivalled "Hawk of the Air-men" is at the zenith of his powers, comes his third adventure, "The Adventure of Love." It is a pleasant little idyl and not badly done,—although Mr. Sinclair has less scope for his natural talent in the confined atmosphere of the ballroom and the boudoir than in the free air of heaven. But, of course, the inevitable happens: the Hawk has his wings clipped, flights are a thing of the past, a confining, although lucrative office position and a conventional apartment on the upper West Side begin to prey upon his nerves; and soon the happy couple are quarreling acrimoniously and often. But, Mr. Sinclair seems to say, you cannot cage a hawk for long; the born nomad must "keep going." So at the end we leave Carl and Ruth, once more adrift, bound haphazard for Buenos Ayres, with their bridges all burned behind them, and with no assurance of what lies ahead. Yet they are supremely happy, because "How bully it is to be living, if you don't have to give up living in order to make a living."

[Review of *The Job*]   H. W. Boynton*

The Job is a feminist document. It sets out to prove, by a particular instance, what obstacles of inheritance and tradition must be faced by the woman who wishes to make her own way; how those obstacles may be overcome; and what the reward may be. This might easily have been a bore, especially as the showman is rather prone to overdo his part. He has little notion of pinning himself down to the business in hand, the telling of his story, the embodying of his idea, but must step aside from it, at will, to lay down the law about all sorts of things. A good many

*Reprinted from the *Bookman* 45 (May 1917):316–17.

of the pages in this book might be cut out to its advantage. But Mr. Lewis has a story to tell, and does fairly embody his idea in interpreting the character of Una Golden. Una is not a striking person, her origin is as commonplace as possible, she has no marked beauty or charm. She is simply an American girl of the "small town," bred in the parasitic theory of woman's sphere, with narrowness all about her, and no hope for the future unless through breaking away and finding a broader atmosphere. That means, of course, New York. It is a quaint theory among current story-tellers that a dingy flat abreast of the elevated, *passim*, offers opportunities for broad and free living such as are unknown to any white cottage on any village street. Mr. Lewis, for one, does not conceal the fact that Una's first experience of New York is an experience of provincialism plus squalour and turmoil. But for one of her courage and sturdiness it does offer a starting-point. Una's ambition is not to achieve happiness or even pleasure, but to make her own way, to be herself to some purpose, "economically"and socially in the human sense. She is a nice little thing, with a basis of sound character to build her life upon. Mr. Lewis takes the easiest way with her, in one respect. The convenient method of emphasising a woman's strength is to surround her with feeble men. Una's father is one of the most pretentious and useless citizens of Panama, Pennsylvania. Her only suitor there is "old Henry Carson, the widower, with catarrh and three children." The men she knows more or less intimately in New York are (in the order of their appearance) (1) Sanford Hunt, an honest but not forceful young fellow-pupil at commercial school; (2) Julius Edward Schwirtz, paint salesman, "ungrammatical and jocose; he panted a good deal, and gurgled his soup"; (3) S. Herbert Ross, advertising manager of the *Motor and Gas Gazette*, a busy and clever piece of business machinery; (4) Walter Babson, roving young male, journalist, advertising man, and what not, with plenty of "temperament" and no moral anchor. It is to Babson that she gives her maiden heart, but he, loving her to the best of his ability, is only strong enough to leave her physically unharmed. His argument is that he has not "found himself" and does not deserve her. Perhaps he is right. After he has vanished westward upon his vague quest, Una marries the gurgling Schwirtz and accepts the parasitic life, until circumstance at last justifies her revolt from it. Then begins her real career; she wins in the open field against all business comers, males preferred; and when Babson turns up again, a made man, he is not, after all, so well made as she. The upshot is that partnership on equal terms—on money terms in particular—which is our current ideal of matrimony. What justifies the book, in the end, is not its "idea," or its incidental cleverness, which is notable, but its portrait of a woman. Una Golden is—herself.

[Review of *The Innocents*]   Anonymous*

The Innocents, by Sinclair Lewis (Harper; $1.25), is nothing to lose one's critical temper over. It will be hailed in hundreds of American homes as a "sweet little story"; and perhaps it should be dismissed as such with a brief and friendly notice. But, somehow, all of it, even Mr. Lewis's disarming preface, which points out that the tale is one "for people who still read Dickens and clip out spring poetry and love old people and children," thus absolving the author of all pretensions to writing for a critical audience, is irritating. One doesn't want Mr. Lewis to write sweet little stories for sentimental ladies to laugh and weep over. One remembers *The Trail of the Hawk* and *The Job*—neither of them a really big book, but both of them warmed by a rich, passionate interest in life and made dignified by a sincere searching after truth. They held out a promise. Some day, one felt, Mr. Lewis would outgrow his crudities and produce for us an American novel to which we might point with pride. Now comes *The Innocents* to break the promise.

The Innocents carries with it the fear that Mr. Lewis has "arrived," but by that easiest way which entices so many of our young American writers. A painted style, as our magazines bear witness, is popular with the crowd. Sentimentality is easier than truth and pays better. It takes a chaste soul—the soul of an artist—to recognize and reject what cheapens and degrades; and Mr. Lewis, one fears, does not even realize where the primrose path is leading him. If he did, he might not have had the courage to dedicate *The Innocents* to that "splendid assembly of young British writers" which includes Compton Mackenzie, Hugh Walpole, Oliver Onions, D. H. Lawrence, J. D. Beresford, Gilbert Cannan, Patrick MacGill, and, looming above them all, H. G. Wells. Any one of them has intellectual sophistication enough to reject the facile smartness of phrase, the essential flimsiness, of Mr. Lewis's latest book, which presents a spectacle made all the sadder by the traces of a better self revealed in it.

Among the well-remembered dislikes of one's childhood is the story of the little boy whose mother gave him loaf sugar with a few drops of rum on it to cure a cough. The little wretch soon learned to cough for the sugar, and, after that first step downward, descended to the gutter, where he died a drunkard's death amid his mother's vain self-accusations. One was familiar with tales of the same type invented, on emergency, by one's elders to illustrate what happened to children who didn't "mind"; so that one could not be intrigued into accepting the loaf-sugar tragedy just because it was in a book with pictures.

It is no longer considered good pedagogy to feed children on tracts,

*Reprinted from the *Dial* 63 (22 November 1917):531.

but tracts for adults, disguised under the more sophisticated title "fact stories," have been popularized long since by the *Saturday Evening Post*. They produce the same irritation that the story of the little boy and the rum produced. One believes in neither the story nor the moral.

[Review of *Free Air*]   Anonymous*

At first reading it is rather difficult to account for the undeniable charm of this novel. The characters and the plot are commonplace to the point of banality. A rich eastern girl taking her invalid father on a trip across the continent in a large machine; a poor but honest and attractive young westerner who attaches himself to the party in Minnesota as an escort and bodyguard; a snobbish suitor of the girl who turns up in Montana and does his best to reveal himself as a disagreeable cad: these are certainly the ingredients of the lightest kind of light fiction. In fact the outlines of such a story are sometimes found in thrillers like *Deadshot Dick* or *Her Western Lover*.

But these reflections do not help to explain the merit and interest of Mr. Lewis's novel. It is always more or less dangerous to speak about the "atmosphere" of a book; but the author really seems to catch the sweep and exhilaration of the great open country over which his characters wind their way. He writes in a spirit of unaffected buoyant joyfulness which is certain to infect the reader sooner or later. And his book is an Odyssey of the Northwest; his pictures of the farmers, hotelkeepers and smalltown merchants whom the travellers meet are distinctly drawn from first hand experience. As for the western boy and eastern girl, even if they are quite obvious, they are also quite human and natural. The author possesses a faculty of smooth and easy narration that makes the story glide along as quickly as the heroine's car, and makes the reader rather sorry when the journey comes to an end.

Mr. Lewis apparently set out to write an oldfashioned love story, with a liberal dash of humor and a rapidly changing scenic background of Middle and Far Western life. He also aimed to make his story entirely free from all serious problems, political, moral and philosophical. It may be said that he has attained all his objectives.

*Reprinted, with permission, from *New Republic* 21 (28 January 1920):275.

Consolation

H. L. Mencken*

After all, Munyon was probably right: there is yet hope. Perhaps Emerson and Whitman were right too; maybe even Sandburg is right. What ails us all is a weakness for rash over-generalization, leading to shooting pains in the psyche and delusions of divine persecution. Observing the steady and precipitate descent of promising postulants in beautiful letters down the steep, greasy chutes of the *Saturday Evening Post*, the *Metropolitan*, the *Cosmopolitan* and the rest of the Hearst and Hearstoid magazines, we are too prone, ass-like, to throw up our hands and bawl that all is lost, including honor. But all the while a contrary movement is in progress, far less noted than it ought to be. Authors with their pockets full of best-seller money are bitten by high ambition, and strive heroically to scramble out of the literary Cloaca Maxima. Now and then one of them succeeds, bursting suddenly into the light of the good red sun with the foul liquors of the depths still streaming from him, like a prisoner loosed from some obscene dungeon. Is it so soon forgotten that Willa Cather used to be one of the editors of *McClure's?* That Dreiser wrote editorials for the *Delineator* and was an editor of dime novels for Street & Smith? That Huneker worked for the *Musical Courier?* That Amy Lowell imitated George E. Woodberry and Felicia Hemans? That E. W. Howe was born a Methodist? That Sandburg was once a Chautauqua orator? That Cabell's first stories were printed in *Harper's Magazine?* ... As I say, they occasionally break out, strange as it may seem. A few months ago I recorded the case of Zona Gale, emerging from her stew of glad books with *Miss Lulu Bett*. Now comes another fugitive, his face blanched by years in the hulks, but his eyes alight with high purpose. His name is Sinclair Lewis, and the work he offers is a novel called *Main Street*. ...

This *Main Street* I commend to your polite attention. It is, in brief, good stuff. It presents characters that are genuinely human, and not only genuinely human but also authentically American; it carries them through a series of transactions that are all interesting and plausible; it exhibits those transactions thoughtfully and acutely, in the light of the social and cultural forces underlying them; it is well written, and full of a sharp sense of comedy, and rich in observation, and competently designed. Superficially, the story of a man and his wife in a small Minnesota town, it is actually the typical story of the American family—that is, of the family in its first stage, before husband and wife have become lost in father and mother. The average American wife, I

*From *Smart Set* 64 (January 1921):138–44. Reprinted by permission of the Enoch Pratt Free Library in accordance with the terms of the will of Henry L. Mencken.

daresay, does not come quite so close to downright revolt as Carol Kennicott, but that is the only exaggeration, and we may well overlook it. Otherwise, she and her Will are triumphs of the national normalcy—she with her vague stirrings, her unintelligible yearnings, her clumsy gropings, and he with his magnificent obtuseness, his childish belief in meaningless phrases, his intellectual deafness and nearsightedness, his pathetic inability to comprehend the turmoil that goes on within her. Here is the essential tragedy of American life, and if not the tragedy, then at least the sardonic farce; the disparate cultural development of male and female, the great strangeness that lies between husband and wife when they begin to function as members of society. The men, sweating at their sordid concerns, have given the women leisure, and out of that leisure the women have fashioned disquieting discontents. To Will Kennicott, as to most other normal American males, life remains simple; do your work, care for your family, buy your Liberty Bonds, root for your home team, help to build up your lodge, venerate the flag. But to Carol it is far more complex and challenging. She has become aware of forces that her husband is wholly unable to comprehend, and that she herself can comprehend only in a dim and muddled way. The ideas of the great world press upon her, confusing her and making her uneasy. She is flustered by strange heresies, by romantic personalities, by exotic images of beauty. To Kennicott she is flighty, illogical, ungrateful for the benefits that he and God have heaped upon her. To her he is dull, narrow, ignoble.

Mr. Lewis depicts the resultant struggle with great penetration. He is far too intelligent to take sides—to turn the thing into a mere harangue against one or the other. Above all, he is too intelligent to take the side of Carol, as nine novelists out of ten would have done. He sees clearly what is too often not seen—that her superior culture is, after all, chiefly bogus—that the oafish Kennicott, in more ways than one, is actually better than she is. Her war upon his Philistinism is carried on with essentially Philistine weapons. Her dream of converting a Minnesota prairie town into a sort of Long Island suburb, with overtones of Greenwich Village and the Harvard campus, is quite as absurd as his dream of converting it into a second Minneapolis, with overtones of Gary, Ind., and Paterson, N. J. When their conflict is made concrete and dramatic by the entrance of a *tertium quid*, the hollowness of her whole case is at once made apparent, for this *tertium quid* is a Swedish trousers-presser who becomes a moving-picture actor. It seems to me that the irony here is delicate and delicious. This, then, is the end-product of the Maeterlinck complex! Needless to say, Carol lacks the courage to decamp with her Scandinavian. Instead, she descends to sheer banality. That is, she departs for Washington, becomes a war-worker, and rubs noses with the suffragettes. In the end, it goes without saying, she returns to Gopher Prarie and the hearth-stone of her Will. The fellow is at least honest. He offers her no ignominious compromise. She comes back under the old rules, and is presently nursing a baby. Thus the true idealism of the Republic, the idealism of its Chambers of Commerce, its Knights of Pythias, its Rotary Clubs and its National Defense Leagues, for which Washington froze at Valley Forge and Our Boys died at Château-Thierry—thus this genuine and unpolluted article conquers the phoney idealism of Nietzsche, Edward W. Bok, Dunsany, George Bernard Shaw, Margaret Anderson, Mrs. Margaret Sanger, Percy MacKaye and the I.W.W.

But the mere story, after all, is nothing; the virtue of the book lies in its packed and brilliant detail. It is an attempt, not to solve the American cultural problem, but simply to depict with great care a group of typical Americans. This attempt is extraordinarily successful. The figures often remain in the flat; the author is quite unable to get that poignancy into them which Dreiser manages so superbly; one seldom sees into them very deeply or feels with them very keenly. But in their externals, at all events, they are done with uncommon skill. In particular, Mr. Lewis represents their speech vividly and accurately. It would be hard to find a false note in the dialogue, and it would be impossible to exceed the verisimilitude of the various extracts from the Gopher Prairie paper, or of the sermon by a Methodist dervish in the Gopher Prairie Wesleyan cathedral, or of a speech by a boomer at a banquet of the Chamber of Commerce. Here Mr. Lewis lays on with obvious malice, but always he keeps within the bounds of probability, always his realism holds up. It is, as I have said, good stuff. I have read no more genuinely amusing novel for a long while. The man who did it deserves a hearty welcome. His apprenticeship in the cellars of the tabernacle was not wasted....

Portrait of an American Citizen   H. L. Mencken*

The theory lately held in Greenwich Village that the merit and success of *Main Street* constituted a sort of double-headed accident, probably to be ascribed to a case of mistaken identity on the part of God—this theory blows up with a frightful roar toward the middle of *Babbitt*. The plain truth is, indeed, that *Babbitt* is at least twice as good a novel as *Main Street* was—that it avoids all the more obvious

*From *Smart Set* 69 (October 1922):138–40. Reprinted by permission of the Enoch Pratt Free Public Library in accordance with the terms of the will of Henry L. Mencken.

faults of that celebrated work, and shows a number of virtues that are quite new. It is better designed than *Main Street*; the action is more logical and coherent; there is more imagination in it and less bald journalism; above all, there is a better grip upon the characters. If Carol Kennicott, at one leap, became as real a figure to most literate Americans as Jane Addams or Nan Patterson; then George F. Babbitt should become as real as Jack Dempsey or Charlie Schwab. The fellow simply drips with human juices. Every one of his joints is movable in all directions. Real freckles are upon his neck and real sweat stands out upon his forehead. I have personally known him since my earliest days as a newspaper reporter, back in the last century. I have heard him make such speeches as Cicero never dreamed of at banquets of the Chamber of Commerce. I have seen him marching in parades. I have observed him advancing upon his Presbyterian tabernacle of a Sunday morning, his somewhat stoutish lady upon his arm. I have watched and heard him crank his Buick. I have noted the effect of alcohol upon him, both before and after Prohibition. And I have seen him, when some convention of Good Fellows was in town, at his innocent sports in the parlors of brothels, grandly ordering wine at $10 a round and bidding the professor play "White Wings."

To me his saga, as Sinclair Lewis has set it down, is fiction only by a sort of courtesy. All the usual fittings of the prose fable seem to be absent. There is no plot whatever, and very little of the hocus-pocus commonly called development of character. Babbitt simply grows two years older as the tale unfolds; otherwise he doesn't change at all— any more than you or I have changed since 1920. Every customary device of the novelist is absent. When Babbitt, revolting against the irksome happiness of his home, takes to a series of low affairs with manicure girls, grass-widows and ladies even more complaisant, nothing overt and melodramatic happens to him. He never meets his young son Teddy in a dubious cabaret; his wife never discovers incriminating correspondence in his pockets; no one tries to blackmail him; he is never present when a joint is raided. The worst punishment that falls upon him is that his old friends at the Athletic Club—cheats exactly like himself—gossip about him a bit. Even so, that gossip goes no further; Mrs. Babbitt does not hear it. When she accuses him of adultery, it is simply the formal accusation of a loving wife: she herself has absolutely no belief in it. Moreover, it does not cause Babbitt to break down, confess and promise to sin no more. Instead, he lies like a major-general, denounces his wife for her evil imagination, and returns forthwith to his carnalities. If, in the end, he abandons them, it is not because they torture his conscience, but because they seem likely to hurt his business. This prospect gives him pause, and the pause saves him. He is, beside, growing old. He is 48, and more than a little bald.

A night out leaves his tongue coated in the morning. As the curtain falls upon him he is back upon the track of rectitude—a sound business man, a faithful Booster, an assiduous Elk, a trustworthy Presbyterian, a good husband, a loving father, a successful and unchallenged fraud.

Let me confess at once that this story has given me vast delight. I know the Babbitt type, I believe, as well as most; for twenty years I have devoted myself to the exploration of its peculiarities. Lewis depicts it with complete and absolute fidelity. There is irony in the picture; irony that is unflagging and unfailing, but nowhere is there any important departure from the essential truth. Babbitt has a great clownishness in him, but he never becomes a mere clown. In the midst of his most extravagant imbecilities he keeps both feet upon the ground. One not only sees him brilliantly; one also understands him; he is made plausible and natural. As an old professor of Babbittry I welcome him as an almost perfect specimen—a genuine museum piece. Every American city swarms with his brothers. They run things in the Republic, East, West, North, South. They are the originators and propagators of the national delusions—all, that is, save those which spring from the farms. They are the palladiums of 100 per cent Americanism; the apostles of the Harding politics; the guardians of the Only True Christianity. They constitute the Chambers of Commerce, the Rotary Clubs, the Kiwanis Clubs, the Watch and Ward Societies, the Men and Religion Forward Movements, the Y.M.C.A. directorates, the Good Citizen Leagues. They are the advertisers who determine what is to go into the American newspapers and what is to stay out. They are the Leading Citizens, the speakers at banquets, the profiteers, the corruptors of politics, the supporters of evangelical Christianity, the peers of the realm. Babbitt is their archetype. He is no worse than most, and no better; he is the average American of the ruling minority in this hundred and forty-sixth year of the Republic. He is America incarnate, exuberant and exquisite. Study him well and you will know better what is the matter with the land we live in than you would know after plowing through a thousand such volumes as Walter Lippmann's *Public Opinion*. What Lippmann tried to do as a professor, laboriously and without imagination, Lewis has here done as an artist with a few vivid strokes. It is a very fine piece of work indeed.

Nor is all its merit in the central figure. It is not Babbitt that shines forth most gaudily, but the whole complex of Babbittry, Babbittism, Babbittismus. In brief, Babbitt is seen as no more than a single member of the society he lives in—a matter far more difficult to handle, obviously, than any mere character sketch. His every act is related to the phenomena of that society. It is not what he feels and aspires to that moves him primarily; it is what the folks about him will think of him. His politics is communal politics, mob politics, herd politics; his

religion is a public rite wholly without subjective significance; his relations to his wife and his children are formalized and standardized;
even his debaucheries are the orthodox debaucheries of a sound business man. The salient thing about him, in truth, is his complete lack of
originality—and that is precisely the salient mark of every American
of his class. What he feels and thinks is what it is currently proper to
feel and think. Only once, during the two years that we have him
under view, does he venture upon an idea that is even remotely original—and that time the heresy almost ruins him. The lesson, you may
be sure, is not lost upon him. If he lives, he will not offend again. No
thought will ever get a lodgment in his mind, even in the wildest de-
liriums following bootleg gin, that will offer offense to the pruderies of
Vergil Gunch, president of the Boosters' Club, or to those of old Mr.
Eathorne, president of the First State Bank, or to those of the Rev.
Dr. John Jennison Drew, pastor of the Chatham Road Presbyterian
Church, or to those of Prof. Pumphrey, head of the Zenith Business
College, or even to those of Miss McGoun, the virtuous stenographer.
He has been rolled through the mill. He emerges the very model and
pattern of a forward-looking, right-thinking Americano.

As I say, this *Babbitt* gives me great delight. It is shrewdly devised;
it is adeptly managed; it is well written. The details, as in *Main Street*,
are extraordinarily vivid—the speech of Babbitt before the Zenith Real
Estate Board, the meeting to consider ways and means of bulging the
Chatham Road Sunday-school, the annual convention of the real-estate
men, Babbitt's amour with the manicure-girl, the episode of Sir Gerald
Doak, the warning visit when Babbitt is suspected of Liberalism, the
New Thought meeting, the elopement of young Theodore Roosevelt
Babbitt and Eunice Littlefield at the end. In all these scenes there is
more than mere humor; there is searching truth. They reveal something; they mean something. I know of no American novel that more
accurately presents the real America. It is a social document of a high
order.

Sinclair Lewis   T. K. Whipple*

In *Arrowsmith*, as in *Main Street* and *Babbitt*, Sinclair Lewis is
interesting chiefly as a social critic, but this has never been his only
interest. He is a recorder as well as a critic of society; he is, after all,
at least at times, a novelist; and he is the product as well as the critic

*Reprinted, with permission, from *New Republic* 42, part 2, Spring Book Section
(15 April 1925):3–5.

of the society which he depicts." When I call him the "product" of it, I mean that he has gone through it and willy-nilly has been affected by it." To reproduce American society, to point out its faults, and to illustrate the effect of this society on a writer who grows up in it—this, surely, is to possess significance. *Arrowsmith*, like its predecessors, has all these elements of interest, but in somewhat different proportions. It pictures and it satirizes American life; its main interest, however, lies in the parallel which it suggests with the author's own life—in that it shows how the American environment affects the creative spirit. Of this theme Sinclair Lewis's whole works may be taken as in a sense illustrations.

Martin Arrowsmith is a physician who becomes a bacteriologist. Before he finally takes refuge in the wilds of Vermont where he can pursue his researches undisturbed, he encounters all the difficulties which the United States puts in the way of a doctor and an investigator who would like to be honest; he struggles with the commercialism of the medical school, the quackery which thrives in the country, the politics and fraud of a Department of Public Health in a small city, the more refined commercialism of a metropolitan clinic, and the social and financial temptations of a great institute for research. He is offered every possible inducement to prostitute himself to an easy success—manifest, worldly success. Nor is he indifferent to the pressures which are brought to bear on him; on the contrary, being a scientist by instinct rather than by reasoned conviction, he wins out in spite of himself. He would like to succeed, he has been contaminated by the success-worship with which he is surrounded, but he is unable to cope with an ineluctable honesty and stubborn drive in himself. In the end he succumbs to his own integrity.

To describe *Arrowsmith* as an attack on the medical profession is utterly inadequate. It is an attack on the United States. It is the story of any scientist, or any seeker for the truth—chemist, economist, historian, philosopher, theologian. Nor does it differ essentially from the story of the artist, of whatever species. It tells, in short, the troubles and obstacles met by all those who in this practical land of ours prefer, in Aristotle's terms, the theoretic to the active life, or, in equivalent terms, the creative to the acquisitive, or the contemplative to the practical life. It deals therefore with the most important theme, in my opinion, of all afforded by American life, and with one of the crucial questions of the ages. The quarrel is a persistent one, because it grows from a fundamental opposition between two types of people; the type on the one hand that cares only for getting on—for making good, for succeeding—and the type on the other that cares less for mere personal advancement and more for taking in the experiences of the journey and for asking "Why?" and "Whither?" The former type, the practical, is opposed to all those disinterested activities which disregard the main chance—the pursuit of knowledge and beauty for their own sake, the wish to investigate or to enjoy—which to the second type constitute the reasons for existence. Practical men, one might say, care only to exploit their environment; theoretic or contemplative men care only to get acquainted with it, to explore and realize and experience it as fully as possible. No one, I suppose, would deny that so far the practical men have had things pretty much their own way in this country—and what they have done with it Lewis has shown in *Main Street* and *Babbitt*.

There is no need of rehearsing in detail the panoramas of Gopher Prairie and of Zenith. Every one is familiar with their ugliness, dullness, hypocrisy, complacency, intolerance, standardization, conformity, inner emptiness, and discontent. Such is the society inevitably produced by whole-hearted devotion to making good, with a corresponding hostility to all activities which by their disinterestedness might interfere with that aim—a society in which science, art, and religion are prostituted and made bond-slaves to practical success, in which poetry becomes heartening doggerel, orchestras are valued as municipal advertisements, and prayer is found to conduce to prosperity. Furthermore, it is a society which stunts and thwarts and starves all who are not in accord with its ethos, which produces Raymie Wutherspoons, Guy Pollocks, Chump Frinks and Paul Rieslings. Of this society *Arrowsmith* also, though less exclusively satirical, is a satire, a national gallery of frauds and fakes; it contains, one might say, all *Main Street* and all *Babbitt*, and much more besides. It too will be invaluable to the future historian of the United States for its close observation and minute detail. Being a vertical rather than a horizonal view, it cuts across all strata of American life except that of the manual laborer, and is therefore more inclusive and more varied than the earlier books. Moreover, having a more sharply defined point of view, it is more positive, and it goes deeper, concerning itself less with the surface and more with a fundamental trait of the national character. It gains enormously from centering its focus, not on the exponents of social aberrations, but on an antagonist and to some extent a victim of them.

The chief importance of *Arrowsmith*, then, is that it shows the extreme difficulty of pursuing the creative or theoretic life in the United States. Furthermore, I should like to suggest that it establishes its thesis in two ways—not only by telling the story of its hero, but also by illustrating that of its author. As a writer Lewis has some curious traits, of which the most striking is his tendency to mimic or to imitate, to give a representation of reality which is the literary equivalent of glass flowers, Mme. Tussaud's waxworks, and barnyard symphonies. Closely allied are his dependence on his own experience and the care with which he gets up subjects, as he has got up medicine and bacteriology

for *Arrowsmith*. All these characteristics, indeed, are abundantly manifested in his latest book; yet *Arrowsmith* is also the best proof that
Lewis is capable of creative writing. It is much more of a novel than
Main Street or *Babbitt*; in characterization, for instance, it is greatly
superior. Leora, Martin's first wife, is by general consent Lewis's mas-
terpiece in the creation of character. Not only is she likable, but she
is indubitably real; though she is portrayed casually and without effort,
no other character I know of in modern American fiction equals her in
absolute final reality. And Martin suffers only in comparison with Leora;
although far more difficult than either Carol or Babbitt, he is more
understandingly and more successfully portrayed. Yet Martin is primarily a type, and reminds one of the preference which Lewis has shown
in all his novels for types rather than individuals. It is characteristic
of Lewis to care more for the representative of a class than for a single
human being as a human being; even Leora interests him less than his
typical fakirs in *Arrowsmith*. That may be why in general he contents
himself with an external treatment of his characters, rarely manifesting
much insight or sympathy or strength of feeling.

All these traits seem to point to a poverty of invention or of imagination—which in turn may be traceable to the influence of Lewis's environment. The growth of a creative mind is a dark and obscure subject,
but the guess may be hazarded that the food on which the creative
mind is nourished is experience and that a practical society operates
in various ways to deprive it of that food. For one thing, the sensuous
and æsthetic, the intellectual, above all the social experience which presumably is most vital to a novelist's development is simply not there—
not in Gopher Prairie, for instance—to be had. But of even graver consequence is the effect of such surroundings on the artist's outlook or
attitude. He needs to be receptive, to welcome experience, to be willing and able to surrender and abandon himself to it, forgetful of himself and absorbed by it. The fatal thing for him is to repel it, to be
on his guard against it. But to wholly practical people any impractical
person is ridiculous, possibly dangerous; and by their hostility they
evoke in him an answering hostility; they make him assume a defensive
attitude toward his environment. Yet for him to do so, for him to resist
experience, is suicidal; unless he can let go and freely yield himself to
it, his mind is denied its proper nutriment and cannot grow and mature
to its full strength. This want of inner substance in turn may entail
further consequences; it may lead to self-distrust, to undue self-consciousness, to a lack of integrity which appears as an unsettled, un-
stable point of view, to the assumption of alien standards in lieu of
authentic personal standards. Besides developing a generally defensive
attitude, an artist in a practical society, a society like that portrayed
in *Main Street*, *Babbitt*, and *Arrowsmith*, is almost certain to return

scorn for scorn, to seek an escape in the refuge of easy romanticism, or to try to deny his own nature and conform to the prevailing opinions.

Every point in the preceding could be profusely illustrated from the writings of Sinclair Lewis. For example, there is that uncanny knack of observation which enables him to mimic or to imitate so exactly to the life: this observation is as watchful as that of a wild animal on the lookout for its foes or as that of a Red Indian in the enemy's country. There is also his keen eye for inconsistencies or weaknesses in his prey—how quickly he pounces! Years of malicious scrutiny must have gone to the making of his last three volumes. Such observation is but one sign of a defensive attitude, an attitude which is also betrayed in the precautions he takes lest his readers misjudge him. He makes greater use of irony as a defensive weapon than any other writer I know of; he early made the discovery that if only he were ironical and showed that he knew better, he could be as romantic and sentimental and playful as he pleased. He writes as if always conscious of a hostile audience. He takes needless pains to make clear that he is more sophisticated than his characters, as if there were danger of our identifying him with them. He makes fun of their ingenuous enthusiasms, even when these enthusiasms have the best of causes. The result of it all is that he often seems unduly afraid of giving himself away.

In this respect he resembles his characters; nothing in them is more striking than their morbid self-consciousness. Only Will Kennicott and Leora are free from it. The others are always wondering what people will think, always suspecting that they are the objects of observation and comment—and in Lewis's novels they are generally right. They are constantly posing and pretending, for the benefit even of waiters and elevator-boys. They do not dare to be natural; they are self-distrustful, uncertain, and insecure. They are self-analytical, and self-contemptuous for their lack of sincerity; yet they continue to pose to themselves, adopting one attitude after another. They have no inner standards of their own, because they are not integral personalities—they have not, in fact, developed any real personality at all.

Lewis himself shifts his point of view so often that finally we come to wonder whether he has any. One of the great advantages of *Arrowsmith* over its forerunners is that in it there begins to emerge an almost established point of view. Otherwise, one would be inclined to call Lewis a man of multiple personality—save that all these personalities have a look of being assumed for effect. All the Lewises are disdainful of each other. When he has been romantic, he throws in a jibe at sentiment lest we think him sentimental; when he has been cynical, he grows tender lest he be thought hard; when he has been severe with a member of the Babbittry, he emphasizes the virtues of the common people and the absurdities of highbrows and social leaders. All his manifold attitudes, however, may be reduced to two basic ones: he is a romanticist, and he is a philistine—each bitterly satirical of the other. That is to say, he has tried to escape from his environment, and he has tried, with more success, to conform to it.

His romanticism is of two kinds. In the first place, there is in him much of the conventional romanticist and even of the sentimentalist. He has said of himself that he is "known publicly as a scolding corn-belt realist, but actually (as betrayed by the samite-yclad, Tennyson-and-water verse which he wrote when he was in college) a yearner over what in private he probably calls 'quaint ivied cottages.'" This is the Lewis who sympathizes with Carol in her dislike of Gopher Prairie and in her longing for "a reed hut built on fantastic piles above the mud of a jungle river," and who invents for Babbitt a dream of a fairy child playmate, "more romantic than scarlet pagodas by a silver sea." There is no essential difference between this romanticist and the more conspicuous one who has taken a tip from Arnold Bennett and gone in for the romance of the commonplace, although the latter despises the former. To establishing the strangeness and beauty of humdrum life Lewis devoted his first four books; he undertook to prove in *Our Mr. Wrenn* that a clerk's life in a Harlem flat is more romantic than travel in foreign lands, and in *The Job* that a stenographer is more romantic than Clytemnestra. This process is really no less an escape from reality than is the old-fashioned romance, for it consists, not in bringing out the essential quality and verity of ordinary life, but in casting a glamor over it and falsifying and sentimentalizing and pretti-fying it. The last three novels look as if most of the romance had worn off the commonplace, but there are traces of it, even in *Arrowsmith*.

Closely akin to the romanticist of the second sort is the Lewis who speaks as a man of the soil, one of the common herd, a Babbitt; he points out the essential goodness of small towns and their inhabitants and of boosters; he is homey and folksy, and strongly opposed to people whom he suspects of thinking that they are "superior." This side of Lewis is especially pronounced in the novels which preceded *Main Street*; long passages in them are sheer glorifications of Main-Streetism and of Babbittry. His whole tendency, when in this mood, is to strengthen and entrench the folk of Zenith and Gopher Prairie in their self-satisfaction and intolerance. In short, he is a philistine. He has not escaped contamination, he has partially conformed to his environment. He speaks, for example, its language. His technique of raillery he has learned from Sam Clark and Vergil Gunch; he merely turns their type of wit and humor back upon themselves; all his satire is a long tu quoque. His irony and sarcasm are of the showy variety popular on Main Street and in the Zenith Athletic Club. His style is founded on the uses of salesmanship, publicity, and advertising. He avails himself of all the tricks of a crack reporter to give a fillip to jaded attention. His people do not run, they "gallop"; instead of speaking, they "warble" or "gurgle" or "carol"; commonplace folk are "vanilla-flavored"; interior decorators are "daffodilic young men," "achingly well-dressed"; dancing becomes "the refined titillations of communal embracing." No wonder Lewis has sold satire to the nation—he has made it attractive with a coat of brilliant if inexpensive varnish. The excellence of his rare intervals of real writing is lost in the general glare.

For there are such intervals; and they bring us back to Lewis, the artist, by no means insensible to beauty or devoid of the tragic sense of life. Save for bits of description and scattered passages, this Lewis was largely obscured in *Main Street* and *Babbitt*; yet no doubt he helped lend animus to the satire of that society which is so fatal to artists. Certainly to him the credit is due for *Arrowsmith*, the story of a man who would rather find out about things than make good. Yet even *Arrowsmith*, though an artist's as well as a scientist's book, is the work of a mangled artist. Perhaps after all it is better so: Lewis's romanticism and philistinism and vulgarity of style make him powerful because they make him popular. The attack on American practicality needs its shock troops—could we afford to give up so effective a critic for a better writer? Perhaps it is worth spoiling an artist to have him take so salutary a revenge. Lewis is the most successful critic of American society because he is himself the best proof that his charges are just.

[Review of *Mantrap*]   D. R.*

Mr. Lewis, who must be forty years old and in whom the flames of revolt are presumably flickering to an even warmth, has distinctly come down from the high tension of *Arrowsmith*. In *Mantrap* he tells a slighter story with his customary deft realism and stacatto progression. A middle-aged New York lawyer on the edge of a nervous breakdown is induced to join a loud-mouthed, witless go-getter in a trip to the woods of northern Canada. Driven to frenzy by the querulous inferiority of his companion, he takes the first opportunity to escape in the company of an Indian trader to the latter's post at the end and finger tip of white civilization. Strangely, they become friends, and the New York lawyer finds himself at last in the abominable position of eloping with his friend's wife, and of being pursued by the injured and homicidal husband. After a weariness of despairing effort, the husband overtakes them; they ask him to shoot them, but he says, no, he has come

*Reprinted from the *Independent* 116 (19 June 1926):721.

to save his friend from his wife, a worthless woman who will destroy him. From that point on the story merely works itself out with the quiet irony of anticlimax. Mr. Lewis is not merely deft, he is almost deadly in the ferocious fidelity of his pictures. He never gives us a rounded man or a stereoscopic woman, but he digs his plate so deeply, he bites in with so caustic an acid, that his black-and-whites are profoundly striking and effective. Like Dickens, he has never succeeded in portraying a gentleman. It is characteristic of his method that the balanced, controlled, unexciting quality of the gentleman—or the lady— is ignored in his concentration on more pungent, eccentric types. The climber, the contented Philistine, the loud-mouthed whelp, the acquisitive, ardent woman—these striking, bold figures he can do superbly. But they are somehow types, rather than people, something to be satirized rather than men and women to be known—and pardoned. The world of his imagining is vivid but bleak; brittle, clean-cut cameo figures execute fantastic gestures like marionettes, independent of their own souls. It is a comedy of manners, not a human comedy of living creatures with all their lusts, selfishnesses, glories, and abnegations on their heads. He plays brilliantly with externals—not with dreams and confused, incoherent visions.

Sinclair Lewis and Blasphemy   Charles W. Ferguson*

In *Elmer Gantry* there is a certain stridor not to be found in the more important novels of Sinclair Lewis. Quite excusably, the man has written from animus, and the result is a glorious lampoon which only a person of Lewis's talent could design. He told the boys at Kansas City: "I'm going off to write a book about you; I'm going to give you hell." It is hell of a vigorous sort that he gave them. His achievement, in fact, lies in the hell he gave and not in the novel he wrote. As a novel, *Elmer Gantry* is simply the kind of story the bad boy of Baltimore would have written if he had turned his thought to fiction. Art has been subordinated to purpose. *Elmer Gantry* was of course inevitable, just as Sinclair Lewis and John Roach Straton were inevitable. Religious has become egregious. Emotions intensified by the war have grown rampant since the war's interrupted termination. Lewis reacted to these emotions in a way that could easily have been predicted. He grew angry at the absurdities of the faithful; he was fortunate enough to be able to carry out the threat so many of us make: to write a book about those who incite our contempt. Evolution produced Bryan, and Bryan pro-

*Reprinted from the *Bookman* 65 (March 1927):216–18.

duced the Lewis of today. Only as we envisage *Elmer Gantry* as the product of social forces can we approach it with any understanding. I do not mean to suggest that it is a lily in a manure lot so much as I mean to say that it is the repercussion of American intolerance and mediocrity. With things as they are, *Elmer Gantry* is a novel which sooner or later must have been written.

It is, I suppose, blasphemous, for blasphemy consists in speaking with disgust of these concepts and practices generally esteemed by any influential class. It is, however, more contumacious than blasphemous; it derides certain American Christians a vast deal more than it blasphemes the name of God. Yet the tone of *Elmer Gantry* will not be appreciated either by religionists or general readers; to the former it will seem irreverent, to the latter it will seem unrestrained.

It would be absurd to say that Mr. Lewis has been fair to ministers. He didn't mean to be and I see no reason why he should have been. We must remember that he is presenting Sinclair Lewis's minister. There is in Lewis enough of the sculptor to keep him from being a photographer. We have here, not ministers as they are, but ministers as Lewis sees them. He has caricatured, it may be, but the base and outlines of the original figure are recognizable. The author means to suggest that Elmer Gantry could live and succeed in America—a land where mediocrity dwells in high places and becomes the *sine qua non* of success. Personally, I have never known a minister quite so frankly disingenuous, quite so overtly given to philandering; but it would be possible, I confess, to take a composite of ministers in American history and in present day life and derive a Gantry. Here again *Elmer Gantry* becomes a social commentary and not a work of fictional art. As a character, Dr. Gantry lacks verisimilitude, and he lacks it more the longer he lives. The story of his conversion and inception into the ministry is unimpeachable. But immediately his seminary days begin, he loses vitality for me and degenerates into a bounder and a rogue in whom all the vices of all the preachers of the ages are incarnated. The dregs of the clergy are vigorously stirred to the top in this bitter concoction, but, Mr. Lewis believes, the dregs are there, and they are important.

It would be a mistake to quarrel with Sinclair Lewis for his view of ministers. If he has chosen to caricature instead of depict, it is his own business. To say that the man has not fairly represented the ministry is to be unfair to him—obviously he never intended to. It would be irrelevant to complain to Covarrubias that his drawing of Coolidge fails to look precisely like the million photographs or the more reverent portraits of our president.

Schmaltz, Babbitt & Co.   Henry Seidel Canby*

I have been reading with a wicked pleasure the monologues of Mr. Lowell Schmaltz which are to appear next week under the title of *The Man Who Knew Coolidge*. Sinclair Lewis, I believe, recites these monologues in his own inimitable fashion, and indeed they are meant to be spoken, as Dickens's *Pickwick* was meant to be read aloud. They have the true colloquialism which solemn naturalistic writers like Mr. Dreiser usually miss. Speech has its own rhythms, so delicate and individual that it takes the nicest ear to reproduce them, and those who accuse Sinclair Lewis of a lack of style have not noticed that, like Mark Twain and Dickens, he is a great artist in the subtlest style of all, the personal speech of highly individual men. Here in America, only Ring Lardner and Booth Tarkington in prose, and Robert Frost in verse, can approach his virtuosity. You must watch such skill as this, for Babbitt and Schmaltz speak with a complete authenticity that makes the truth of their satiric self-portraitures seem self-evident.

I would not give up a sentence of Mr. Schmaltz's self-story. He can keep me from a poker game as long as he held up his friends in the hotel while he gave them a close-up of Zenith's most admired mortician as a background of a story of which he forgot the point. I enjoy reading of his wife, Mame, and his spaniel and her canary, and the pert children. That he was a 100 per cent American I knew as soon as I read his name (Pennsylvania Dutch, *not* German), and he never disappoints me in his comments on the radio, Christianity (and the Reverend Elmer Gantry), hunkies, the Security League, California, and the difficulties of a pious he-man with sexual morality. He has, as they say, everything that belongs to his kind, and if I need to know anything of life beyond the Alleghenies (Mr. Schmaltz hates New York) he will tell me. Listen to him—

> And the picture he gave of California in the days before it was combined with the main streams and currents of American destiny— Say, it certainly'd make a fellow stop and think.
> Here was this great country. Here was these titanic mountains— well, I don't want to get highfalutin and poetic, but as I said in my little talk that I gave to the Kiwanis Club on my return from California, here was these titanic mountains with their snow-crowned tops kissing the eternal blue of that Western sky. And here, as Reverend Sieffer pointed out in his book, were those great canyons, stretching their silent but pine-filled depths up to the higher and unknown divides. And here was vast plains ready for the happy plow of

*From the *Saturday Review of Literature* 4 (24 March 1928):[697]–98. Copyright 1928, *Saturday Review*, reprinted by permission.

civilized man but as yet filled with nothing but the howl of the coyote. And here was this great big huge long seacoast with the waves of the blue Pacific beating against it but without one single solitary real-estate development or even a resort to prepare it for the coming and use of civilized men.

And then what happened? What happened!

Say, to my mind, what happened in California, and that within just a few years, mind you, is one of the miracles that to a *thinking* man proves the providence and care of God that has always guided the destinies of the American people.

Some guy—and say, it's a damn shame but I don't suppose his name will ever be known to history—some guy in Iowa (or it might have been Minnesota or Wisconsin or Illinois or even Missouri, yes, or for that matter he might have come from Kansas)—but anyway, this fellow, he saw that when the great Middle Western population had finished their efforts in growing corn and those equally valuable and constructive efforts in selling supplies to the farmers who are, after all, say what you may, the great backbone and strength of our nation—he saw that it would be the proper caper for these gentlemen to retire to that lovely and you might say idyllic California coast and there in their old age enjoy the fruits of a lifetime of arduous and frugal toil.

And then what happened? What happened!

All along that barren land, lovely little bungalows began to spring up. Where formerly there hadn't been one single darn' thing but seashore and mountain valleys, there sprung up, almost overnight you might say, a whole kit and bilin' of dandy little bungalows and where formerly, as Reverend Sieffer says, you couldn't hear a blasted thing but the sullen roaring of the breakers on the shore, you could hear phonographs going, radios tuned in on Chicago, nice jolly normal young folks dancing to the sound of jazz, and the sound of Fords and motor cars as the folks started off for a nice picnic in some canyon.

Say, you take it from one who's traveled! I've seen it and I know! I've seen beauty spots in California where even twenty years ago there couldn't 've been hardly a single human being in sight—some point of interest filled with holy quiet between the eternal hills; and now you'll find there, especially on a Sunday, no less than maybe a couple hundred cars parked, and all the folks out looking at the scenery.

And please listen once more—

Service is imagination. Service is that something extra, aside from the mere buying, stocking, and delivery of goods, that so tickles the comfort and self-esteem of a customer that he will feel friendly and come back for more. Service is, in fact, the poetry, the swell manners, the high adventure of business.

And this is the first time in history that a nation has conceived the massive, the daring and glittering idea, that you can do more than just sell the customer the goods he wants—that you can, in fact, tie him to you by that subtle form of friendliness known as Service, so that, without its really costing you much of anything, you can make him feel that he's getting double value for his money.

Service! If the Rotarians and Kiwanians had done nothing else, they would have justified themselves and made their place secure in history for all time by their insistence on the value and beauty—the, in fact, if I may without sacrilege say so, *religion* of Service.

Lowell Schmaltz is too convincing. He is a human victrola purring on in a monotone about laundry-machines, Calvin Coolidge, cafeterias, the kiddies at home, Americanization, birth-control, with now and then a song or a story. He is as informative as a radio, and his mind is like the air on a busy evening, buzzing with platitudes, quotations, statistics, stories on the wife, sales talk, and mixed ideals. He is the behaviorists' ideal man, a machine that reacts to dogs, sex (within limits), and business; his brain is plastered with advertising posters that tell him what to think. Philosophically considered, he is a low variety of the human race, successfully adapted to life in an industrial civilization, with the morals of a domestic animal, the culture of a housebroken barbarian, and the soul of a flea. Only his heart is large and pulpy—but for dogs and children, not women—women, or at least familiar women, annoy and puzzle him. In short, Lowell Schmaltz is the satirist's conception of the American bourgeois, model 1928. He is what happened after George F. Babbitt.

I do not know why Sinclair Lewis has not been more often compared with Charles Dickens. Dickens could do those immensely humorous figures, who express a philosophy of life in monologues that never seem funny to them. Schmaltz is as convincing as Tony Weller, and for the same reason. He exists; he is one of the comic gallery to which we turn for reassurance when real men and women seem dull and inanimate. I believe more thoroughly in the existence of Falstaff and Tony Lumpkin and Winkle and Babbitt than in some of my own boyhood acquaintances who have lost the living principle in growing older. Lowell Schmaltz is not to be doubted for a moment—but he is far surer than I am that he represents America.

In so far as Art is concerned, we may rest content. Sinclair Lewis has it; Lowell Schmaltz is a creation. But Sinclair Lewis will let neither his critics nor himself (and this is sometimes a misfortune) stop with Art. He challenges investigations as a sociologist and historian—and so did Dickens—and raises questions which will make a good deal of trouble for future writers of theses on "The Truth to Contemporary Fact in Sinclair Lewis's Satires."

Fiction allows only the very great and the very small to escape with Art as their only criterion. Even Shakespeare is at least one-third an Elizabethan, if two-thirds a man for all the ages, and his borrowed theory of kingship will sometimes quite offset his first-hand studies of human nature. Dickens's humanitarianism makes him unreliable whenever he encounters social injustice. The cause was good, but that does not excuse his sentimentalism. Nor does Sinclair Lewis's art justify or explain his irritable discontent with where we have got to now in America.

There is more indignation than discontent in Dickens. Messrs. Dodson and Fogg indicate a deplorable condition of legal morality, and one learns, even in *Pickwick*, that medicine, the army, innkeeping, and the prisons were in sad need of reform, yet it is a jolly old England nevertheless, there are good beer, good jokes, honest and honorable men, good talk, good living. While much needs changing, more had better stay as it is, and indeed we have been running educational tours to England ever since in the hope of still finding some of it as it was—an inn, a dinner, or Sam Weller's descendants.

Mark Twain, to introduce a still more relevant name into this discussion, was also not discontented with his country, although his bitter distress over life in general (not just America) increased as he aged, until it far exceeded in depth of pessimism Sinclair Lewis's petulance. He too, like Dickens, like Lewis, could create characters that stepped from his books to testify to their own reality—Huckleberry Finn, Tom Sawyer, Col. Sellers. He, too, like Lewis, dealt with homely colloquialism, and was more interested in the barroom of a Mississippi packet than in high talk of Fifth Avenue. But Twain liked his America, liked it almost too well, as *Innocents Abroad* naively testifies. His Americans boast (like Mr. Schmaltz) of their country, they cheat their neighbors in the name of progress, are sentimental over women and children while condemning both to unlovely lives. In this they resemble Lewis's twentieth century bourgeoisie, and also in their easy intoxication by words—and if instead of "service" and "practicalness," they rolled their lips over "progress" and "liberty," the self-deception is identical. I am thinking particularly of that lovable blow-hard, the grandfather of all American boosters, Col. Sellers, and his dream world of the immediate future gilding a present of poverty-stricken, whiskey-soaked, rough-and-tumble frontier. But Mark Twain loved Col. Sellers and so did the friends and relatives he deluded, and there is no bitterness in the description of the Colonel's family dining on turnips for their health's sake.

But no one loves our American bourgeoisie. Schmaltz has the kind heart of the American democrat—he fights for his dog and spoils his children—but his boasting would be an intolerable bore except for Lewis's irony, and his ideas on man's place in the universe have not even the merits of an illusory dream. Sellers lived in an impossible future, but Schmaltz is content with an ugly present, where "dandy" gas-filling stations, automobiles that don't squeak, wives that patronize culture, and a Zenith that resembles the New Jerusalem in that all the inhabitants congratulate each other on being there instead of in New York or Paris, completely satisfy the longings of 100 per cent man. If he wants anything more, he is a Bolshevik.

Why does Lewis so bitterly hate this smug bourgeoisie, whose round faces (no longer lean and long—that was Mark Twain's type) one has seen before in Dutch pictures and in frescoes of late Rome? Why do we all take a malicious joy in reading of Schmaltz; and how he lied about his friendship with Coolidge, and how his cousin called his bluff when he tried to borrow money, and how he muddled ideas like a shrewd ape just taught to talk? For no one, probably not even Lewis, believes that the everyday American is as bad as all that. Only Europeans and a few Easterners admitted that George F. Babbitt was a true summary of the Middle West. You will not find him in Willa Cather, or in Booth Tarkington, or in Dreiser, or Anderson, and they know their America and can cut and slash when they wish. Men trying to be Babbitts, men on the way to become Lowell Schmaltz, are alas, too common, but few achieve; there is much more to the American story than a degeneration into an adding machine with an upper row of platitudes for thought.

I repeat, whence comes a bitterness that can be elicited only by a type not an individual? Why are Lewis's figures not ugly, as Dickens's so often are, not crude, absurd, or malignant, like Mark Twain's, but gross, unlovely, contemptible, ridiculous, petty, mean, without a single redeeming feature except a weak will to be good?

There is one answer worth giving, if only because it avoids the complexities of personal attitude, the difference between Dickens's incorrigible jollity, Mark Twain's exaggeration, and Lewis's sociological view of a world for which science has made a new pattern. Dickens loved his England as much as he hated its Scrooges and Heeps. As for Mark Twain, his America was all in the making, and, whatever the realities, its hopes were far nobler than the actualities of the historic past. The Yankee in King Arthur's Court was vulgar, but he was an idealist. Col. Sellers dealt in impossibilities, but impossibilities for his generation only. Above the dirt of a Missouri cabin, the mud of a prairie street, the quaint intellectuality of a primitive people, rose a vision that was certainly not Zenith, but nearer imperial Rome on a democratic basis. It was impossible to despise (as Lewis despises) men and women who lived on hog and hominy, yet talked of Zion, and named their towns Athens, Ithaca, and Rome.

But Babbitt and Schmaltz live in a civilization that in mechanism has gone beyond the wildest dreams. They roll upon asphalt, bathe in porcelain, draw music from the air, read the world's news (or can read it) every morning, profit by a credit system that stretches across the oceans, are lapped about by insurance, guarded by a public security that makes hazard an accident, can do with words for religion since fear is far off, and their souls are too fat to yearn. Education—or at least the body of knowledge which teaches how to live by machinery— is had for the asking. The Romans, who conquered the world, had no decent transportation and made no single improvement for centuries in the art of war, but Babbitt and Schmaltz (and please compare *their* features with those powerful faces of the Romans of the great period) have everything auxiliary to power, progress, and one might suppose happiness. Yet they remain Schmaltz and Babbitt!

And this is what makes Lewis, and his kind, so sarcastic, so ironical, so unjust to the everyday American. For Lewis has no pity, he can have no pity, for these men who have everything—except intelligence, idealism, and a soul. You pity the poor, the oppressed, the hopeful who cannot achieve; but men with prosperity bubbling about them, with a button to push or a lever to move for every desire, you scorn, you despise them for remaining swine when their pig pen has been tiled, piped, and wired, with a runway to Europe, and a loud speaker installed over the trough.

Are they swine? No more than Dickens's England was all pettifoggers, and Twain's America all cheats and blow-hards. Lowell Schmaltz is an ass, but that is his individual not his generic quality. He represents a true tendency, but he is not a true type. Even in his fatuous asininity he wonders sometimes—

> I tell you, Walt, I'm kind of puzzled. Sometimes I almost kind of wonder (though I wouldn't want to be quoted) whether with all the great things we got in this greatest nation in the world, with more autos and radios and furnaces and suits of clothes and miles of cement pavements and skyscrapers than the rest of the world put together, and with more deep learning—hundreds of thousands of students studying Latin and bookkeeping and doctoring and domestic science and literature and banking and window-dressing—even with all of this, I wonder if we don't lack something in American life when you consider that you almost never see an American married couple that really like each other and like to be with each other?
>
> I wonder. But I guess it's too much for me. I just don't understand—

And that wonder is more significant than Lewis will admit.

The vital question, of course, is whether American man, and European man, is going to rise to the level of his environment. He is a child now, wondering at his radios, complacent over his automobiles, fascinated by his success with capitalism, just as his grandfather on the Mississippi marvelled at his millions of free acres, was complacent over his weedy streets, and rejoiced at his thousands where ten Indians roamed before. Acres, roads, population, are an old story in the history of the race, and even when our grandfathers were young one could laugh tolerantly at their obsessions. But we are dazzled by the wonders of the machine world and a little afraid—even Sinclair Lewis. It piques us to see man, with his finger on the lightnings and his foot on power, smugger than ever before, and still content to take his thinking from the dark ages and his morality from words. We expose him for the petty fool he is by comparison, not with his own past, but with that machine which works so smoothly beneath him, having adapted itself to power and power to it.

And Sinclair Lewis would have been a wiser novelist if in this new book, and in *Elmer Gantry*, he had realized the nature of the reforming passion which makes him hot. His irony is salutary and I believe in it; he scores again and again; but his estimate of the contemporary American is no fairer than Swift's study of the Yahoos. They might have been horses, said Swift, but they chose to be apes. They might be the ideal men of H. G. Wells's Utopian state, says that idealist, Lewis, but look at Lowell Schmaltz—look at him, and grind your teeth, and swear!

Well, I see him. He seems to me absurd, pathetic, but still human. I think that Lewis himself has had too much machinery in his cosmos. He has whirled through Gopher Prairie at sixty miles an hour, making notes. He has taken the American bourgeoisie at its own expressed valuation, which is a mistake Dickens and Twain never made. He would judge men by their opportunities, which is a doubtful proceeding. He forgets that presumably the first result of primitive man's discovery of iron was more slaughter. He takes a sow's ear (if Mr. Schmaltz will pardon the epithet), mercerizes it, and then spits on the meretricious thing because it is not a silk purse.

Have charity, Mr. Lewis, and a little more humor (wit you have never lacked), and patience, and don't expect human nature to keep up with its inventions, for it never has, nor will. We see why you hate *homo Americanus*—and why many more are going to hate him, if, living on gold floors, he continues to eat with his fingers and think with his feet; but that you understand, or properly estimate, all of him, in the round, with that sympathy which is indispensable to understanding—well, thank heaven, you don't! There is more to him than that posterior which you so justly drub.

Samson Agonistes   Frances Lamont Robbins[*]

If Sinclair Lewis lives long enough there should be no type of American whose braveries, frailties and frustrations he will not have investi-
gated and disclosed. Each of his books has come home to a great many
readers. *Dodsworth* will do so with painful insistence. It has left us
more profoundly depressed than the most hysterical Russian novel. Only
once or twice in *Babbitt* has Lewis written anything so sad as this book.
In tempo it is slower than his previous work. But, if less strident, only
in that is it less American. Whatever one may think of Lewis's creative
and literary gifts, one is bound to acknowledge his understanding of the
American idiom, character and scene.

Sam Dodsworth, at fifty, is persuaded partly by his restless wife
and partly by a recrudescence of his boyhood longing to walk distant
roads, to sell his extremely successful and self-created automobile business and go to Europe. Leaving their daughter married and their son
at Yale, the Dodsworths proceed to England where the agony of Samuel Dodsworth begins. Sam and Fran, his wife, are upper-class Americans: that is, materially, they are successful, educated, intelligent,
useful; spiritually, they are children, requiring coddling and toys. The
Sams of America are Samsons, easily shorn of their strength by the
shears which the Frans, their brummagem Delilahs, wield. When the
Dodsworths were married Sam was a warm-hearted, handsome foot-
ball player; Fran, a lovely, over-nurtured doll. Sam idealized and had
a normal physical appetite for her. Fran had a clinging and a domineer-
ing affection for Sam—and not enough children. When Sam, having released his emotions in work and play, woke Fran at two in the morning
after poker, he had a simple passion for her. But she having used
energies and no emotions on society and good works, needed a scene,
and had only anger for him. He turned her into a pretty pet goddess:
she turned him into a reliable easy-chair. When he left work, she was
no refuge to him, and when she left social occupations, he was no playmate to her. That, and the loneliness of Europe destroyed them both.
Fran, ineffectually romantic, slipped into verbal flirtations which eventually had to become more than verbal but which demanded and received no more emotion than a new hat. Sam, with nothing to make
him feel big and important, wandered like a lost soul through the most
ghastly of Europes, not the homely Europe of the sight-seer but the
Europe of social climbing expatriates, shady hangers-on and Europeans
alternately patronizing and covetous. He left Fran twice, once to go
back to an America that had forgotten him, once to eat lotus with a
woman clever enough to nourish his ego with fair words. As each of

*Reprinted from *Outlook and Independent* 151 (20 March 1929):466–67.

Fran's affairs collapsed, she called for him and he went to her. Finally, he perceived too plainly the shears she used. He took her home and returned himself to the woman who could make him believe that his shorn head was covered once more with manly curls. But the light of his eyes had been put out. Sometimes, if she tried hard, Edith, mother and nurse, could make him forget Fran for two whole days.

In *Dodsworth*, Lewis is lost in the tragedy of his story He does not patronize his characters, nor is he detached from them. There is frank sentimentality in his pity for Sam, personal vindictiveness in his scorn for Fran. His unfailing observation and facility in the minute reporting of character have peopled his book with authentic types. Every person, every place, every situation is photographically clear. There is no more beauty in *Dodsworth* than in an ordinary newspaper story. There is no subtlety and no irony. It is a mistake to think of Lewis as an ironist. He is the cameraman and producer of the great American movie serial. This instalment is called "Samson Agonistes." And there is a moral. Many of Lewis's critics will complain that he exposes a painful situation and suggests no remedies although they would accept eagerly any symposium of learned opinion on "What is Wrong With American Marriage." But the particular is always more poignant than the general, and Lewis's book opens up a wide field for speculation. Men, here, retain the pioneer dread of spiritual entanglements. Women have not succeeded in adjusting unchanging biological needs to changed economic and cultural conditions. The machine age subjects both men and women to too great nervous and mental strains and offers them too few small emotional outlets. The fierce personal pride of the Nordic demands the "stiff upper lip," the "whistling to keep up courage" which gives a false sense of security. All these things go to make husbands and wives for whom Samson and Delilah are prototypes. Obviously they must be thought about for they must be remedied. Somehow Samson must be kept from his agony, the shears taken from Delilah's hands. The man is young and strong and guileless. What if he does lay about him with the jawbone of an ass? He has work to do in the world. And Delilah must remember that, even shorn and blind, Samson pulled the temple down.

Sinclair Lewis

Bernard DeVoto[*]

The truth is that Sinclair Lewis is a warring marriage, a divided soul, a novelist and a satirist forever at each other's throats. The virtues

[*]From the *Saturday Review of Literature* 9 (28 January 1933):398. Copyright 1933, *Saturday Review*, reprinted by permission.

of the satirist are the defects of the novelist. He has never yet succeeded in creating a complex character nor, in the best sense of the word, a sophisticated one. He has not given us a person of mature intellect or one in whom the passions of the mind or of the spirit seem credible. When he draws a college professor, he manipulates a cliché from the comic strips with the single-minded enjoyment of Booth Tarkington drawing a silly young dramatist of a later day than his own. If he should draw a duchess, we would be aware of her red flannels. When he essays a scientist we get only Martin Arrowsmith, a Babbitt touched with inspiration, or Sondelius, a study in advanced glee-club portraiture, or Gottlieb, an adventure in pure tears. The pastels, the chiaroscuro of personality are quite beyond him. He has made his way through the American scene with a naïveté, a simplicity of point of view, a limpidity, and even a shallowness which it is now time to pronounce invincible. And yet these qualities have enhanced his satire. Simplicity enables him to concentrate his superhuman energy; insensitiveness to chiaroscuro prevents the doubt that would be fatal. He becomes a flaming hate, and out of that hate he has written the most vigorous sociological fiction of our time, in America or anywhere else. Be sure that it is accompanied by a corresponding admiration, which gave us Gottlieb and Sondelius and Ann Vickers, but that admiration too is a simple passion and they also are creatures of simplicity, who exist primarily as channels for the hate directed at the milieu that they struggle against.

Ann Vickers, Lewis's first novel in four years (it appears that he chucked the labor manifesto about which rumors once circulated), makes all this plain. For what has been said above merely announces that Sinclair Lewis was shaped by the Herbert Croly age in American thinking—the pioneer era in Greenwich Village, the days of generous, idealistic thinking about the future in America, the last generation of American hope. He is Randolph Bourne writing novels, and in his novels that liberal hope meets the reality of post-war America and, its eyes opened, goes the way of all optimism. So he turns now to hagiology, giving us a saint of that movement, a nun of the sisterhood most consecrated and most esteemed in that happy noon. Her legend has all the fecundity, all the gusto, all the hate that gave life to the earlier novels. It is Lewis writing, in matters of mere style, rather better than he ever wrote before. It is magnificently informed—instinct with a hundred qualities of the time it deals with that only Lewis could seize and fuse. A comparison is just: the novel partly coincides, in time and intention, with Forty-second Parallel, and of the two Lewis's is much more alive, much deeper, and infinitely more aware. Beside it, the work of Dos Passos seems precious, somehow inert and more than a little flat.

Ann Vickers is a sister of Martin Arrowsmith—simple-minded and single-minded, dogged, undeluded, honest with herself, capable of the tumultuous activity that gets things done in the world. She is a suffragette, a social worker, a "penologist," and finally the superintendent of a prison. Unlike her predecessors in Mr. Lewis's biography, she does not originate in Winnemac, that state which no one who is sensitive to the feel of words could have named, but in Illinois. First converted to reform by a cobbler who is a sentimental socialist, she experiments with debating and "leadership" in college, joins a suffrage flying-squadron, and is jailed for biting a policeman, works in settlement houses, has a fling at charity, spends some time as a matron in a Southern penitentiary, and eventually becomes both the head of a women's prison and a national authority on reform, ending by seeing her lover, a dishonest judge, condemned to the system she hates and delivered from it by methods she has denounced. Her story is loosely strung, panoramic, and headlong, like all its predecessors. Ann's is somewhat more biological—in the earlier Lewis novels people seldom went to bed together except in *Elmer Gantry*, and there only meretriciously—but the biology is as simple and unromantic as Ann herself. Passion, even sentiment, as a human motive eludes Mr. Lewis. He is better at hate.

It is hate that has made his earlier novels memorable, and it is hate that provides most of what is good in this one. It is spent lavishly on the politicians and reformers who are to *Ann Vickers* what pastors were to *Elmer Gantry* and doctors and bacteriologists to *Arrowsmith*, and it rises to the finest rhapsody he has yet given us when Ann goes to the State penitentiary at Copperhead Gap. Those pages are Lewis at his purest, most concentrated, most powerful—hurling at our naked nerves cruelty and stupidity, ugliness, graft, bribery, wretchedness, hopelessness, despair. Public attention will probably concern itself mostly with Copperhead Gap—approval and resentment will center there. And yet those pages and the magnificent hatred that produces them are not all. For Ann's career covers most of the thinking that was going on in America during its time. Constantly interrupted by Mr. Lewis's scolding and by his frankly Thackerayan essays on a myriad liberal themes—published separately, they would make a year's output for any Foundation—it does project Our Times, and on the whole more truly than Mr. Sullivan. It is an America violently caricatured by a satirist and further distorted by the lens of the hopeful generation, and yet it is the America we know, more profoundly seen and more vigorously rendered than anywhere else in our fiction.

There you have him. Too unscrupulous a satirist, too defective a technician, too limited by the intellectual and emotional clichés of his generation, too naïve and too earnest, Sinclair Lewis is nevertheless the best novelist of his generation in America. He knows America better than any of the others, and he has conspicuously what they lack, fecundity and strength. Mr. Van Doren is right in calling him masculine. But why be euphemistic? The word is "male." He has extraordinary power, virility, boisterousness, and sheer nervous and muscular energy. They are qualities which dissolve away his shortcomings and which cannot be spared from fiction, these days of anemic invention and querulous estheticism.

Still, he is no sun god. Mr. Van Doren's expectation that *Babbitt* will live on long after Detroit is dust seems to me a little silly. Mr. Van Doren, not I, is responsible for the appeal to Mark Twain who, he feels, had as wide a sweep as Mr. Lewis but was otherwise inferior to him. But *The Adventures of Huckleberry Finn* possesses, besides an infinitely deeper and wiser knowledge of America, a serenity that makes the anger of the Lewis novels seem a trivial and somewhat hysterical yell. In that serenity, not elsewhere, immortality resides. The shadow of a period is already on Lewis—already he seems, even in *Ann Vickers*, a little shrill. Public preference moves on to novels written with a firmer technique, to themes whose tragic despair goes deeper spiritually than his basic optimism, to methods more rigorous and ideas more skeptical. That, no doubt, is a fashion and will pass, but first it will establish a sense of proportion about Sinclair Lewis. The Detroiters of that day, in their unfallen city, will say truly that he was the finest American novelist of his period, but in that day no American of genius was writing novels.

Including Sinclair Lewis   T. S. Matthews*

It is interesting to watch your elders and betters grow older. If they happen to have been heroes of yours, you observe them with a feeling more emotional than curious—you make pitying excuses for their "mellowness," their "ripe fulfilment of their early promise"; as their spurious colors fade you may even see some "grandeur" in their "starkness." But Sinclair Lewis has never been one of my heroes. I have always thought his reputation as a great American satirist was a great American joke; he always seemed to me as defenseless a romantic as one of his own Babbitt-businessmen. A satirist has to feel superior, and Sinclair Lewis has not felt superior since *Main Street*. Being uncomfortable, and angry with the things that make you uncomfortable, is not the same thing as feeling superior. His "satire" has become a rudderless indignation, a stale and whimsical, turn-the-rascals-out liberalism, which has taken the specific form of caricaturing individual types he happens

*Reprinted from *New Republic* 77 (31 January 1934):343.

to dislike. His restless spirit is that of a high-pressure journalist, a roving reporter who covers one assignment after another, usually in a critical spirit but never from a critical point of view.

For the subject of *Work of Art* he has not sought very far. Arnold Bennett did it before him, in a longer book that seems shorter. But Bennett's *Imperial Palace* was simply a *tour de force* glorifying his lifelong love, the luxury hotel; he was too sensible a man and too competent a writer to preach a sermon on so dubious a text. Sinclair Lewis, on the other hand, not content with reëstablishing the already labored point that hotel-keeping is an arduous, highly technical and expert profession, must try to shock the bourgeois a little further by insisting that hotel-keeping can be a high and holy pursuit, and that literature as she is usually written is in comparison a scummy racket.

Work of Art tells of two brothers, Myron and Ora Weagle, sons of a country hotel-keeper in New England. Myron was a serious, priggish, hard-working lad; Ora a self-confessed "genius." Their ambition took different forms: Ora left home for the sites of Greenwich Village, the ultimate glories of Hollywood, while Myron went into the hotel business from the bottom, aiming for the top. Like the Horatio Alger hero his brother used to call him, he got there; but even after he was a big man in the hotel world he never forgot his ambition to run the Perfect Inn. After sinking all his money, experience and reputation in the project, bad luck and the venality of associates robbed him of success. Once more he had to begin almost from the bottom; the end of his story finds him running a country hotel in Kansas and revolving schemes for the Perfect Tourist Camp.

As a novel, *Work of Art* is second rate, in spots almost dull. It is, however, not only as a novel that we should consider it, but as a message. To the Nobel Prize Committee Sinclair Lewis stands as the leader of American letters, and though he is without that honor in his own country, we are still interested in what he is trying to say. What he is trying to say in *Work of Art* is that there is no substitute for honest work. But what he has succeeded in saying is that Babbitt is right. He has been writing about Babbitt so long that he is suffering from the effects of total immersion.

Mr. Lewis and the Primitive American

Howard Mumford Jones*

While the Marxist critics seek whom they may devour and the proletarian novelists compass us about with gall and travail, Mr. Sinclair Lewis continues to stalk what may be called the Primitive American of the Pre-Alphabet Era. He is not at ease in the Roosevelt Zion. "I wonder," he says apologetically in the introduction, "if this American optimism, this hope and courage, so submerged now in 1935, are not authentic parts of American life." Somewhere in Elysium the shade of William Dean Howells is hopefully cutting an extra branch of laurel and picking out a comfortable stretch of grass for Mr. Lewis to repose on. Mr. Howells, it will be remembered, thought that the more smiling aspects of life are the more American.

The . . . stories in [Selected Short Stories] were originally published between 1917 and 1931. Mr. Lewis now thinks that the earlier ones "belong to an era distant now and strange as the days of Queen Victoria." The earlier ones may be described as O. Henry with trimmings. In "The Kidnapped Memorial" a Confederate veteran kidnaps a G. A. R. Memorial Day parade for the benefit of a forgotten Unionist widow, and, being offered a Northerner's sword, buckles it on, crying: "This isn't a Northerner's sword any more, nor a Southerner's, ma'am. It's an American's! Forward! March!"

"The Cat of the Stars" is devoted to the proposition, beloved of O. Henry, that mighty contests rise from trivial things. "Go East, Young Man" proves that honest go-getter business activities are preferable to sham estheticism. "Things" develops an analogous theme. Mr. Lewis is right. These stories date.

The author himself prefers three later tales: "Let's Play Kings," "The Willow Walk," and "A Letter from the Queen." They are more mature; yet the first is a variant of the boy story, this time with a Hollywood aura, the second is the sort of thing Irvin Cobb has often turned out, and the third, though able, is not striking. "The Willow Walk" is memorable because of a kind of grim precision in its structure. "A Letter from the Queen" might be more nearly memorable if it were not stuffed with various typical Lewis excrescences.

Even in his better work, it appears that Mr. Lewis is content with a simple and conventional technique. In what, then, does the interest of the volume lie? I should say that here, as in the novels, there is an infectious zest which carries the author triumphantly through rudimentary plots and facile characterization. Mr. Lewis is always amazingly alive.

*From the Saturday Review of Literature 12 (6 July 1935):7. Copyright 1935 Saturday Review, reprinted by permission.

And this liveliness is coupled with a kind of queer jollity. Even when travesty seems to be verging on bitterness, the effect is as if he stuck his head around the side of the Punch-and-Judy box to remark: "Look here! Don't be frightened. It's all a part of the show, you know!" Like Thackeray, Mr. Lewis is incapable of hate. He shyly reveals from time to time a healthy longing for romance. Describing the researches of Dr. Selig in "A Letter from the Queen," Mr. Lewis writes:

"He had touched a world romantic and little known. Hidden in old documents . . . he found the story of Franklin, who in his mousy fur cap was the Don Juan of Paris, of Adams fighting the British Government to prevent their recognizing the Confederacy, of Benjamin Thompson, the Massachusetts Yankee who in 1791 was chief counselor of Bavaria, with the title of Count Rumford."

This is the E. Phillips Oppenheim interpretation of history, likable and boyish. As Mr. Lewis remarks, optimism, hope, and courage, "so submerged . . . in 1935" are, for him, authentic parts of American life. I should add to these, sentiment. Mr. Lewis satirizes sentimentality, but there is in him this honest vein of sentiment, a possession which puts him apart from most contemporary fiction. Amid the tortured souls who frequent our fiction just now, it is refreshing to have this belated but healthy objectivity, this telling of stories for the fun of it. In the long run it is just possible that Mr. Lewis may be wiser than the sophisticated.

[Review of *It Can't Happen Here*]   Herschel Brickell*

Sinclair Lewis' latest novel, *It Can't Happen Here*, which takes its title from the typical American remark concerning the possibility of a dictatorship in this country, is a piece of journalistic fiction in every page of which is the sound of a swiftly pounded typewriter. In fact, without listening, the attentive reader will catch in its pages the rattle of the flying keys and the tinkle of the bell at the end of the line.

Written at a white heat, the novel is filled with feeling, as well as with the sharp and accurate observation that has always marked Mr. Lewis' work even when it has failed, as has often been the case, to reach his top mark. One might naturally suppose that such a book would call for the exercise of a good deal of creative imagination, but actually Mr. Lewis has saved himself from the exercise of a faculty for which he has never been noted by the simple expedient of transferring what has happened in other countries to this; there is a striking resemblance

*Reprinted, with permission, from *North American Review* 240 (December 1935): 543–46.

to our dictatorship in that of Hitler—too striking, in fact, for credible accuracy.

The parts of the book that relate to the actual operations of the dictatorship are but little more than rewritten passages from the many volumes that have told of hardships and cruelties in Nazi Germany. Here again, as in the whole plan and tempo of the novel, the author is writing as a journalist, taking available material and reshaping it, but not enough so to suit his own purposes.

His descriptions of concentration camps, for example, parallel exactly similar descriptions of such institutions in Germany, and when he insists upon the widespread existence of homosexuality from the top to the bottom of the dictatorship, it is seen that he is merely following an established pattern, rather than trying to work out an American version.

The principal virtue of the work, aside from the fact that it represents Mr. Lewis as a tale-teller, the writer of exciting and even gripping narrative which carries the reader along at a breathless speed, lies in its re-statement of the liberal principles that belong to the generation of Americans of which Mr. Lewis himself is a member. For, without laboring the point too much, he makes it clear that both fascism and communism will inevitably find hard going in this country merely because of the existence of a large number of people who do not have to rationalize their belief in freedom of thought and expression, as well as in the exercise of the kindlier virtues, but whose minds are set on these matters in such a way that nothing but death can change them.

In other words, Mr. Lewis again makes it apparent that as much as he has scolded his fellow-Americans—even in the present book he finds them relieved of their dictatorship but uncertain what they want—there has never been any doubt in his mind that certain Americans are possessed of admirable qualities. Toward these he can be as gentle, almost sentimental, as he can be brutal to the whole tribe of hypocrites and stuffed shirts. Hence, while the present book is filled with rude and raucous laughter at many of our follies, it is also tender toward what Mr. Lewis considers our best in both men and women.

The spokesman for his own opinions is Doremus Jessup, a sixty-odd-year-old newspaper editor in the Vermont town of Fort Jessup. Mr. Lewis remains loyal to his own Middle West in having the "radical" territory lead in the revolt against the dictatorship, but his real tribute is to the state of his adoption. Jessup is shrewd, whimsical and liberal to the bone, quite a "character."

Often in his cogitations the accents of Mr. Lewis himself are unmistakable. This is a familiar Lewis trick, of course, elbowing the character aside to do the talking himself. In fact, there is one place where the phrase, "meditated Jessup," seems purely an interpolation, an afterthought, as if Mr. Lewis in making his revision had decided that it would be more in accordance with the rules of fiction if he retired a little more from the center of the stage.

His plan for the establishment of the dictatorship is not by the use of force and arms, which the Communists declare is the only possible method. On the contrary, he prophesies the next presidential election as resulting in the choice of one Buzz Windrip, who more nearly resembles the dead Huey Long than anyone else at present in the political picture. (The death of Long takes some of the punch out of Mr. Lewis's book, incidentally.) Windrip is full of fair promises, $5,000 a year for everybody, and so on; and he is greatly aided by Bishop Prang, the famous broadcaster, who is a Methodist Father Coughlin. The real devil in the Windrip administration is Lee Sarason, who more nearly resembles Hitler than he does an American. Windrip is in the main a sort of poker-playing, whiskey-drinking Harding, a good-natured, not very shrewd politician, who knows how to rouse the rabble and to play "Man-of-the-People" with finish and effect.

The League of Forgotten Men is the basis of Windrip's strength, and his administration is backed by the Minute Men, who are Hitler's Brown Shirts or Mussolini's Black Shirts all over again, taking the trick of beating with steel tapes from one and the use of castor oil from the other.

Eventually, after the dictatorship has grown in severity, and has resulted in what might be expected in the way of suppression of all freedom, Sarason, the diabolical, succeeds in getting rid of Windrip by sending him off to France. Then Sarason is killed by Haik, another member of the group, and things go from bad to worse the country over until the reaction sets in and the curtain falls, with our old friend Doremus Jessup active in what seems to be an excellent chance of the reëstablishment of democratic government, with an honest liberal Republican, Walt Trowbridge, as its head.

While all this is happening, Jessup has lost his paper, and is sent away to a concentration camp for his subversive activities in printing and distributing anti-Windrip propaganda. His daughter Mary, whose husband has been murdered, takes her melodramatic revenge by diving her airplane into a ship carrying the judge who sentenced her husband. His sweetheart, Lorinda, who is another one of Mr. Lewis's "free women," is done with complete sympathy—the same sort of tender affection as Sissy, the youngest Jessup child, who sounds, one must admit, slightly antiquated, as if she were a left-over flapper from the post-war revolt of youth.

It is easy to see that in describing the course of the dictatorship alone, with the German pattern at hand, Mr. Lewis is handling essentially dramatic material. This, coupled with his satirical jibes, his sketches of many living people, particularly of politicians—one way he has of dodging the identification of his characters with the living, or the freshly dead, as in the case of Huey Long, is to put in both—his joshing of patriotic songs, and the warm friendliness of his treatment of the Vermonters he likes, makes his book quite as readable as anything he has ever done. It is not literature, nor is it in any sense profound. But it is unadulterated Sinclair Lewis, and it represents him perfectly as the essential journalist he has always been.

I may add, as a personal observation, that the book left me unconvinced of the possibility of a dictatorship's arriving any time soon, or in the manner described by Mr. Lewis. The difference between us is that I have more faith in the Doremus Jessups than he has; I still think they would go into action before a Buzz Windrip and a Lee Sarason got as far as the White House.

Red Menace   Anonymous*

Two years ago, when Sinclair Lewis published *It Can't Happen Here*, a miscellaneous group of left-wing writers hailed that anti-Fascist novel with a dinner in a small Italian restaurant on Manhattan's East Side. There in an upstairs room Sinclair Lewis sat at the head of a long table facing a row of radical poets, proletarian novelists and dramatists, defenders of civil liberties, pamphleteers, listening uncomfortably to their speeches that welcomed him to their ranks. Said *New Masses* Editor Granville Hicks: "When I read *Work of Art* I wondered—is Red Lewis with us or against us? But when I read *It Can't Happen Here*, I knew—Lewis is with us."

Last week, if he read Lewis' *The Prodigal Parents*, Granville Hicks must have been wondering again. A brief, inconsequential book, more typical of Lewis' choppy short stories than of his novels, *The Prodigal Parents* is notable only for the stern tone it adopts toward the Communist Party and for its sympathetic portrait of the type of U. S. businessman Lewis has previously satirized. The story revolves around the rebellion of Frederick William Cornplow, a plump, prosperous, middle-aged automobile dealer of Sachem Falls, N. Y., who is a dead ringer for Babbitt.

But unlike Babbitt, Fred Cornplow is harassed by two extraordinarily rude, extravagant, self-centered children who almost drive him crazy and then try to lock him in a sanitarium so he can recover the mental

*From *Time* 31 (24 January 1938):61–62. Copyright 1938, Time Inc. All rights reserved. Reprinted by permission from *Time*.

balance they have destroyed. Son Howard is a handsome, stupid, un-principled college boy who is always borrowing money, wrecking his father's cars, and trying to lie his way out. Daughter Sara is a handsome, ill-natured poseur who becomes a Communist, falls in love with an agitator, overdraws her allowance of $1,000 a year and spends most of her time making poisonous remarks about her father. Thus, although it contains the story of Cornplow's flight to Europe and the eventual reconciliation of his family as a result, most of *The Prodigal Parents* is given over to scenes in which Howard or Sara bait Cornplow. Cornplow gets mad, the children make wild speeches about youth and Communism and Cornplow answers with speeches defending businessmen. When Cornplow refuses to give $500 to the Spanish government, Sara snarls at him, "Heaven knows I can't give anything with my wretched income," and Cornplow snarls right back, "I know I'm just a millionaire capitalist . . . only I don't expect to contribute for the privilege of being destroyed!" With a dozen of the 40 brief chapters in *The Prodigal Parents* sounding variations of that theme in varying degrees of abruptness, crudity, animosity, all the characters emerge as too intense to be as funny as the situation warrants. But if it adds nothing to Lewis' reputation as a humorist, *The Prodigal Parents* makes it reasonably certain that this time there will be no left-wing dinner at which he will listen uncomfortably to the praise of radical critics.

[Review of *Bethel Merriday*]   Harry Lorin Binsse[*]

Mr. Lewis has always written to a pattern—or almost always. And it is a pretty sure-fire pattern. You pick a trade or profession, steep yourself in it, write a novel pack-jam full of its jargon, its local color. If you have Mr. Lewis's powers of observation and expression, his ability to suck up into himself all the things that give character to his theme, you are pretty sure to write an interesting novel.

Bethel Merriday, like everything Sinclair Lewis has ever written, has that sort of interest. Some people will, perhaps, find it a little tedious because Bethel's trade—acting—doesn't appeal to them, but to anyone in the slightest degree stagestruck, to anyone who really cares anything for the theatre, the book will inevitably seem good.

A reviewer is forced into comparisons. Is this latest opus as well done as *Arrowsmith*, *Babbitt*? On the negative side one must admit that *Bethel Merriday* just hasn't got as much stuff in it as one expects of its author. What there is is of the old quality, but quantity is a

*Reprinted, with permission, from *Commonweal* 31 (22 March 1940):477.

definite part of Lewis's quality, and it is the quantity that is lacking. *Elmer Gantry*, for example, covered a pretty wide range of the activities of a certain kind of evangelical preacher. *Babbitt* gives you about as complete a picture of a rotarian real estate man as you can stand. *Bethel Merriday* seems, by contrast, a pretty thin slice of an actress's possible variety of experiences. The heroine acts at college. She is an apprentice in a summer theatre. She goes through the ordeal of a road company that fails. And there the book ends, with Bethel back in New York starting rehearsals on a Broadway comedy. How would success affect her? And maybe a touch of Hollywood?

But on the positive side there is much to be said. Evidently the author himself loves and respects the theatrical profession. He sees its sillinesses, its petty jealousies, its real faults, but he loves it. So he approaches it as a lover rather than as a critic. The result is happy. There is none of the bitterness, the scorn that in some sense hurt many of his other novels. And then, too, the characters in this book seem to have a little more life, a little more humanity. One could not help feeling that Gantry and Babbitt and even Dodsworth were caricatures in some sense. Bethel Merriday is a very human girl with a passion for the stage. Of course Lewis cannot altogether deny his talent for subtle exaggeration. Mrs. Lumley Boyle, the wickedly clever, slightly alcoholic, utterly competent leading lady, with her incredibly awful dog, never quite existed on land or sea, yet always will exist so long as there is a theatre.

The plot of *Bethel Merriday*, like most of Lewis's plots, counts for little. Indeed, it is weaker, perhaps, than is usual with him. His heroine's "love-life" is in spots about as improbable as anything you can imagine. But if you like Lewis, you will forgive all that. His philosophy also seems to have mellowed a little. Less cracks, more gentle kidding seems to be the ticket, which may be a result of the author's growing older, may be the result of his love for the stage. In any case, a pleasant book.

Young Sinclair Lewis
and Old Dos Passos   Maxwell Geismar*

Spring marks the revival also of two of our ranking American novelists, out of about six now going. There have been solid novels, this winter, like James Cozzens' *The Just and the Unjust*, promising

*Reprinted from *American Mercury* 56 (May 1943):624–28. By permission of Mrs. Maxwell Geismar.

novels like Nancy Hale's *The Prodigal Women*, extraordinary novels like Upton Sinclair's *Wide Is the Gate*, talented novels like Prokosch's *The Conspirators* and disappointing novels like Eudora Welty's *The Robber Bridegroom*. And just now there is William Saroyan's first novel, *The Human Comedy*, which is talented, promising, extraordinary and disappointing at the same time, like nearly all his work. But until these new books by Sinclair Lewis [*Gideon Planish*] and John Dos Passos [*Number One*] none of our first rate authors has published anything of consequence for more than a year. The interest of these two novels is heightened by the fact that both Lewis, who has had perhaps the largest influence among an older generation, and Dos Passos, who fills much the same rôle among the newer writers, seem to be at the crossroads of their careers.

Now some might say, and have said, after *The Prodigal Parents* in 1938, or after *Work of Art* in 1934, or after *Elmer Gantry* in 1927, that Lewis is well beyond the crossroads. For the last fifteen years, in fact, from *Arrowsmith* on, Lewis has figured in the minds of some commentators as a sort of literary ghost. But since he has insisted on reappearing, with a new title, every two or three years, his reputation has had to be reappraised periodically. And since every so often—with *It Can't Happen Here* in 1935 and now again with *Gideon Planish*—the ghost has given amazing proof of living and even rambunctious vitality, the whole process of judging Lewis's novels is getting cumbersome and probably should be simplified.

If the work of Sinclair Lewis has not noticeably matured, it often seems, on the other hand, as youthful as ever. The chief quality of *Gideon Planish* is certainly its immense energy, in construction as well as in phrasing. Lewis remains one of our most vivid and wittiest and most stimulating novelists. In the matter of material, his latest novel is in a sense less fresh. He again portrays typical characters in American life. His country doctor, small businessman, scientist, politician, career women of one sort of another (career women have haunted Lewis's thoughts)—all these national types are now followed by the study of a modern public-relations expert in the era of "scientific philanthropy." Perhaps Dr. Gideon Planish is not exactly that; it is difficult to tell just what he is; the more vague his direction becomes, the faster he tries to get there.

The good Doctor starts merely as an ordinary professor at Kinnickinick College, having an ordinary affair with Teckla Schaum, daughter of a college trustee. But Planish, heavy in manner and light in head, a provincial who like all provincials considers himself superior to his provincial habitat, keeps his eye on the Main Chance wherever his tongue may wobble. Peony, his new wife, with her very mature flesh, her adolescent values and infantile morals gets her "Gidjums" really moving. Soon he is Dean of Kinnickinick, Editor of *Rural Adult Educa-tion* (Des Moines), Secretary of the Heskett Rural School Foundation (Chicago), Member of the True American Federation to Attack Racial Prejudice (New York), Assistant General Manager of the Citizens' Con-ference on Constitutional Crises (Washington), and Director of Dyna-mos of Democratic Direction (USA). Around this familiar American motif of Getting On, Lewis has elaborated a powerful array of practi-tioners in the national art: among others, the Reverend Dr. Christian Stern and Msgr. Fish; William T. Knife, devout prohibitionist and pro-prietor of Okey-Dokey, a soft (caffein) drink; and Dr. Elmer Gantry, a manly New York clergyman sponsored by Phosphorated Chewing Gum. Higher up on the list of genus Exploiter are Winifred Homeward the Talking Woman, who bears a suspicious resemblance to two or three over-articulate females now in the public eye or ear; a Colonel Charles B. Marduc of Marduc, Syco and Sagg; and Marduc's group of young Yale journalists, who only suggest a particular magazine combine.

The eccentrics, cranks, fanatics and professional operators who fill the pages of *Gideon Planish*—these Lardnerian suckers and Faulknerian slickers, these smooth guys and wise guys and tough guys (and girls, like Winifred, who at sight of any two persons congregating will mount her imaginary platform and start a fervent address full of imaginary Conditions and Implications)—are often quite brilliant character studies. But the wholly admirable youthful energy with which Lewis once again describes, satirizes, ridicules, parodies and lambastes his typical Amer-ican scene has concomitant limitations. *Gideon Planish* assumes, as Dos Passos almost does in *Number One*, that all co-operative movements, like all "organizators," are either hopelessly inefficient or quite hopefully vicious. There is no mean, there is even no minimum, of those groups whose very inefficiency perhaps is a token of their sincerity. *Gideon Planish* takes its stand, as Lewis's "Mr. Johnson of Minneapolis" states it, on "anarchy and the comics," and Lewis's satire is apparently based on no conviction but that of pure negation.

Because of this Lewis's work has sometimes and superficially been termed reactionary, whereas it approaches more nearly the destructivity of precocious adolescence; and I am willing to contend that Lewis re-mains our foremost youthful iconoclast, though the time for mere icono-clasm is probably long past. Lewis, moreover, is by temperament a human and generous artist who often knows more than he seems to know, and sometimes believes more than he may think he believes. *Gideon Planish*, on the whole, still leaves us in the dark as to the future of the young Mr. Lewis, but it is a dark that is still violent, acrid, and entertaining, and by no means that of the sepulchre. . . .

Salute to an Old Landmark:
Sinclair Lewis
Edmund Wilson*

This review of Sinclair Lewis's new novel—*Cass Timberlane* (Random House)—is, I am afraid, going to be one of those articles in which the reviewer talks about himself, so if this irritates you, you might skip to the middle, where I really get to work on the book. Coming back a month ago to New York after visiting several countries of Europe, I found myself more alienated from the United States than I ever remembered to have been after any similar trip. This may have been due partly to the fact that in Europe I had constantly been thinking how much better off we were at home and had built up an ideal picture, and partly to the fact that making the trip by plane in two days from Naples to New York does not, if you are accustomed to the old-fashioned kind of travel, give you time to prepare yourself for the change from one continent to another. The old reflexes, conditioned by sea voyages, do not tell you that you are home again, and you feel that you are not really there, that the new place in which you seem to have alighted is some sort of simulacrum or mirage. In any case, it was almost like arriving in another foreign country. I noticed characteristics of the Americans of which I had not been aware when I left: they were much larger than Europeans, enormous; their faces seemed lacking in focus and their personalities devoid of flavor; and most of the things that they were doing seemed to me done in a boring way. I had looked forward to picking up my old interests and was baffled and disconcerted when I discovered that these no longer seemed interesting.

Then I saw that I had to make an adjustment quite different from the kind of adjustment that is involved in going abroad and learning one's way about. I already knew my way about at home, yet I could not find the values I had known, the values on which I depended; and I realized that what made the difference was that abroad you were always in the position of a spectator for whom the inhabitants were putting on a show. This show consists of their being foreigners and behaving in a foreign way, and it provides you with entertainment without your needing to do anything yourself. But at home you are no longer in the audience, you have to be one of the actors, and there will not be the old show unless you get back into your rôle. You have to contribute, yourself, to creating the interest and the value, and I was still in the state of mind of the passive looker-on. I had not begun working yet.

At this moment I read Sinclair Lewis, and I appreciated him in

*From the *New Yorker* 21 (13 October 1945):98, 101-2, 104. Reprinted by permission of Farrar, Straus and Giroux, Inc.

certain ways as I had never done before and as I perhaps should not otherwise have done. We have had Lewis around for so long, so consistently being himself, that he has become a familiar object, like Henry Ford or the Statue of Liberty, about which, if one has been living in America, one does not think very much. Up to his novel before this last one, I had not read him for years, and had heard little about him except routine complaints that he was repeating himself or going to pot. I did read his book before last, *Gideon Planish*, because I had heard it was about foundations and I had had enough experience of foundation workers to want to see Sinclair Lewis turned loose on them. *Gideon Planish* was an extremely funny caricature, and I saw that Lewis's writing had improved: he moved more swiftly, made his points with less effort, and had mastered a not common art of introducing colloquial American, with style, into literary prose. But I found in his new book, *Cass Timberlane*, some qualities that were new to me and that I had not expected. Lewis has returned to Minnesota to live and he has written about a small Middle Western city in a way that is quite distinct from anything in *Main Street* or *Babbitt*. These northern Middle Western cities, with their big lakes and their raw business buildings, their gloomy old houses of the eighties that run to fancy windows and towers, and their people playing bridge and drinking cocktails, kept warm by a new oil furnace, in the midst of their terrific winters, have a peculiar impressiveness and pathos which is sometimes rather hard to account for in terms of their constituent elements but which, despite all the crassness and dullness, is inherent in the relation of the people to the country. This Lewis has got into his novel. Gopher Prairie, of *Main Street*, he hated; Zenith, of *Babbitt*, he ridiculed; but Grand Republic, Minnesota, the scene of *Cass Timberlane*, has really been lived in and loved. And the book made me feel, when I read it, that I was back in touch with home again and made me realize that Sinclair Lewis, in spite of his notorious faults, is one of the people in the literary field who do create interest and value, that he has still gone on working at this when many others have broken down or quit, and that he is, in fact, at his best—what I never quite believed before—one of the national poets.

And what about the story itself? It is a story about a husband and wife and is very much the same sort of thing as such novels as H. G. Wells's *Marriage* and Arnold Bennett's *These Twain*, of the literary era in which Lewis grew up and to which he still more or less belongs. A judge in his early forties, a serious and upright man, falls in love with and succeeds in marrying a girl in her early twenties, pretty, clever, and rather perverse. They do all the usual things—there are clashes of taste and interest, quarrels and reconciliations, she has flirtations with other men and he makes her jealous scenes, she gives birth to a baby, which dies, and has a period of ill health and depression. When she recovers, he takes her to New York, and there she is unfaithful to him with an old friend turned city slicker. Back in middle-class Grand Republic, she decides that she will divorce the Judge and marry the other man, but when she goes to New York, she finds out that her lover has never taken her seriously. She falls ill; the Judge comes on and rescues her and takes her back to Grand Republic. She has learned to appreciate her husband and is prepared to like their neighbors better, and we assume that all will now go well.

What is new in Sinclair Lewis's picture is an attempt on the author's part to deal with a typical bright young woman of the forties, so different from the emancipated woman of the earlier decades of the century, the "Woman Who Did," that heroine who dared to get herself a job or be a social or political worker or desert her conventional husband for the unconventional man she loved. The new young girl wants to compete with the man without learning any trade, is rebellious against marriage but does not want a job, leaves her husband but does not stick to her lover. Lewis is trying to get hold of this type, and his perception of social phenomena is always alert and sharp; but the truth is that he does not like Jinny, is too old-fashioned, perhaps, to sympathize with her. He works hard to make her attractive, but her relentless cuteness and cleverness always sound off key and self-conscious. Does he know how obnoxious he has made her? At one point he remarks that if the Judge had not been so much in love, he might not have cared for her whimsicality; and we have an uncomfortable feeling that if the author changed his tone only a little, we should get one of his frank female caricatures, like the wife of Gideon Planish. Here is Jinny being cute in Florida: "Jinny eyed the crêpe myrtle, the roses, the obese wonder of a grapefruit growing, and looked at the Cass who had worked this magic for her. 'My Merlin!' she said." And here she is being clever on the subject of their going to New York: The Judge says, " 'We'll pick up New York and shake it.' 'Oh, but that headwaiter at the Marmoset Club, with eyes like a wet old dishrag, who looks at you just once and guesses exactly what your income is, and do you know any Astors.' 'Maybe we'd get to know a few Class B Astors, if we wanted to, which I doubt.' 'I'd love to know *lots* of Astors—big fat juicy ones, and little diamond-studded ones in sables!'... 'Jinny, you shall have all the Astors you want. Have Astors with your corn flakes.' 'And cream.' 'And extra cream, from the Ritz. God knows even a very rich Astor or Vanderbilt or Morgan, one nine feet tall with a robe made of securities, couldn't be more chilly than our local John William Prutts. Let's look their lodge over. I mean, before we actually decide whether

I ever shall resign, I think we ought to go to New York and study it, to see whether, if we had a real home of our own there, we wouldn't enjoy the place.' 'And Cleo?' 'Naturally.' "

Cleo is an intolerable kitten, who goes all through the book and reflects the moods of their marriage.

The ending is absolutely Victorian. Lewis stacks the cards against Jinny by making her lover such a cold-hearted scoundrel—he has the currish name of Bradd Criley—as has hardly been seen in serious fiction for a century, and he has her develop diabetes so that she will become a chronic invalid. Scorned by her seducer and confined to her bed, she has no choice but to go home with the Judge, and Lewis evades the problem of finding out what such a girl would do if she were well and had pleasanter friends. He leaves her reading *Dombey & Son*, where, in the story of Edith Dombey and Carker, she must have found a singular parallel to the destiny which her creator has invented for her.

But with *Judge Timberlane*, Sinclair Lewis is much better. Here he has something he intimately knows, and the Judge in relation to his town is really thoroughly and admirably done. The most satisfactory section of the book is the early part, in which we see Timberlane, divorced from his first, worthless wife, living alone in his sombre house, hearing cases and dining with friends, working out chess problems at home, and discovering the birdlike young girl, living among the local Bohemia, whom he is passionate enough to pursue but not young enough or supple enough to meet on her own ground. The best and subtlest thing in the novel is the effect, on the Judge's behavior with his wife and his treacherous friend, of the conception of justice and individual rights to which he has trained himself in the law. Judge Timberlane, too, in his personal as well as in his official life, is creating interest and value for his less conscious and responsible neighbors.

These neighbors, the social organism of Grand Republic, are shown not only in relation to the Timberlanes but also by a series of brief histories, interspersed through the book, of the married lives of certain selected citizens. Some are funny, some are touching, some are implausible or superficial. But the general effect is successful. These sketches build up the community and serve to set the Timberlanes off. Nor can it nowadays be said of Lewis—as Sherwood Anderson used to do—that he does not see inside his characters and appreciate their human merits. He does not slight their commonness and ugliness any more than he did in *Main Street*, but Grand Republic, Minnesota, is a place in which one can imagine living, not, like Main Street, a circle of Hell.

Problem Novel

Malcolm Cowley*

Problem novels are problems for critics, too. What is to be said, for example, about Sinclair Lewis's new book, *Kingsblood Royal*, published by Random House? Should we admire it because it is an effective tract, written in the best of causes; because it is angry and accurate about the indignities suffered by Negroes even here, in the supposedly open-minded North; because, since it is being distributed by the Literary Guild, some of the group's million and a quarter members will be forced to think about racial prejudice in a more worried and personal fashion? Or should we throw the book aside because, though important in view of the facts it presents, it is less important as a work of fiction; because it is a long step down the ladder from *Arrowsmith* and the four other big novels that Lewis wrote between 1920 and 1929, when he was making his contribution to American letters? One's sense of social justice and one's literary conscience don't always agree. Which of them should govern one's opinion of *Kingsblood Royal?*

The story deals with a young Minnesota banker and war veteran, Neil Kingsblood, who accidentally learns that one of his thirty-two great-great-great-grandparents was a Negro. Shaken by this revelation—more shaken than it is probable he would be in real life—he begins to investigate the Negro colony in his native city of Grand Republic. He meets so many Negro intellectuals whom he likes better than his white neighbors, and is so angered by the stupidities they have to endure, that he decides, as a matter of principle, to reveal his secret. The result is that he loses his job in his bank, and, at the end of the book, is assailed in his home by a white mob and dragged off to jail with his wholly Caucasian wife. For a problem or propaganda novel, Lewis has probably found the best approach to this particular subject. He couldn't have made his hero completely a Negro without arousing the suspicion in his readers that he didn't know what really went on in the hero's mind, and he couldn't have made him lily white without spoiling the story. By selecting a conventional hero who switches midway in life from the white to the colored world, he gives his conventional readers a sense of identity with Kingsblood that makes them share his discoveries about the things Negroes are forced to accept and shudder each time a white man's door is closed in his face.

The story is convincing, in that one feels it *could* happen in Grand Republic or any other city north of the Ohio (what would happen in the South is a different matter). Yet one also feels that it wouldn't be likely to happen quite as Lewis sets it down. Kingsblood, at the begin-

*From the *New Yorker* 23 (24 May 1947):100–101. Reprinted by permission. Copyright 1947, © 1975, the *New Yorker* Magazine, Inc.

ning of the novel, is a little too charming and self-satisfied for us to expect the feat of honesty he will soon perform. His wife has told him, "You're so absolutely just what you are: a one-hundred-per-cent normal, white, Protestant, male, middle-class, efficient, golf-loving, bound-to-succeed, wife-pampering, Scotch-English Middlewestern American. I wouldn't believe that you were anything else, not if you brought me papers signed by General Eisenhower to prove it." A few weeks later, Neil elects to join the colored race, as if it were a church that could save his soul, but there is nothing in his character or his intellectual concerns to mark him as a man ripe for conversion. There is something psychologically wrong, too, with the action ascribed to Neil's neighbors, most of whom seem to have moved to Grand Republic from one or another of Lewis's earlier novels. Having known Kingsblood for years, they would, it is true, be amazed to learn that a thirty-second part of his blood was Negro, but I can't believe that the fact in itself would have led them, within the space of a few weeks, to cut him dead on the street, abuse his child, kill his dog, and finally storm his Colonial cottage. Eventually they might have done all this, just as disgracefully, but only after months or years, and then chiefly because Neil kept speaking of himself as a Negro and entertaining Negro guests, and the neighbors had begun to think the value of their property was threatened.

Sinclair Lewis has been writing novels since 1914 and has learned more tricks about them than he is willing to forget. After choosing a new subject and collecting a mass of information—such as his facts here about Negro life—he seems to feel that he can slip back into one of his old routines and still turn out a better story than most of his competitors. *Kingsblood Royal* is at times a very good story, and I suppose we shouldn't complain that it has the same setting as *Cass Timberlane*, but it also has characters borrowed largely from *It Can't Happen Here*, with nothing changed but their names; and the plot, so far as it deals with a businessman's revolt, is much like that of *Babbitt*. Lewis would have had to work harder on Neil Kingsblood and his neighbors to make the book a serious work of fiction. Perhaps the answer to the questions I began by asking is that problem novels have to be judged by the same standards as all novels; they are good if their characters live after them. *Babbitt* was a problem novel, in its milder fashion, and some of the satire has lost its point, but Babbitt himself was patiently brought to life, and he will be remembered longer than Neil Kingsblood.

Lament for a Novelist

John Woodburn*

Even the most benign appraisal of the novels Sinclair Lewis has been turning out over the last fifteen years might give the impression of a man trying to cover his tracks. While it is true that his earlier work had a tendency to be almost rhythmically uneven, there was at least a pendulum movement and an element of surprise: if *Arrowsmith* was followed by *Mantrap, Dodsworth* came along to redeem *The Man Who Knew Coolidge.* Somewhere about 1934 or 1935, depending upon how you felt about *It Can't Happen Here,* the pendulum got stuck on the down stroke. The last six novels, including the one under review, have been monotonously bad, a soggy mishmash of sentimentality and half-digested social consciousness, through which one looks in vain for the robust rancor, the boisterous humor and the broad but often lethal satire that won Lewis the 1930 Nobel Prize. If these novels articulate what might be generously called his period of affirmation, they also constitute a negation of the attitudes and abilities which gave him stature. In fact, it has become increasingly clear that Lewis' work began to decline rapidly as soon as he removed his thumb from his nose and placed it against his brow.

His new book, which is about religion (old-time), is a historical novel, in line with the author's recent interest in America's pioneer past. *The God-Seeker* is not only colossally bad; it is colossal, with Indians. It begins in 1830, in northern Massachusetts, with a little backwoods jackanapes named Aaron Gadd. Aaron's father is a psalm-singing curmudgeon who shoots dogs, pinches pennies and runs a station of the Underground Railroad for biblical rather than humanitarian reasons. At the age of eighteen, when he is by way of becoming a village toss pot, Aaron is converted at a revival meeting and determines to carry the bible to the indifferent Sioux. He also falls in love with a beautiful half-breed Indian maiden, Selene, whose father, Caesar Lanark, is a wealthy Indian trader in the Territory, an arrogant, sneering, cynical character apparently on loan to *The God-Seeker* from a Frank Yerby novel.

Aaron's religious zeal suffers a degree of deterioration during a few seasons with the missionaries, and he becomes deeply concerned with the Indian Problem. He is abetted in this by a preposterous young college-bred brave named Black Wolf (whose mother Lewis, in what I take to be a spirit of *blague,* has named Her Door) who is imbued with Red chauvinism and who spouts anachronistic social anthropology. When Selene returns to the reservation, Aaron defies her father, eludes the amorous clutches of a young female missionary, and sets off east-

*Reprinted, with permission, from *New Republic* 120 (16 May 1949):16–17.

ward with Selene across the snow. At the frontier settlement which was to become St. Paul the two are married and decide to stay and grow up with the town. When the book ends, in 1856, Aaron is a wealthy contractor in partnership with the chastened Lanark, a fearless liberal and an honorary member of the St. Paul Building Workers' Fraternity and Union, which he has helped to found.

There is almost nothing of the old Lewis here, and certainly none of his best. The gusto is forced and hollow, applied, as it is, to alien themes. The satire has become in some instances sarcasm—and heavy sarcasm at that ("'I simply cannot abide these ugly, awkward foreign names,' said Mrs. Tryphosa Bopp Boogus, who came from Gahgosh Falls.")—and now that Lewis has laid his candid camera down, the characters appear like pictures cut from old bill-posters. There is nothing left but the old, clumsy, often lurid style, and the bones of the faults which we excused in the good books he wrote. *The God-Seeker* is an embarrassingly bad book by a reformed satirist. With it, I fear, Sinclair Lewis has joined the ranks of the less promising older writers.

Sauk Centre Was Home Still   Harold C. Gardiner*

It was always a moot point—if an uncharitable suspicion—whether one reason Mr. Lewis could capture so neatly and pillory so mercilessly the U. S. provincial mind was that he himself was the quintessence of that mentality. And since provincialism springs from or leads to some sort of isolationism, it is likewise debatable whether Lewis was not always a cultural isolationist. Whether he was politically is hard to say, because politics rarely found place in the Lewis canon, save in the unsuccessful *It Can't Happen Here.*

At any rate, the captions that have been appearing on reviews of this posthumously published book have been somewhat misleading on this point, I believe. They have been saying that for Lewis the United States, no matter how much he poked fun at its follies, was still home. I believe that Sauk Center was still home, because I don't believe that Lewis ever truly knew the United States, save in a caricature of it of his own making as the gol-darnest, grandest and most glorious, cantankerous and perversely lovable of all the countries on God's green earth.

This tone is dominant in *World So Wide*. It is roughly the story of

*Reprinted, with permission, from *America* 85 (7 April 1951):19–20.

American innocents abroad, wide-eyed and suspicious of the devious Italians (Florence is the scene), somehow bright and shining and naive jewels in a murky setting of an older and more cynical civilization.

The story is simple. Hayden Chart goes abroad to recuperate after the motor accident that killed his wife. He falls in love—somewhat superficially—with the beauty of Florence (he is a young architect), hobnobs with the American expatriate set (among them Sam Dodsworth), is attracted by an American woman scholar. He learns of her fickleness when she has an affair with a brash, four-flushing American university professor who is going to streamline European history courses for Midwestern students, and finally is saved from too much Europeanization by marrying a breezy girl reporter from his home town.

The Lewis idiom is unchanged, and reads now for all the world like foreigners trying to use U. S. slang—they are always about ten years behind time, though they think they are right on the ball when they proclaim "yes-sir, she's the cat's pajamas." Lewis' Americanese is dated.

All in all, this is a sorry book at the end of a career that did make at least some aspects of U. S. life known to the world, to ourselves and thereby managed to cauterize some of our more obvious excesses. The pathetic reflection *World So Wide* occasions is that here Lewis gives a hint that his talent might have been on the verge of taking a new turn. He was getting interested in a world so very much wider than Sauk Centre. That interest might have taken on depth as well. But the end came too soon and Lewis, so innocent about many aspects of American life, remained, like his characters, an innocent abroad.

The Lewis Letters   Anonymous*

From Main Street to Stockholm, the letters of Sinclair Lewis during the period 1919–1930 to his friends and associates in the firm of "Alf" Harcourt, "Don" Brace, and "Hal" Smith, interspersed with their replies to "Red" Lewis, are a blow-by-blow description of the author's career, obscure and precarious at the outset, but leading to the Nobel Prize. They have been edited by Harrison Smith, and the volume includes a few letters from Grace Hegger Lewis, the author's first wife, sent to the publishers, with replies from other staff members.

The book is therefore chiefly concerned with business and professional matters, covering only eleven years, in a time already remote to

*Reprinted, with permission, from *Newsweek* 40 (24 November 1952):102–3. Copyright 1952 by Newsweek, Inc.

the publishing industry. The reader who does not have some knowledge of that small, capricious world, both then and today, may find its pre-occupation with rights, royalties, promotion, as well as with an author at work, merely statistical. But to the reader who does know something of the process of writing (and then selling) fiction, these letters are charged with drama.

For in those eleven years Sinclair Lewis was a superb aerialist of the high trapeze, perpetually facing the leap to the next book, and after that, the equally risky business of grasping its financial success or fail-ure. Lewis's first published book with the new firm of Harcourt, Brace, *Free Air*, was not much of either, despite his copious and frequently skillful suggestions about promoting it. But he was off to the races with *Main Street*, in a line that included *Babbitt*, *Arrowsmith*, *Elmer Gantry*, and *Dodsworth*. However, even as *Main Street* began to roll with the public he had to appeal to "Dear Alf" for advance royalties. (A national magazine unexpectedly rejected a story he had designed for it.) There is exactly the same flamboyant, indomitable tone of the protagonists which he so fondly lampooned as he writes: "We're going to do, to-gether, Alf, the biggest job of novelizing in the country."

This chronic battle, utterly disastrous to many of Lewis's genera-tion, was inevitably bound up with the personal life led by the author. In the letters, there is no warning of the crisis in the marriage of Sinclair and Grace until it suddenly occurs. He is in a sanatorium, and she is ready for one. Similarly, there is no hint of the break between Alf and Red until Red makes it, closing the act with a somber bang.

Babbitt has entered the language, and the casual reader may have some hair-raising moments as he learns that that word might have been Pumphrey. But Pumphrey lost ground to Babbitt, and Babbitt, in turn, seemed losing to Fitch, right down to the photofinish.

Mr. Lewis as Essayist   John W. Aldridge*

Sinclair Lewis had, at the time of his death in 1951, a somewhat insecure reputation as a writer of serious fiction and practically none as an essayist and critic. Of the twenty-two novels he had produced in the thirty-seven years of his active career, five had been forgotten before the publication of *Main Street* in 1920; perhaps four had had genuine literary merit; six were readable; three were nearly unreadable; and the

*Reprinted, with permission, from the *New York Times Book Review*, 15 February 1953, 6, 23. Copyright 1953 by The New York Times Company.

remaining four, of which the posthumously published *World So Wide* was regrettably one, were the sheerest trash.

As for non-fiction, one scarcely imagined he had the time or inclination for it or, if he did, that it could be of a very high order. There had of course been the famous and penetrating literary essay which he had read before the Swedish Academy in Stockholm shortly after receiving the Nobel Prize in 1930; and one had here heard of the furor occasioned by his brilliant exposé of labor conditions in Marion, N. C., during the mill strikes of 1929. But it was generally assumed that, in the main, what ideas he had he had used in his novels, and that outside his novels he had no ideas.

That this was as gross an underestimation of Lewis as it was an overestimation of his fiction is made clear in the range and depth of the writings which Harry Maule and Melville Cane have brought together here [*The Man from Main Street*] from the nearly a million words of non-fiction which we now learn Lewis wrote during his lifetime. Many of the pieces are occasional essays, fragmentary, inconclusive, and deliberately limited to the short view. Others are personal reminiscences.

Still others are remarkably astute critical studies and portraits of writers he admired—Thoreau, H. G. Wells, William Lyon Phelps, his close friend Carl Van Doren—and of critics he quarreled with or despised, like Bernard De Voto who once made the mistake of attacking Van Wyck Brooks. All of them suggest the surprising breadth of his intellectual interests, the generosity of his mind, his passionate concern—amounting at times to a mother-hen fussiness—with every manifestation of the creative spirit of his age. But they also suggest, in their very richness and vitality, the reason for the startling failure of his novelistic career.

Lewis had, it is now plain, a first-rate practical mind coupled with an arrested and largely third-rate creative sensibility. His mind was continually expending in controversy and journalism what his sensibility could not express in art. It was the defect of his fiction, as well as the source of its popular appeal, that it was always dominated by an extravagant sense of the actual, always threatening to spill over the bounds of artifice into the banality of life. If this sense had been less strong in Lewis and his creative power had been greater, he might have succumbed to that necessary befuddlement, the elision of the practical intelligence and memory, which Pascal once defined as the "holy stupidity" of the artist, and as the result of which many lesser minds than Lewis' have blundered into greatness. But it was his abiding misfortune to be always intelligent, to be always under the control of a sense of reality so keen that, once established, it could never be shaken.

In the end this betrayed him; for when the world he knew in his youth, with its expanding social frontiers, its village chauvinism, and its cult of business success, ceased after 1930 to be quite real, he continued for years to write of it as if its conventions were still intact, berating stupidities and injustices that were dead and pointing angrily at a king who had long since put his clothes back on.

ESSAYS

A Long Way to Gopher Prairie:
Sinclair Lewis's Apprenticeship   John T. Flanagan[*]

When Sinclair Lewis's *Main Street* burst upon the American public in October, 1920, it not only provided a fictional channel for the
stream of public discontent with economic and social conditions, but
it initiated a series of realistic books which have collectively been called
the revolt from the village. Obviously it was not the first attempt of
this kind in American fiction. Hamlin Garland and E. W. Howe several
decades before, Dreiser at the turn of the century, Zona Gale only two
years before Lewis—all had anticipated *Main Street* in their naturalistic
representations of ordinary people against a shabby background, and
all had produced significant books which were quite as effective as
Lewis's indictment of Gopher Prairie even though they lacked his
peculiar combination of satire and caustic humor. But there can be no
question that Lewis's novel was the first factual treatment of the American rural community to attract large public response.

The ripeness of the time was a major factor in the success of *Main
Street*. The novel appeared at the precise hour when readers suddenly
freed from the tensions of a world war and conscious of the need for
self-examination were willing and almost avid to learn the truth about
themselves. A decade earlier *Main Street* would have made small impression upon the complacency of a public dedicated to material gain
and convinced of the justice of the status quo, even as Zona Gale's
Birth attracted little attention as late as 1918. In 1920 Lewis's reportorial
skill, his gusto, his grand scorn, and his intimate knowledge of the small
town persuaded people to read *Main Street* even though it mirrored their
own banalities.

All this is not to deny the solid merits of the novel, which remains

*Reprinted, with permission, from *Southwest Review* 32 (Autumn 1947):403–13.
Copyright 1947 by the *Southwest Review*.

one of Lewis's best achievements and one of the influential novels of the twentieth century. Nevertheless, although Lewis's literary photography was both accurate and full and although his skill made the small town the temporary cynosure of the American reading public, the enormous and sudden success of *Main Street* was partly circumstantial. The really surprising thing about the novel is not its popular reception but the fact that it was the author's sixth published work of fiction under his own name and that in substance, in treatment, and in tone it is a far cry from the five novels that preceded it. [Flanagan includes *Hike and the Aeroplane* (1912), a book for boys, written under the pseudonymn of Tom Graham.] One may well wonder why Sinclair Lewis at the age of thirty-five suddenly reversed his field.

As a youth in Sauk Centre, Minnesota, as an undergraduate at Yale, as an enthusiastic if temporary partisan of Upton Sinclair's Helicon Hall community, as a free-lance writer submitting poetry and prose to any kind of magazine which would publish him, Lewis was essentially a romantic. The Sauk Centre of his boyhood, a small community on the fringe of the Minnesota prairie, lay in a region notable for woods and lakes. Presumably Lewis saw and understood less of nature than did the poet Wordsworth; certainly he never rhapsodized over it and was congenitally incapable of pantheistic reverence. But like any normal lad in a small town he was aware of it and possibly became conscious of it at unusual times and places through his habit of occasionally accompanying his father, a country physician, on his calls. For excitement Lewis persistently turned away from the street and the playground to books and read widely in much the same sort of literature that had appealed to young William Dean Howells in Hamilton, Ohio. Indeed, Sherwood Anderson remarked in his *Memoirs* that Lewis seemed never to have participated in the thrills and pleasures of the small town. There was certainly less of the rebel than of the escapist in the tall, freckled, red-headed graduate of the Sauk Centre High School who, after an interlude of exploratory reading at Oberlin Academy, matriculated at Yale in 1903.

At New Haven Lewis was notable for habits of seclusion and an addiction to poetry. He roomed off the campus in an old boarding-house, cut off from the garrulities of the undergraduates, and he lived a little apart from the eddies of campus life. Geographical separation probably implemented the social separation induced by Lewis's reputation as socialist and agnostic. But he was already famous for his voracious passion for books—William Rose Benét, later his roommate in California, doubts that any undergraduate ever withdrew as many volumes from the Yale library—and it was romantic poetry, even medieval tales and legends, which held his fancy. A Yale classmate, Leonard Bacon, claims that he always expected Lewis to earn fame as a poet rather than as a satirical novelist, and that at one time Lewis seriously considered composing an epic. Even his early contributions to the *Yale Courant* and the *Yale Literary Magazine* were usually metrical, and his first work to appear in general periodicals was lyric or descriptive verse of a commonplace sort which he contributed to magazines like the *Sunset*, the *Overland*, and the *Century*.

The reader to whom Lewis is known only as caustic reporter would hardly trust his eyes were he to turn back to the files of the *Minneapolis Bellman* of 1911 and there read a tale entitled "The Way to Rome." Set in the days of Pope Boniface, the story concerns two travelers en route to Rome to participate in the papal jubilee. One wayfarer is a jongleur, who talks blithely and freely about the charms of his way of living; the other is a minor cleric who is convinced that the monk's position in life is ideal. But as each listens to the unfolding of the other's story he begins to question his own choice of vocation, and the story ends with the two travelers exchanging their professions. The road to Rome is certainly more than an ocean removed from the highway leading to Gopher Prairie.

This strong streak of literary romanticism only confirmed in Lewis his passion for travel and his curiosity about the other side of the thoroughfare. Even before graduation a feverish restlessness afflicted him. Like the Mr. Wrenn of his novel he worked his way across the Atlantic on a cattle boat and thus made his first acquaintance with Europe. In 1907 he took time off from college to journey steerage to Panama in the hope of finding a job in the Canal Zone. His interest in utopian experimentation led him to flee from the classroom to try out socialistic living. And after permanently departing from Yale he left a trail of jobs behind him across the continent. One of the minor paradoxes in Lewis's career is that he even looked with interest once on an academic career and toyed with the notion of taking a Ph.D. in English.

Lewis's years as a free-lance writer, publisher's reader, editor, and feature writer saw him located on both coasts and doing a wide variety of hackwork. In the summer of 1908 he worked on the Waterloo, Iowa, *Courier*. In Carmel, California, he roomed, picnicked, and wrote with William Rose Benét, who has testified to the amazing fertility of the Lewis imagination even in those days, a fertility paralleled only by the spate of words poured out by the embryonic novelist. He contributed verse and prose to west coast periodicals and was a telegraphic editor in San Francisco until discharged for incompetence. Back in New York he read manuscripts for a publishing firm, wrote advertising, and worked at a novel piecemeal while commuting daily from Port Washington. It was only after several stories had been accepted by the *Saturday*

Evening Post that Lewis was financially and physically stable enough to settle down anywhere. He himself has asserted that until he purchased a farm in Vermont in 1928 he had never owned any real estate.

This febrile instability has remained dominant throughout his life. If he never equalled Mark Twain's record of crossing the Atlantic twenty or more times, he has certainly roamed up and down the land until his familiarity with city and crossroads hamlet can be assumed. Only recently Lewis bought a house in Duluth and announced that he was returning to Minnesota to live, a decision quite in harmony with his known penchant for collecting books dealing with the history and culture of his native state. But not long after the publication of *Cass Timberlane* Lewis sold his house in Duluth and returned to New York. As Carl Van Doren once pointed out, Lewis is bored and disgusted by society, yet his temperament unfits him for solitude so that an occasional return to metropolitan life is imperative. Lewis's passion for novelty and excitement has led him from place to place in his physical life just as it has induced him to try twenty or more different themes in his fiction. Continuity and long-time devotion to place or subject have never been his forte.

Lewis's first romance, *Our Mr. Wrenn*, appeared in 1914. The protagonist is an underpaid clerk in a New York novelty house, a lonely man of thirty-four who craves friendship and whose longing for glamor and romance impels him to feed upon travel literature. He devours steamship company brochures, timetables, advertising pamphlets. Finally when the sale of an inherited farm brings him a thousand dollars he determines to take the great adventure. He gives up his job and secures passage to England on a cattle boat as butler to the steers. His voyage is somewhat more successful than might be anticipated, since he does his share of the chores and not only stands the ribbing to which he is submitted but actually outfights a bully who has been annoying him. In England, however, he has little money left and small knowledge of what to see or do. Something of a lost figure, William Wrenn eventually gets to London and mopes around boardinghouses until he meets Istra Nash, a disappointed American artist who out of pure ennui takes up Wrenn and patronizes him. For a time his meek devotion satisfies her and he is enraptured by her attention, but when she flees back to Paris, there is nothing for Wrenn to do but to return to New York and ask for his old job again. Occasional flurries of dissatisfaction occur but on the whole Wrenn's wanderlust has been curbed; he has seen Europe and is a traveled man. The rest of the novel—showing him reoccupying his New York niche, changing boardinghouses, meeting Istra Nash once again, and finally marrying a fellow boarder—adds little to the portrait. Wrenn is the romanticist and rebel, however inoffensive he may seem, ultimately conforming to pattern.

The basic romantic mould of his four subsequent novels Lewis established here. There is the lowly protagonist without education or wealth feebly protesting against life as it is, bored by daily routine yet rarely able to escape from it, constantly envisaging a rosy and exciting future. There is the sense of restlessness, with the implied need of change. There is the one affirmation of protest, the one act of rebellion, after which the character sinks back into his rut with wings slightly scorched. Above all there is the novelist's sympathy and compassion for his protagonist. William Wrenn is pathetic and shabby and a bit moronic, but he is not ridiculous. Lewis saved his scorn for Babbitt and Elmer Gantry.

In *The Trail of the Hawk*, 1915, Lewis through the medium of the airplane wrote a novelized travelog quite in keeping with his own instability. Carl Ericson, a small town lad from Joralemon, Minnesota, has no prospects save an interest in and a way with machinery. He does reasonably well in school and endures part of a year at Plato College until its narrow sectarianism drives him to revolt. Subsequently he is an automobile mechanic and chauffeur in Chicago, a stock company actor in Virginia, a saloon porter in New York, a jobhunter in Panama, and an aviation student in California. Machinery and speed fascinate him and in short order he becomes a pilot, then a barnstorming performer at fairs and race tracks, and eventually the winner of a cross-country race. Carl Ericson the blond country boy has become Hawk Ericson the famous flier. But various factors such as fatal accidents to his former associates, the general dubiety in which aviation is held, and the outbreak of the World War cause him to retire from competitive flying and to resort to the less hazardous work of promoting an automobile equipped with camping devices. At the end of the novel, as the guns boom in Europe, Carl and his bride start off on a selling trip to South America.

The Trail of the Hawk has much of the gusto commonly found in Lewis's fiction. There is incessant movement, frequent change of locale, the excitement of a new transportational medium, the romance of the new air age. Ericson, a confirmed extrovert, lives for the moment only. As he tells his wife, "For us, I believe, it's change and *keep going.*" Savoring life deeply, he spends his own energy recklessly. As he expresses it, "How bully it is to be living, if you don't have to give up living in order to make a living." Conceivably this approximates the philosophy of Lewis himself in 1915 as he developed it in one of his most nearly autobiographical novels. *The Trail of the Hawk* as a story bounces along from one scene to another without much causality. Characterization suffers because Lewis does not bother to give his people dimensions and because he is so eager to dart to something new. Like his protagonist he is so bespelled by the glamor and novelty of flying that the backgrounds become blurred. Even a Lewis narrative seldom gallops as it does here.

The next novel, *The Job*, 1916, is Lewis's best achievement before *Main Street* and of all the early books comes closest to the later realistic portrayals. It is the story of Una Golden, daughter of a lawyer in a small Pennsylvania town, who through her father's early death is thrown upon her own resources. The Goldens were members of the town's aristocracy despite Lew Golden's improvidence, and when Una begins to look for a job she finds that there are certain things a genteel young lady cannot do. Panama, Pennsylvania, offers little that is both respectable and remunerative, and eventually friends urge Una to come to New York. There she prepares herself for office life by studying stenography; necessity, not choice, compels her to become a career woman. Una holds various positions, gradually bettering herself, and by a combination of persistence and intelligence establishes herself in the business world. Once indeed she tries marriage as an escape but discovers that her husband is both grossly sensual in his tastes and consistently unfaithful to her. When Una consents to marry an advertising man whom she once youthfully admired it is only upon the understanding that neither his career nor hers shall be interrupted. Already deeply hurt by certain personal experiences. Una is unwilling to sacrifice the independence and the economic security which life has compelled her to achieve under the threat of perishing. It is notable that Una is neither a feminist nor a materialist by conviction; she is exposed to much socialist talk and her own observations produce a mild belligerence in her, but she never becomes a crusader for the rights of women, like a Floyd Dell heroine, nor an esthetic reformer, like Lewis's own Carol Kennicott. Her creed is a defense mechanism produced by external forces.

Woman in the business world was a theme that definitely interested Lewis. In no other early novel did he hew so close to the main line and limit himself so strictly in locale. Una is typical of thousands of girls, not unusually gifted and without distinct attractiveness, who as typists, clerks, or secretaries make a dreary living and struggle for small advances in pay. Each enjoys her small romance, even as Una finds Walter Babson, but in general they succumb to endless and debilitating routine. The various jobs that Una holds until she becomes manager of a hotel chain allow Lewis to picture different facets of business life and at the same time to capitalize on his reportorial skill. If Una is not an engaging heroine, she is convincingly and faithfully drawn.

Two other novels preceded *Main Street: The Innocents*, 1917, and *Free Air*, 1919. The first of these was written, according to the author's prefatory note, for those who still enjoy Dickens and still love old people and children. An innocuous and strangely naïve tale, it deals with the Applebys, "almost old," who live in a New York flat and are devoted to each other. Seth Appleby has clerked in a shoestore for many years and has earned a modest living. Annually the couple spend a summer vacation with the Tubbs's on Cape Cod, the men catching crabs and playing cribbage together, the women cooking and cleaning and gossiping about millinery fads. But Seth enjoys these two-week outings so much that it occurs to him that he and his wife might operate a tea-shop on the Cape and thus spend all their time in rural surroundings instead of only visiting there once a year. The Applebys plunge into this venture enthusiastically but quickly discover that the successful operation of a teashop exceeds both their experience and their capacity. When one of the local celebrities loudly ridicules their establishment they decide to close up the shop and for the time being visit their daughter in upstate New York. But life with the daughter and her vulgarly successful husband proves likewise unpleasant. The Applebys sneak back to New York, where for some time they live meagerly and so close to starvation that once they go to sleep with the gas jet open. Seth, however, determines not to die by asphyxiation, and then he and his wife make their great decision, resolving to take a pedestrian tour to the South and West, living on the bounty of farmers, doing small chores in return for meals, trusting their future destiny to providence.

The rest of the book is sheer romance. The apple-cheeked old man with the high spirits and the grandmotherly old woman find farmers, housewives, and merchants alike compassionate, and only seldom do they suffer real hardship. Perhaps the most fantastic incident is their stumbling upon a hobo jungle, where Mother Appleby takes over, supervises the cooking, does the sewing and cleaning, and inaugurates a moral as well as a physical regeneration. Lewis brings the book to a triumphant conclusion by having the Applebys become famous pedestrians, whose very appearance brings celebrity to a small town, and by allowing Seth to become a partner, without capital, in a small shoe-shop to which he brings instant prosperity. The Appleby trek to fortune has finally proved successful.

Free Air as a piece of art is even less plausible than *The Innocents*, but coming only a year before Lewis's presentation of Gopher Prairie it has considerable interest. Here a transcontinental automobile trip (following closely, as a matter of fact, Lewis's own route to Seattle) supplants the aviation theme of *The Trail of the Hawk*, but there is the same emphasis on travel and rapid shift of scene. In addition *Free Air* has a conventional boy-meets-girl and boy-pursues-girl plot. Claire Boltwood, driving her father from New York to Seattle, finds her roadster bogged down in prairie gumbo somewhere between Schoenstrom and Gopher Prairie, Minnesota. A German farmer is about to extricate the car at an exorbitant price when Milt Daggett, a Schoenstrom mechanic, comes along in his flivver and hastens to the rescue. The Boltwoods are duly grateful and casually drive on, but Milt is fascinated and impetuously decides to follow them to Seattle. He becomes the feudal knight, jalopy style. When Claire's car develops motor trouble Milt appears out of nowhere to oil the distributor and send the roadster on ahead. When Claire gives a wandering hobo a lift and then finds herself unable to get rid of him, Milt again materializes out of the horizon and knocks the man off the running board. In Yellowstone Park a bear becomes unpleasantly intimate with the Boltwoods, but Milt gallantly removes the intruder; and subsequently when the roadster's brakes fail, Milt devises a logdrag to slow the car's descent. These practical tests Milt passes easily; things are different in Seattle when he is flung into a concert-attending, tea-drinking society and when he has to compete with a Princeton graduate for Claire's affections. But Milt is indefatigable and Sinclair Lewis is generous to his hero. Obviously Milt's devotion cannot go unrewarded, and in a burst of resentment at Jeff Saxton's superciliousness Claire decides to marry Milt. Presumably the girl from Brooklyn Heights and the boy from Schoenstrom will live happily ever after.

This tale offers nothing but conventional romance against a background of automobiling with, in 1919, the concomitants of bad roads, highway obstacles, and motor trouble. The story of the western swain who by his practicality and persistence won the eastern girl away from her social-register suitor was trite long before Lewis attempted it. But there is some originality in making the hero a garage mechanic, even though his impulsive pursuit of a transient girl to Seattle seems highly implausible; and the use of the Minnesota background in the initial chapters of the book is significant in Lewis's later development.

It is obvious that none of these novels quite explains Lewis's sudden blossoming forth as a realist. He had some years previously begun a story about the village virus which was to use the lawyer Guy Pollock as protagonist, but this was thrown aside, and the jejune characterization and stereotyped plots of his published novels hardly prepare the way for *Main Street*. Yet no artist ever springs forth from the sea of time in full control of his powers, and there are signs in even the flimsiest of his early novels that point to his mature work. Amid banality and crudeness, there are streaks of vivid realism and touches of satire that anticipate the later Lewis. Individual portraits, parenthetical remarks, bits of observation, expository synopses frequently suggest the maturing satirist and prove, as Carl Van Doren asserted, that Lewis was becoming saturated with knowledge of American life. Before this saturation point was reached Lewis was unable to present his complete picture of the American village and perforce contented himself with popular fiction. Before he was ready to depict hypocrites and charlatans and bores he chose such feeble protagonists as William Wrenn and Carl Ericson and

Milt Daggett, but in the very act of telling their stories he revealed occasional touches of his later craftsmanship.

Thus little in the more famous novels can eclipse the terse characterization of Lew Golden on the first page of *The Job:*

> He carried a quite visible moustache-comb and wore a collar, but no tie. On warm days he appeared on the street in his shirtsleeves, and discussed the comparative temperatures of the past thirty years with Doctor Smith and the Mansion House 'bus driver. He never used the word "beauty" except in reference to a setter-dog—beauty of words or music, of faith or rebellion, did not exist for him. He rather fancied large, ambitious, banal, red-and-gold sunsets, but he merely glanced at them as he straggled home, and remarked that they were "nice." He believed that all Parisians, artists, millionaires, and Socialists were immoral. His entire system of theology was comprised in the Bible, which he never read, and the Methodist Church, which he rarely attended; and he desired no system of economics beyond the current platform of the Republican party. He was aimlessly industrious, crotchety but kind, and almost quixotically honest.

Lew Golden promptly disappears from the novel, which is Una's story, but his portrait is a clear adumbration of the George F. Babbitt to come.

In similar fashion S. Alcott Wood, president of Plato College in *The Trail of the Hawk*, anticipates Lewis's later strictures on the clergy.

> President Wood was an honest, anxious body, something like a small, learned, Scotch linen-draper. He was given to being worried and advisory and to sitting up till midnight in his unventilated library, grinding at the task of putting new wrong meanings into perfectly obvious statements in the Bible. He was a series of circles—round head with smooth gray hair that hung in a bang over his round forehead; round face with round red cheeks; absurdly heavy gray mustache that almost made a circle about his puerile mouth; round button of a nose; round heavy shoulders; round little stomach in a gray sacksuit; round dumplings of feet in congress shoes that were never quite fresh-blacked or quite dusty. A harassed, honorable, studious, ignorant, humorless, joke-popping, genuinely conscientious thumb of a man. His prayers were long and intimate.

This president of a small Baptist college was rigidly orthodox in religion and morals; the doctrine of evolution horrified him and smoking was a cardinal sin. He exemplifies the Bible Belt educator who for years was H. L. Mencken's special target (and *Elmer Gantry* was dedicated to Mencken).

Two minor portraits from *The Trail of the Hawk* further confirm this early satirical tendency. The dean at Plato College was "a young, collegiate climber, with a clipped mustache, a gold eye-glass chain over one ear, a curt voice, many facts, a spurious appreciation of music, and no mellowness. He was a graduate of the University of Chicago, and aggressively proud of it." A schoolteacher who taught youthful Carl Ericson did not hesitate to use feminine weapons upon the lad. "For after irritating a self-respecting boy into rudeness by pawing his soul with damp, puffy hands, she would weep. She was a kind, honest, and reverent bovine."

Almost equally revealing of the Lewis to come is the type of character of whom he approves or the occasional characteristic which he ascribes to certain figures as a kind of leaven. Hawk Ericson, extrovert that he is, intermittently reflects on life and develops a mild agnosticism which his creator relishes. It was also his acceptance of socialistic doctrines and his support of the teacher who espoused them that led to his departure from Plato College. Istra Nash, the artist and Bohemian who so fascinated William Wrenn and whom Lewis reintroduces in *The Trail of the Hawk*, represents urban sophistication in opposition to the small town insularity of Gertrude Cowles. And in Bone Stillman, the agnostic farmer who lives alone in a dirty house and reads Karl Marx to his dogs, Lewis pictures the social rebel who challenges all conventions and is both feared and ostracized. There is a close identity between Stillman and Miles Bjornstam, the red-headed Swedish plumber in *Main Street* who scandalizes the town but who is too handy with tools to be ignored. If Lewis devoted considerable space to bourgeois dullness he also praised with consistency the occasional rebels who scorned social tyranny and boiler-plate thinking.

All the Lewis novels have been notable for their rapid narrative, but even in the earliest the novelist took time to underscore certain scenes or to suggest the tone of locality in a flashing phrase. Walter Babson, in *The Job*, attends Jonathan Edwards College in Iowa and is expelled for boisterous conduct, but he could get little nourishment from college classes "which were as hard and unpalatable as dried codfish." Carl Ericson was equally displeased at Plato College where he found the classwork pure rot: "arbitrary mathematics, antiquated botany, hesitating German, and a veritable military drill in the conjugation of Greek verbs conducted by a man with a non-com. soul, a pompous, sandy-whiskered manikin with cold eyes and a perpetual cold in the nose, who had inflicted upon a patient world the four-millionth commentary on Xenophon." Boardinghouse scenes in *Our Mr. Wrenn* and business offices in *The Job* give Lewis ample opportunity to picture bilious wallpaper, moth-eaten furniture, stale-smelling rooms, and heavily jocular minor executives. A further example of this kind is the collection of tearoom furnishings foisted upon the innocent Applebys just before they inaugurate their ill-fated restaurant on Cape Cod.

Tea-cups and saucers gilded like shaving-mugs and equally thick. Golden-oak chairs of mid-Chautauquan patterns, with backs of saw-mill Heppelwhite; chairs of cane and rattan with fussy scrolls and curlicues of wicker, the backs set askew. Reed tables with gollops of wicker; plain black wooden tables that were like kitchen tables once removed; folding-tables that may have been suitable to card-playing, if you didn't play anything more exciting than casino. Flat silver that was heavily plated except where it was likely to wear . . . Dark blue plates with warts on the edges and melancholy landscapes painted in the centers . . . Tea-cartons that had the most inspiring labels; cocoa that was bitter and pepper that was mild; preserves that were generous with hayseed and glucose.

But in connection with the major novels the attempts of Lewis to picture small town life in the early stories are most revealing. The first dozen chapters of *The Trail of the Hawk* picture the small Minnesota community of Joralemon and the college community of Plato. The opening pages of *Free Air* introduce the reader to the hamlet of Schoenstrom, a village with a brick general store, a frame hotel, a farm-machinery agency, a church, three saloons, and the Red Trail Garage which services cars, repairs binders and sewing machines, and offers weekly the skill of a veterinarian. In chapter four Lewis sketches Gopher Prairie, a town of five thousand people, the same Gopher Prairie with muddy roads and bathless hotel rooms which was to become the cynosure of thousands of readers. These four small towns, incompletely limned as they are, came to represent the archetype of the American fictional hamlet. They crouch on the edge of the prairie gumbo, which Lewis defines as "mud mixed with tar, flypaper, fish glue, and well-chewed, chocolate-covered caramels." They offer markets and bright lights and places of entertainment to the adjacent farmers whose labors support them. They are dull and stolid, inquisitive and censorious, garish and crude. To a visiting Claire Boltwood looking for a room with a bath or to the newcomer Carol Kennicott hoping to reform a community they are insufferably dreary. On the other hand, a Dr. Will Kennicott finds them friendly and comfortable, and when they are inflated to the size of Zenith in the state of Winnemac they become the natural habitat of the species Babbitt.

It is notable that Lewis seldom ridiculed the protagonists of his apprentice novels. William Wrenn and Hawk Ericson and Milt Daggett and even Father and Mother Appleby are not made absurd, probably because the genuine romanticist was a figure too close to the author's own character. Wrenn's pathetic visions of escape from routine, Ericson's passion to fly, Daggett's fascination with a girl who suddenly appeared on his horizon—these Lewis could sympathize with because they were genuine and because they represented an effort to grasp something new and something exciting. The desire for change, for travel, for freedom was always close to his own heart and epitomized much of his own past life. Lewis even allows Babbitt a thin romantic touch when he pictures him visualizing a little fairy who seems to beckon him into a different existence. Perhaps the fairy sometimes assumes the semblance of Babbitt's stenographer, an inescapably anthropomorphic touch, but she is constantly there to suggest flight from the dreary present. The romantic, sanguinely assured that over the horizon or around the corner things are better or at least more exciting, is not the target of Lewis's ire; he reserved his corrosive photography for different game. The best known figures of Lewis's later fiction are those with whom the author has least sympathy: Elmer Gantry, Dodsworth, Ann Vickers.

Pretense, hypocrisy, demagoguery, the traditional butts of the satirist and Lewis's prime concern in the later novels, do not figure largely in the books preceding *Main Street.* Nor had he then begun to level his sights obviously on the businessmen and the clergy. Occasional malicious thrusts are directed at teachers, college executives, salesmen, farmers—particularly at those whose training or whose profession should have made them skeptical and alert; but there are no full-dimensioned portraits. Possibly this is in part the result of differences in method. The typical Lewis novel after 1920 is a biography, a major segment of the protagonist's life story being told in great fulness of detail, and everything else—other characters, situations, background—being subordinated to the chief purpose. As a consequence the story is somewhat impeded in narrative speed, and although the character is still presented externally he is given breadth and form. Indeed, one of the sharpest differences between Lewis's early novels and his later ones is the change of tempo. Where *The Trail of the Hawk* hurtles along with the speed of Carl Ericson's airplane, a mass of relevant but static details slows up *Arrowsmith* or *It Can't Happen Here.* Lewis even requires two chapters merely to show Babbitt arising, shaving, dressing, and preparing to leave for the office—incidentally one of the memorable passages in modern American fiction.

There is one other way in which Lewis's early novels possess more than a superficial connection with those that succeeded them. Just as the author's satirical observation, his command of caustic humor, and his enormous vitality reveal themselves intermittently, so is Lewis's later style anticipated. Here in embryonic but unmistakable form is the exaggeration, the periodic distortion for effect, the extravagant analogies, the deliberate use of slang, and—to a lesser extent—the accurate mimicry, which distinguish both Lewis's writing and his conversation. That none of these qualities is developed enough to be conspicuous may be attributed to Lewis's careless composition, possibly to his conviction that his real task was not the writing of these intermediate volumes but the absorbing of a tremendous fund of information about American life which he was to spew out in *Main Street* and its sequels.

For in the final analysis all of Lewis's published fiction, even the relatively unsuccessful novels published before 1920, forms part of an American comedy which embraces the world of business, religion, politics, industry, education, and farming—an impressive whole with twenty or more parts picturing the national scene. It was Lewis's decision to present this scene with the accent on scorn, on ridicule, on satire. He may even be, in Robert Cantwell's phrase, the historian of America's catastrophic going-to-pieces, with no remedy to offer for the decline he records. But no American novelist has planned more, and few have achieved so much.

Most people will readily forget the five novels that Sinclair Lewis published before he hit his stride, or will at least dismiss them casually as amateurish work. Their imperfections admitted, they still reveal something about the direction and the quality of the novelist's later fiction. In another age than the post-war 1920's, with readers perhaps hungering for pleasant legends and heart-warming romances, Sinclair Lewis might have continued the tendencies of his youth. But the realistic and satiric undercurrents, as well as the prevalent tone of the period, suggest that his evolution into a realist was inevitable. Possibly the permanent value of his five apprenticeship novels is that they taught him what not to do in writing *Main Street*.

How Good Is Sinclair Lewis?   Warren Beck*

Sinclair Lewis' latest novel, his twentieth in thirty-four years, has somewhat revived him as big name and literary property. The theme of *Kingsblood Royal*, one man's crucial involvement in the race problem, is the most portentous Lewis has attempted. Nevertheless, this book seems to prolong in his grotesque career that apparent anticlimax following *Main Street* (1920), *Babbitt* (1922), and *Arrowsmith* (1925). It would be a lenient judgment that *Kingsblood Royal*, together with *Dodsworth* (1929) and *It Can't Happen Here* (1935), rounds out a trio of second magnitude widely spaced in the gloom since his half-decade of greatest success. Through twenty-two years and a dozen novels many reviewers and readers have gone on shaking their heads in regretful surprise over Lewis' failure to come back. It seems time to discard

*Reprinted, with permission, from *College English* 9 (January 1948):173–80.

this built-up indulgence of a perennially disappointing writer and to take another look.

For one thing, the most important, how much of an artist has Lewis ever been? He can pace off a narrative of detailed event and hack out blunt caricatures, but can he characterize consistently and penetratingly or clarify his themes and transmute them into sustained and moving drama? For all their energy, do his novels have power over the imagination? Is their vaunted realism more than sketchy? What dignity is there in Lewis' work—either the dignity of human nature or that of art itself— and what real pathos? With all his pretensions as satirist, is there either high comedy or subtle irony? In spite of its long decline, is not Lewis' still the most extravagantly inflated reputation in contemporary American fiction? That inflation sprang from the historical accident of his tapping, with his three most notable books, a swollen mood of iconoclasm and escapism among millions of readers, a peculiarly American nihilism, expressing a second and third generations' edgy revolt against the platitudinous materialism their pioneer fathers had settled for, but lacking any compensatory aims, being without roots in a vital culture. Lewis' self-winding fame was strengthened further by the outrageous award of the Nobel prize. A critical minority, however, have thought his amazing succession of books increasingly perfunctory; others have decided that, while he has been as serious as his nature permits, his practice has remained inept. In any case, if it may not be said that *Kingsblood Royal* adds nothing to Lewis' reputation, it should be seen that what is added is more of the same.

Lewis begins his twentieth novel thus: "Mr. Blingham, and may he fry in his own cooking-oil, was assistant treasurer of the Flaver-Saver Company." Such violence seems to mark Blingham as a chief target, but he is discarded after four pages in which Lewis lets his fingers wander idly over the yellowing keys. Blingham is the boastful businessman, allegedly from New York, yet really from nowhere on earth but from Zenith, and he has with him a wife and daughter of standard odiousness, to Lewis' fancy. Motoring along, they chat with that raucous malevolence and elephantine facetiousness which Lewis uses to brand any who knew Coolidge. They stop in Grand Republic, Minnesota, to lunch and leave the reader there, having glimpsed for him, in their cockeyed way, a Negro headwaiter, a junior bank officer—Neil Kingsblood, and Neil's glamorous wife and daughter by their new suburban house-beautiful. The novel could have begun more honestly and effectively at the second chapter. Whether those first stereotyped pages disclose an author's mounting anxiety over his output or exhibit the routine brashness of an old trouper is a question to be held over for a psychographer who may one day analyze this novelist stranger than any of his fictions.

Whatever the reason, throughout *Kingsblood Royal* Lewis relies on his customary lines, not only Babbitt-families, but hypocritical clerics, mock-heroic men's clubs, mutually boring relatives, and jerry-built social situations, all patched with incongruous scraps of hearsay culture and eked out by incredibly banal dialogue or else that forced slang and cant which Lewis has so long palmed off as lively colloquialism. Rodney Aldwick, a graduate of the Harvard law school and a tank-corps major, speaks thus of the war injury which left Captain Neil Kingsblood with a slight limp: "Neilly, I've heard how gallantly you took your wound." Not only is Major Aldwick said to reminisce about "the Other Side"; Lewis heartily writes down the Kingsbloods as "a Happy Young American Married Couple." And just who is being ostentatious when at Rodney's party, where his talk with Neil is a "recollection of juvenile basketball" and a reviling of Negro soldiers, the "four-piece orchestra played Delius and Copland"? What will one who does not know *Hamlet* make of Rod's appearance as "a soldier, a gentleman adventurer, a hawk, a handsaw, a hero," and what indeed can be made of it by any who recall Hamlet's distinction between hawk and handsaw? If the reader is to excuse the arch description of a suburb with "forests ancient as the hills enclosing sunny spots of greenery," then when an interior decorator thinking of a publicity stunt allegedly "waved his china cigarette-holder in a magic circle and closed his eyes in holy dread, for he on honey dew had fed and had been demoniacally possessed of an Idea," may not the reader too be excused if his mind wanders to surmise that Mr. Lewis of all people had been reading a certain poem?

What else, though, has Lewis fed on besides his own works that he continues to write so badly? His irresponsible exaggerations not only offend common sense but devastate fictional illusion. College presidents, the knowing author says without qualification, believe "that if anyone with .000001 per cent of Negro genes married anyone fair as alabaster (which is notoriously fair) their children were more than likely to be all of them as black as the heart of a dictator." Anonymous letters, we learn from Lewis, are "written in painful ecstasy by neurotics who spend the rest of their time in sneaking along back alleys, after midnight, poisoning small cats." Even granting the Nobel novelist those small cats, could not the poisoners have been spared "the rest of their time" once the hours of poisoning had been fixed at "after midnight"; or do they write anonymously up to the stroke of twelve and resume the pen the moment they lay down the poison; or does Lewis never look back, once he has started a sentence? Furthermore, is Lewis' knowledge of what the anonymous do, especially after midnight in back alleys, based on more of that meticulous documentation he has been widely noted for? And does it take the Horatian perspectives of nine years to bring on revision of a description of icy sidewalks on which "everybody in town, practically, broke an ankle or at least sat down hard and looked around indignant"?

Such minutiae are not insignificant. Crudity in detail not only flaws sentences but can prevent the whole work of art, which constantly depends upon relevant substance regulated in the perspectives of theme and mood. This is especially true in characterization, where credibility, proportion, and consistency are essential, and it is here that Lewis is most at fault. Neil's remark that he "used to laugh at the Southern fellows in the Army" who said that Negroes "don't quite belong to the same human race" leaves the reader to reconcile two discrepant facts: first, that this hitherto tolerant young man is, strangely, the product of a northern town preoccupied with racial prejudices; and, second, that all it then requires to make him "guess" the southern fellows were "right" is the Kingsbloods' dissatisfaction with their unreliable colored maid. Neil's inconsistencies, however, run deeper than such instances. Discovering that he has one-thirty-second part Negro blood, he is so troubled whether to avow it that he asks his pastor's advice; yet, when the Negro Brazenstar suggests that, considering errant human nature, every white person probably has some trace of Negro blood, Neil is "offended," because such a general leveling would threaten what he now cherishes as "the whole careful structure of his unhappiness." This case typifies Lewis' tendency to betray his protagonists into incongruities which discompose theme and shatter the reader's evolving illusion. Such reversals, if not the result of Lewis' caprice, must be charged to his confusion and loss of grip on subjects he had never conceived profoundly. Neil's inclination to proclaim his Negro blood is an arbitrary and scarcely credible detail; most men of his class and circumstances would have tried concealment, for motives not altogether selfish. Lewis could have told the story that way with greater psychological and emotional depth, making Neil faithful to his family's welfare and yet increasingly kindly toward his discovered brothers and letting the revelation come more dramatically, by accident or another's malice. It was Lewis' prerogative to pass by this subtler treatment and make Neil the hotheaded little hero in that grotesque clubroom scene when the intolerance of fellow-members provokes his defiant confession; but it was also Lewis' duty either to make Neil substantially a morbid feeder on his own unhappiness or else not suddenly ridicule and abandon him as such after trying to represent his struggle as one of conscience.

The denouement of *Kingsblood Royal* also typifies its author's superficiality and evasiveness. In Grand Republic there has been a plot to crowd out Negro workers, both skilled and unskilled; there is pressure to force Neil out of his "restricted" neighborhood. Such injustices are credible and deplorable, and to show them applied stealthily and hypocritically would come close to the race problem in the North. This would require deft treatment, however, especially in characterization. Lewis takes the broader and seemingly easier way of melodrama. Neil's friends, Negro and white, gather armed to ward off a mob, and there is even some shooting, but no one is killed. One wild shot merely grazed the arm of Neil's wife, while another "nipped off a toe" of an attacker "and sent him home howling." From this shamefully irresponsible reduction of the fact of mob violence to farcical terms Lewis hurries to a sentimentally cheerful close; Neil's wife insists on being arrested along with the Negroes, and, when police tell them to keep moving, she says, "We're moving." These closing words might have been powerfully thematic had they been preceded by realistic characterization and logically evolving drama, but they merely cap the novel with a dab of saccharine. To some readers that "We're moving" may suggest a parallel with Steinbeck's Okies on the road at the close of *The Grapes of Wrath* or Dos Passos' Vag thumbing a ride at the close of *U.S.A.*; but the example of these two broadly conceived and powerfully executed novels shows off *Kingsblood Royal* by contrast as an inadvertent parody of socially significant fiction. Lewis' grotesque plots and distorted characterizations have hitherto been aesthetically annoying to some readers; when he turns such irresponsible treatment upon the race problem, blunting great issues until he removes them from the area of earnest and perceptive consideration, his whole career is brought further into question.

A backward glance by the light of Lewis' latest work discovers in his most admired books similar basic faults. Carol Kennicott of *Main Street* is another character betrayed. Lewis' preponderant attitude is that she has aspired and gone down in "tragedy devoid of palls and chanting, the humdrum inevitable tragedy of struggle against inertia." At her first party, attempting to break up the "circle of mourners" seated in languishing conversation, Carol dresses her guests in Chinese paper costumes, and she herself appears in green brocade, announcing "The Princess Winky Poo salutes her court!" Then music is made with combs and tissue paper. This creepy episode Lewis actually seems to take straight, for when Gopher Prairie relapses into its more stolid ways after so shining an example, he represents it as a setback to beauty and the higher life. In another passage Carol reflects that the village needs stimulation by the exotic: "Strindberg plays," she says, "and classic dancers—exquisite legs beneath tulle—and (I can see him so clearly) a thick black-bearded Frenchman who would sit about and drink and sing opera and tell bawdy stories and laugh at our proprieties and quote Rabelais and not be ashamed to kiss my hand." Since Carol is a midwesterner familiar with no more cosmopolitan spot than the Minneapolis Public Library, any Frenchman she sees so clearly would be all in her eye—a synthetic product, perhaps, of the Alphonso-Gaston comic strip (current in Lewis' youth) and the sophomoric lore that all Gauls are superfluously naughty. Yet here too her creator seems to approve of Carol, for her thirst for the exotic as incarnate in that ersatz Frenchman is expressed in the midst of ten pages where, with phrases like "Carol thought," "reflected," "told herself," Lewis uses her as a mouthpiece in earnest assault against village mores. Apparently his concept is serious too when, during her escape to a war job in a Washington office, Carol reputedly enjoys conversational evenings with intellectuals, though Lewis does not show how she connected with what kind of intellectuals or what they found to say to her. What, then, is Carol at her best—what are her positive criteria beyond bearded Frenchmen and Winky Poo parties? "Criticism, perhaps, for the beginning of the beginning," she declares. "There's nothing that attacks the tribal god Mediocrity that doesn't help a little. . . . and probably there's nothing that helps very much. Perhaps some day the farmers will build their own market towns." Her notion that any sort of attack helps and her shallow discontent spending itself in shifty utopianism are not uncommon American faults, which could be tellingly satirized, but, even presented with Lewis' naïveté and lack of humor, they cancel out Carol as a heroine of tragedy. Did Lewis dimly feel that his hand had slipped and cut her down into a shrill little ingénue? And was it to sublimate his sense of failure that he abandoned her in this guise at the birth of her daughter: "Carol couldn't decide whether she was to become a feminist leader or marry a scientist or both, but did settle on Vassar and a tricolette suit with a small black hat for her Freshman year"? The self-appointed Princess may deserve that, but not from her formerly earnest impresario, of whom it is easier to believe that he was quite taken with Winky Poo than that he would use irony or any other satire too faintly or subtly.

Lewis must be credited, however, with projecting two substantial and consistent characters, Babbitt and Arrowsmith. Indeed, though the style in _Babbitt_ is typically vociferous and the satire heavy, George Babbitt is recognizably human, and his case is viewed with some artistic detachment and even an enhancing touch of compassion. However, Babbitt is no hero; he is indeed ridiculous almost throughout and at other moments merely pitiable. And Martin Arrowsmith, though consistently portrayed, is not an equally well-controlled characterization. He has run off not only with many a reader but with his author, for in glorifying Arrowsmith as scientist Lewis seems unaware of what a crude and lopsided human being he had made of him. Dodsworth, who at moments comes as near being a matured and rounded personality as any of Lewis' characters, suffers a betrayal like Carol's; he is sometimes idealized in protest against Babbittry and in search of a satisfying culture, but he is also caricatured as the intolerant big shot and the blustering tourist. Sometimes Lewis feels that nothing is too good for his midwestern industrialist, as when Dodsworth is said to have "thought rather well of Dreiser, Cabell, and so much of Proust as he had rather laboriously mastered," and yet in answer to the charge that Americans "don't love earth," he is made to rant, "Oh, look here now! What about our millions of acres of plowed fields? Nothing *like* it, outside of maybe Russia! What about our most important men, that get out in the fresh air and motor and golf?" While Babbitt and Arrowsmith are convincing characterizations, they are not cultivated men; and Dodsworth, being refined but part of the time, lacks reality.

Where indeed among Lewis' dramatis personae is there a compelling and sustained manifestation of cultured intelligence, to say nothing of human graciousness, dignity, humor, charm, or an elevated sense of life, whether joyful or tragic? Such characterizations must lie beyond Lewis' grasp, for certainly in his argument of the individual's case against a materialistic conventionality he would put up the best protagonists he could command. If Carol is a typical victim, if here is a representative "tragedy," the case against Gopher Prairie was not as damning as Lewis felt it to be. The naïve, flabby, and morbid Neil Kingsblood revives suspicion that the limitations of Lewis' characters are inherited from their only begetter. At a most august and conspicuous moment, receiving the Nobel prize and speaking in his own right and on his own responsibility as man of letters and man of the world, Lewis characterized himself by choosing to emphasize as a shaping policy his doubt that

> all American men are tall, handsome, rich, honest, and powerful at golf; that all country towns are filled with neighbors who do nothing from day to day save go about being kind to one another; that although American girls may be wild, they change always into perfect wives and mothers; and that, geographically, America is composed solely of New York, which is inhabited entirely by millionaires; of the West, which keeps unchanged all the boisterous heroism of 1870, and of the South, where everyone lives on a plantation perpetually glossy with moonlight and scented with magnolias.

All this is symptomatic: the preoccupation with the obvious, the reliance on a line, the degeneration of humor into labored caricature, the harsh zeal outrunning judiciousness, the easy triumph that is really an evasion, the dissatisfied and vindictive tone. One is tempted to imagine, by contrast, some other American writer on that platform, with the world's intellectuals and artists listening in. How much more humanely would Robert Frost have spoken, or Willa Cather, or John Dos Passos, or E. B. White, or, a better satirist than Lewis, John Marquand, or, a much better realist in Lewis' own territory, Ruth Suckow?

The examples of Miss Suckow and Marquand suggest more particularly that the realist can judge folly and meanness without succumbing to chronic jaundice and that human imperfections can be chided without resort to ridicule and even without loss of compassion. Once Lewis indicated deep sympathy for a defeated character in the notably human scene when Babbitt sobs at his wife's sickbed, made to repent his strayings by the claims of personal loyalties, which even in that drab domesticity evoke the pathos of the familiar and the mutual. Here Lewis approached the ancient springs which sustain humans in the desert of habit and under the inescapable glare of conventions. This radiating episode which brings Babbitt's story full circle and relates it representatively to the life of man may yet be seen to place this novel above the widely admired *Arrowsmith.* In the latter, Lewis consistently glorifies a hero and satirizes his opposites, yet Dr. Arrowsmith's only virtue is a devotion to scientific method and truth. His too is an escape story, after his passing grief for Leora, through increasing specialization to a laboratory in the woods, where he goes flannel-shirted, free of feminine domination, social intrusions, or even any friction with colleagues. The terms under which Arrowsmith succeeds are thus less significant, humanly speaking, than those under which Babbitt is said to have failed. And it is notable that even while idealizing the objective scientist, perhaps in compensation for his own hasty emotionalism and habit of exaggeration, Lewis could not forego the theme of escape. Similarly in *It Can't Happen Here* the brave antifascist editor worships liberty, not only as political principle, but in pursuit of another woman for whom he leaves his wife. Similarly, *Kingsblood Royal* is blurred as a view of race relations in that Neil so often seems motivated by desire for emancipation from a Babbitt-society into the intellectually livelier and more cordial company of his new-found Negro friends, though to suggest this Lewis sentimentalizes the Negroes and caricatures the Caucasians, setting the latter up in waxworks parties as incredible as those Carol opposed.

Kingsblood Royal suggests that Lewis knows little of Negroes (who are more like white people and also more charmingly themselves than he lets them be) just as he knows little of research scientists (who may have cultural interests and social inclinations) or of businessmen and industrialists (who may possess some dignity based on personal integrity). What Lewis does know, and cannot forget, is a rage against convention, as apparently his temperament and conditioning made him see it in middle-class midwestern society, and a fantasy of escape to places and associations reputedly more sophisticated and glamorous. Lewis generously bequeaths these two attributes to his characters, but there his gifts end. It is small capital indeed upon which to have done such spectacular literary business. Lewis is often praised as realist, but realism presupposes an objectivity he has never achieved. Possibly it is himself he laments or loathes when in morbid escapism he runs out even on his own characters; perhaps, on the other hand, he flatters and gratifies himself even in his irresponsibility as artist. Nevertheless, he must be judged finally in terms of his professed intention, the satirical. Satire implies certain artistic and intellectual qualities—a genuinely objective treatment, contrasting human conduct realistically viewed with human life as it might be, not in egoistic escape, but under its actual terms and yet improved by reason. It follows that the satirist must be a philosophical man of the world, able in the strategic practice of idealism. Hence, in the best satire a subtle control typically finds logical and aesthetic fulfilment in irony. Great satire always implies comprehensive value-judgments, which in turn depend upon the equation of human sympathy and cultivated insight. Pseudosatirists, lacking personal integration and urbane judgment, oppose the aberrations of other men with their own caprice and largely out of their own frustrations or vanities.

In *Arrowsmith* the pure scientist Gottlieb advocated his specialization as an ignoring of both American booster and European aristocrat and an equal opposition to "the capitalists who t'ink their silly money-grabbing is a system and the liberals who t'ink man is not a fighting animal." Ten years later in *It Can't Happen Here* Lewis tried to respond fashionably to the times' demand for something beyond the sterile neutrality and escapism of science sentimentalized. *Kingsblood Royal* is one more up-and-coming attempt at a timely and socially implicative matter. Still spreading himself in his callow way, however, Lewis has further confused a complex problem by arbitrary caricature, has denied his protagonist consistency and dignity, to the nullification of theme, and has injected into social drama the debasing tone of farce and the disrupting element of personal escape. His view of the race problem lacks both social and psychological penetration, as did his tale of fascism in America, and he had not the intuitive sympathy and artistic power to enhance Neil Kingsblood's story with a pity and terror potential in it. He could bring to it only his old bag of tricks. His latest book emphasizes how shabby with long use those devices are and how lacking in either conscience or percipience he can be in applying them to momentous subjects. By this time readers should know what not to expect of Sinclair Lewis, who seems to have forgotten nothing but the humanity of Babbitt and to have learned nothing except perhaps a greater recklessness.

Sinclair Lewis:
Apostle to the Philistines   George J. Becker*

Thirty years ago, most Americans lived in, came from, or at least had had fairly intimate experience with small towns. Village America dominated patterns of thought and of behavior to an extent that seems scarcely credible today. Although that dominance was being rapidly undermined by the growth of great industrial cities and their dormitory suburbs, so that the census of 1930 would establish that nearly half of our population lived in metropolitan areas—in 1920, the village was still glorified as "Friendship Village," the cradle of democracy, the nursery of individuality and genius, the repository of all the abiding virtues.

Then, within a few months, there came blasts from two new writers, Sherwood Anderson and Sinclair Lewis, which forever shattered that image, creating a literary phenomenon known as "the revolt from the village" and precipitating a controversy whose alarms and excursions have become largely meaningless as the village has been reduced to impotence in national life, sapped of its youth by the automobile and the factory, sterilized in its culture by the movies and the radio. The chief figure of that controversy was Lewis, who, for thirty years, whooped periodically down Main Street, shooting wildly to right and left while the citizens took cover.

Sinclair Lewis was filled with crusading zeal. His attack on contemporary society was overt, tireless and hyperbolic. He blew up huge balloons labeled "Babbitt," "Gantry," "Planish," and then punctured them with howling glee. He had little sense of social process, little concern for the detailed workings of institutions. Like his own Carol Kennicott, he began everywhere at once and turned himself, if not the world, topsy-turvy, without indicating specifically what he wanted done. Always in the back of his mind was the biting reminder that the half-men whom he pictured were not those promised to this Eden—that when the pioneering fathers sailed in thought and aspiration to the far Hesperides, it was a vision of the transcendent man that led them on. For thirty years, Lewis lambasted, cajoled, ridiculed and threatened without arriving at any definitive diagnosis of what was wrong with his country or his countrymen. All his life, he was seeking the cause of the multiple malaise which he encountered everywhere. He never isolated the virus, although some of his novels filtered very fine.

The best statement he ever made is one contained in the speech accepting the Nobel Prize at Stockholm, when he spoke of himself as "a writer whose most anarchistic assertion has been that America, with

*Reprinted, with permission, from the *American Scholar* 21 (Autumn 1952):423–32.

all her wealth and power, has not yet produced a civilization good enough to satisfy the deepest wants of human creatures."

It may be that Lewis has played a strong and decisive part in shaping constructive changes. It may be that his countrymen have shed the crude vesture of a Babbitt for a Brooks Brothers number equally inappropriate to men of destiny. It may be that he has had little or no effect on his countrymen, whose enthusiastic reception of his writing may have merely indicated their own readiness to turn away from the attitudes and antics he ridiculed. In any event, it is the amplitude of his evaluation, rather than its profundity, which makes him a significant figure in America's coming of age.

Of the five novels before *Main Street*, only *Our Mr. Wrenn* (1914) and *The Job* (1917) show much evidence of social concern. They gave a tentative enunciation to a theme which was to become important in our literature, although Lewis left its development to others. Both novels explore the concept of the tyranny of the job, the whole business system and the business myth over the individual. *The Job* also touches on two ideas which were to engross Lewis's attention for the rest of his life: feminism, the struggle of the partially emancipated woman for self-hood, her effort to humanize her "existence of loveless routine"; and the shoddy quality of our civilization.

Although these early works are often high-spirited, they do not give any clear indication of the direction their author was to take. In view of the stereotyped criticism of the economy which they contain, Lewis might have been expected to produce increasingly tendentious studies in the manner of the writers of the 1930's. Perhaps the tremendous success of *Main Street* was decisive in setting his course, but it must not be forgotten that he had for some years been meditating such a work, to be entitled *The Village Virus*, and had been collecting examples of stupidity for that purpose. At any rate, he found himself amazingly at home in the broad depiction and sweeping denunciation of a whole way of life. His success encouraged him to use the discursive chronicle as a frame tale for a multitude of sketches of what Mencken called the "Boobus Americanus"; he never really had to channel his thought or subject himself to the discipline of a narrow focus. It may be, as E. M. Forster has said, that he lodged "a piece of a continent in our imagination," but its outlines are vague, its hills and watercourses only approximate, and its geologic strata completely uncharted.

Whatever the deficiencies of *Main Street* as a novel—and it is bound to suffer by the inevitable comparison with its prototype, *Madame Bovary*—it is important as the original trumpeting of Lewis' discontent, as his first gesture of flinging open every window and door and letting the fresh air of the prairie turn smugness and conventionality head over heels. His quarrel with the village is set forth as a challenge in the epigraph:

> Main Street is the climax of civilization. That this Ford car might stand in front of the Bon Ton Store, Hannibal invaded Rome and Erasmus wrote in Oxford cloisters. What Ole Jensen the grocer says to Ezra Stowbody the banker is the new law for London, Prague, and the unprofitable isles of the sea; whatsoever Ezra does not know and sanction, that thing is heresy, worthless for knowing and wicked to consider.
>
> Our railway station is the final aspiration of architecture. Sam Clark's annual hardware turnover is the envy of the four counties which constitute God's Country. In the sensitive art of the Rosebud Movie Palace there is a Message, and humor strictly moral.
>
> Such is our comfortable tradition and sure faith. Would he not betray himself an alien cynic who should otherwise portray Main Street, or distress the citizens by speculating whether there may not be other faiths?

Carol Kennicott, the alien, though no cynic, does indeed distress the citizens of Gopher Prairie. Her faith, like Lewis', is uncertain and ill-defined, but of one thing she is sure: there are other, more gracious ways of feeling and of living. Once we reconcile ourselves to the fact that Carol is not an Emma Bovary—animated by an authentic though minor daemon—and accept her as the convenient mouthpiece for all the discontents the author wishes to discharge, we can see that the village is the real protagonist, and Carol no more than the stimulus which sets off its reactions. It is difficult to work up any concern over her sufferings; it is a matter of indifference at the end whether she returns or stays away. What is important is the exhibition of village life and the judgment passed upon it.

In a long summary passage in the middle of the book, Carol-Lewis topples village complacency with an explosive comment:

> It is an unimaginatively standardized background, a sluggishness of speech and manners, a rigid ruling of the spirit by the desire to appear respectable. It is ... the contentment of the quiet dead, who are scornful of the living for their restless walking. It is negation canonized as the one positive virtue. It is the prohibition of happiness. It is slavery self-sought and self-defended. It is dullness made God.

In this general atmosphere of drabness and dullness, there are four principal targets. First of all, there is moral and religious inhibition, dominated by a philosophy of "dull safety," turning in frantic reprisal on anyone whose behavior departs from the limited and unimaginative norm. Second, there is thralldom to a crude materialism. The village values knowledge only as it is the visible avenue to money or to social distinction. It divides people into clubs, churches and schools on a basis of income and punishes those who dare to ignore such lines. Third, and most appalling, this mentality is pawing at world dominion, "not satisfied until the entire world also admits that the end and joyous purpose of living is to ride in flivvers, to make advertising-pictures of dollar watches, and in the twilight to sit talking not of love and courage but of the convenience of safety razors," demanding, moreover, that foreigners give up their own heritage so that they may be "ironed into glossy mediocrity."

It is this fourth point, this "glossy mediocrity," which is the climax and epitome of Lewis's grievance. The attitudes he pillories have become institutionalized, and any adventurer of the spirit must combat Polite Society, the Family, the Church, Sound Business, the Party, the Superior White Race—and, when his strength gives out, he must succumb to the Village Virus, which is the deadly distillation of all these.

There are other themes in *Main Street*; that is one of its difficulties: it starts more hares than it can conviently follow. It is often hard to determine how much of Carol's revolt is against Main Street and how much against her condition as woman. The author is also disposed to seek nobility in the soil, to find among the farmers of the bounteous countryside the greatness and dignity absent from the village, and to speculate as to where the original promise of a pioneer region was lost and we began to incur the risk of "the ancient stale inequalities . . . the tedious maturity of other empires." Certainly all of Lewis' later writing is implicit in the tangled and multitudinous skein of this novel. Once he had described the milieu *in extenso*, he turned to the unlovely seed which it spawned.

Babbitt (1922) shows the pitiful product of a crude and adolescent civilization, but one that is not entirely despicable or completely beyond hope. As we first see the protagonist going through the routine of meaningless and repetitive activity which for him constitutes living, we find him a comic figure. We laugh at his addiction to gadgets, to the cliché in speech and thought; at his tagging his values with dollar signs and sanctifying them with advertising slogans; at the clumsy gregariousness necessary to give him even a faint sense of being. In spite of mitigating touches—such as his unadvantaged loyalty to Paul Riesling—when we begin to look beneath the comic exterior, we find him distasteful, even faintly evil: a portent of the mass man and of the mentality that turns others into mass men or expels them from the community.

The cruelest of Lewis' darts are reserved for those minor figures, Verg Gunch, Chum Frink, and the rest, whose very names are an affront to the sense of human dignity. Such a figure is Lowell Schmaltz, the monologuist of *The Man Who Knew Coolidge* (1928), the emptiness of whose mind and heart is turned inside out in the six meandering conversations which make up that book. He is a windbag, a boaster, a boor. He is a coward with an underhand streak of cruelty. He has drunk deep of Main Street's class consciousness and cultural chauvinism. His vision of the New World is summed up in his ideals of Service and Practicality. The first consists of selling a fellow something he does not want or need and cannot afford; the latter involves the elimination of those "intangibles" which normally constitute the glory of a civilization.

If *Elmer Gantry* (1927) is a less devastating portrait, it is only because we see the whole man in action over a period of years and not just the fetid essence of his mind. This novel, above all others, was lovingly contrived to shock. It begins, "Elmer Gantry was drunk." It ends with a crashing demonstration of his hypocrisy. Throughout, it is a debunking, of the sort popular in the 1920's, of the claims of a certain type of minister and a certain type of religion to sanctity and godliness. The author is careful to sketch more godly men, true priests, but the novel is focused on the fakery of religion as exhibited in the America of the boom period.

In contrast with such figures, Martin Arrowsmith is a success, even by Lewis' exacting standards. After being subjected to every kind of temptation, every kind of blind alley his vocation affords, Martin strides firmly down the path of righteousness and follows his vision of "serene spaciousness of mind." Though the novel is severely restricted in action to the medical profession, it has wider application and embraces all vocations, all efforts to be a complete human being. Here, institutions, human needs and incapacities, approximate values and delusory ambitions are drawn up in implacable enmity, ready to smite the individual who dares run the gauntlet. Much of the book's popularity is probably founded on the fact that, in a wasteland of abortive human beings, Arrowsmith succeeds—the nature of the Grail which he seeks being less important than the fact that he is a Parsifal.

Lewis' limitations as a critic of society are well exhibited by these works. Good or bad, his heroes are largely static, being little more than incarnations of qualities of which the author approves or disapproves. Their very excesses discredit the novels as criticisms of society. In our horrified amusement or disgust, we lose sight of the social matrix which forms these human caricatures and find it impossible to believe that they are typical products of that matrix, even though we adopt their names as household words. It is interesting, therefore, to find that *Dodsworth* (1929), in which Lewis succeeds in creating a more credible human being, also comes more nearly to grips with those problems of our society which trouble him.

This novel, more than any other by Lewis, has a symbolic structure. Edith Cortright is an expatriate who has fled the crudity and harshness of existence in her homeland because she lacks courage for the crude but potentially fruitful life on the American continent. Sam Dodsworth, on the other hand, is a vindication of his country's promise. Although his perspective has been limited by years of pursuing money, he is not a Babbitt; he has status in his own mind as a *maker*, a savant; he is not intimidated by the culture of Europe but is able to assimilate and evaluate it without stooping, as his wife does, to sterile imitation. His integrity alienates his wife, whom he is forced to put aside as a childish encumbrance, but his qualities give hope to Edith, who finds that American life can be a richer amalgam than she has dared to dream. Thus we come to the conclusion that the American adventure is to Lewis the bigger for his discovery of Europe, a timely fertilization coming when "we're no longer satisfied with the log cabin and the corn pone."

By 1930, then, the date of the international recognition attested by the Nobel Prize, Lewis was beginning to give closer and more thoughtful scrutiny to the problems with which he was concerned. Main Street had become less localized in his mind, and he was willing to accord somewhat more dignity and promise to its product than some of the earlier portraits had indicated. For example, a few years later he says of Ann Vickers, a latter-day Carol Kennicott, that the small town and its ways would enter into everything she would do in life and that she was fortunate to be related to "the bourgeois colony which, up to 1917, was the only America," and to be alive "in the magnificent though appalling moment when the United States began awkwardly to see itself not as an illegitimate child of Europe but as the master of its own proud house."

As we look back on the novels of his last two decades, however, it seems that Lewis was seeking desperately for a subject adequate to the evaluation he wished to make, and that he failed to find such a subject. His affirmative statements, such as *Work of Art* (1934), are shallow and sentimental; attempts to reach his former high-spirited vein of mockery are forced; and, on those occasions when he does at last take hold of a specific social problem, his habitual diffuseness defeats him. Nonetheless, *It Can't Happen Here* (1935) and *Kingsblood Royal* (1947) are the most interesting works in this last period because they do attempt to come to grips with the most serious social manifestation of our time: the vindicive limitation of human sympathy which produces authoritarianism and racial discrimination.

Kingsblood Royal is decidedly the most bitter of his books, ending with a battle to the death between the Kingsbloods and the forces of bigotry which are determined to drive them out of the neighborhood in which they had been accepted when Neil Kingsblood thought he was a white man. The author runs into two difficulties with this book. First, he makes discussion of a deeply serious social issue depend on a capricious mechanism, that of Neil's sudden change from white man to Negro. Secondly, if such a mechanism is to be employed with any effectiveness, it must be used consistently so that the whole work becomes a comedy of errors with only the edge of bitterness showing. Lacking such treatment, the book becomes the author's most outright social tract and the least characterisic of his works. It bespeaks a patience worn thin, a bitterness of judgment on "the whole damned human race" reminiscent of Mark Twain in *The Mysterious Stranger.* It pulls the reader up short, making him wonder if, in the end, the roistering Lewis had become convinced of the fundamental unregeneracy of man, and had despaired of the future.

A more characteristic work in terms of both technique and attitude is *It Can't Happen Here,* published twelve years earlier. Reversing Lewis' former strictures, it comes closer to veneration of the small town as the focus of democracy and individuality, the only hope of a world increasingly subjugated to the sterile forces of propaganda and mass emotion. Doremus Jessup, the Vermont newspaper editor who is the hero of this novel, is characterized by the author in terms not applicable to himself:

> ... far from being a left-wing radical, he was at most a mild, rather indolent and somewhat sentimental Liberal, who disliked pomposity, the heavy humor of public men, and the itch for notoriety. ... But for all cruelty and intolerance, and for the contempt of the fortunate for the unfortunate, he had not mere dislike but testy hatred.

He maintains that, "with scandalous exceptions," democracy in this country has given the ordinary man more dignity than he has ever had elsewhere, but he is not blind to repressive and authoritarian tendencies as manifest in Red scares and Catholic scares, White Supremacy, peonage in the South and wage-slavery in the North.

Not the least of Jessup's antagonism toward the imaginary fascist regime is that, if it is against communism, he has to be for communism, and he doesn't want to be. He has no use for any of the patent solutions, doubting that there will ever be a state of society which will come anywhere near perfection. He comes to realize that the struggle going on in the world is not that of communism against fascism, but of "tolerance against bigotry that was preached equally by Communism and Fascism," and he sees that he must stand by himself, a "Liberal," scorned and abused by all parties for insisting on privacy and the right to think and criticize as he pleases:

> More and more, as I think about history, I am convinced that everything that is worth while in the world has been accomplished by the free, inquiring, critical spirit, and that the preservation of this

spirit is more important than any social system whatsoever. But the men of ritual and the men of barbarism are capable of shutting up the men of science and of silencing them forever.

This is the most meaningful statement that Lewis made, and it is even more pertinent today than it was in 1935. Here at last he approached a definition of the social evil which had provoked his attacks in the earlier novels. Here he made the necessary distinction between imperfection of behavior and imperfection of the spirit. Here he recorded the eternal warfare between aspiration and habit.

At long last, Lewis seemed to discern what his countrymen at large must learn if they are to survive and flourish: growth, though organic, is not automatic. There are impeding forces—some within the organism, some within the environment—which must be countered with directive energy, not by simple fiat. It is not enough to mount a pillar and proclaim on high: Be ye no longer Babbitts. There are worse fates than being immured in Main Street, though we must fight on Main Street those germs which multiply to plague in Babylon. When conflicting forces which would harden the heart and mutilate the will bring all the resources of bell, book and terror to subjugate the individual, we must be as resolute against the one as against the other. Tyranny is one and the same, whether it be the mediocrity of the village, the stultifying gregariousness of the herd, the privileged exclusiveness of the institution, the snobbish imitation of the hallowed and esoteric, or a dogmatism whose means are the antithesis of its ends. Perhaps Lewis should have learned this sooner, so that he might have begun where, in fact, his thought came to an end. If that be the case, he has provided inadvertently still another measure of our adolescent shallowness and, as long as we are honest with ourselves, he will be remembered as the image of our salad days.

Sinclair Lewis and the
Method of Half-Truths   Mark Schorer*

Let us begin with a pair of quotations that are concerned with the conception of the novel as a social instrument. The two conceptions are opposed, but the author of each is led by his conception to conclude that because of it the novel is the most important literary form in the modern

*From *Society and Self in the Novel: English Institute Essays, 1955*, ed. Mark Schorer (New York: Columbia University Press, 1956), 117–44. © 1956, Columbia University Press. Reprinted by permission of the publisher.

world, and *for* the modern world. The first is from D. H. Lawrence, and it is, I believe, a unique conception:

> It is the way our sympathy flows and recoils that really de-termines our lives. And here lies the vast importance of the novel, properly handled. It can inform and lead into new places the flow of our sympathetic consciousness, and it can lead our sympathy away in recoil from things gone dead. Therefore, the novel, properly han-dled, can reveal the most secret places of life: for it is in the *passional* secret places of life, above all, that the tide of sensitive awareness needs to ebb and flow, cleansing and freshening.
>
> But the novel, like gossip, can also excite spurious sympathies and recoils, mechanical and deadening to the psyche. The novel can glorify the most corrupt feelings, so long as they are *conventionally* "pure." Then the novel, like gossip, becomes at last vicious, and, like gossip, all the more vicious because it is always ostensibly on the side of the angels.[1]

Lawrence's conception implies a novel that will admit us directly into the life-affirming activities of the integrated consciousness of his own ideal man; a novel that, concerned with the formed individual consciousness, reforms ours; a novel that is not about society or the social character but that is ultimately indispensable to the health of both. We know whose fiction he has in mind; we know, too, with what exasperation he achieved the first term of his exalted ambition, the writing itself, and how impos-sible it is to achieve the second, the therapy.

Our second quotation is a commonplace in the annals of American naturalism, and we could find it, in substance, in any of a dozen writers. Frank Norris will serve. I quote first from his essay, "The Responsibilities of the Novelist," an attack on what he calls "lying novels," novels of sentiment and romance.

> Today is the day of the novel. In no other day and by no other vehicle is contemporaneous life so adequately expressed; and the critics of the twenty-second century, reviewing our times, striving to reconstruct our civilization, will look not to the painters, not to the architects nor dramatists, but to the novelists to find our idiosyn-crasy. . . . If the novel . . . is popular it is popular with a reason, a vital, inherent reason; that is to say, it is essential . . . it is an instru-ment, a tool, a weapon, a vehicle. Public opinion is made no one can say how, by infinitesimal accretions, by a multitude of minutest elements. Lying novels, surely in this day and age of indiscriminate reading, contribute to this more than all other influences of present-day activity . . . The People have a right to the Truth as they have a right to life, liberty and the pursuit of happiness. It is *not* right that they be exploited and deceived with false views of life, false charac-ters, false sentiment, false morality, false history, false philosophy,

false emotions, false heroism, false notions of self-sacrifice, false views of religion, of duty, of conduct and of manners.[2]

And where do we find the truth-telling novel? In the novel with a "purpose," as it is discussed in the essay of that name.

> Every novel must do one of three things—it must (1) tell something, (2) show something, or (3) prove something. Some novels do all three of these. . . . The third, and what we hold to be the best class, proves something, draws conclusions from a whole congeries of forces, social tendencies, race impulses, devotes itself not to a study of men but of man. . . . Take this element from fiction, take from it the power and opportunity to prove that injustice, crime and inequality do exist, and what is left? Just the amusing novels, the novels that entertain . . . the modern novel . . . may be a flippant paper-covered thing of swords and cloaks, to be carried on a railway journey and to be thrown out the window when read, together with the sucked oranges and peanut shells. Or it may be a great force, that works together with the pulpit and the universities for the good of the people, fearlessly proving that power is abused, that the strong grind the faces of the weak, that an evil tree is still growing in the midst of the garden, that undoing follows hard upon righteousness, that the course of Empire is not yet finished, and that the races of men have yet to work out their destiny in those great and terrible movements that crush and grind and rend asunder the pillars of the houses of the nation.[3]

It is within this somewhat crude conception of "the novel with a purpose" that we are accustomed to place the novels that brought Sinclair Lewis his fame. Lewis himself was not content to have his work thus located. In a heavily playful refutation of the charge that he was "a raging reformer, an embittered satirist, a realist dreary as cold gravy," he said:

> I should have thought Brother Lewis was essentially a story-teller— just as naive, excited, unselfconscious as the Arab story-tellers about the caravan fires seven hundred years ago, or as O. Henry in a hotel room on Twenty-third Street furiously turning out tales for dinner and red-ink money. In his stories Lewis does not happen to be amused only by the sea or by midnight encounters on the Avenue, but oftener by the adventure of the soul in religion and patriotism and social climbing. But they are essentially stories just the same.[4]

The fact is that the novels we have in mind are not "essentially stories," that the "story" element is secondary and quite feebly managed; and that if they are not quite the "novel with a purpose" as Norris conceived it—motivated by an outraged sense of justice and executed with naturalistic fulness—their impulse is plainly the exposition of social folly.

H. L. Mencken, some years after he had ceased to be a well-known literary critic, takes us to the center of Lewis's imaginative uniqueness when, in 1945, he congratulates him on a poor novel called *Cass Timberlane*, an exposure of the corruptions of marriage in the middle class:

> I am not going to tell you that "Cass Timberlane" is comparable to "Babbitt" or "Elmer Gantry" (all except the last 30,000 words, which you wrote in a state of liquor), but it seems to me to be the best thing you have done, and by long odds, since "Dodsworth." . . . In brief, a well-planned and well-executed book, with a fine surface. . . . The country swarms with subjects for your future researches. You did the vermin of the Coolidge era, but those of the Roosevelt and post-Roosevelt eras are still open—the rich radical, the bogus expert, the numskull newspaper proprietor (or editor), the career-jobholder, the lady publicist, the crooked (or, more usually, idiotic) labor leader, the press-agent, and so on. This, I believe, is your job, and you have been neglecting it long enough. There are plenty of writers of love stories and Freudian documents, though not many as good at it as you are, but there is only one real anatomist of the American Kultur. I think it stinks, but whether it stinks or not is immaterial. It deserves to be done as you alone can do it.[5]

The catalogue of social types is the significant item in this letter. Each of these, with its implied section of social life in the United States, could have become a Lewis novel. Some already had. With Lewis, the subject, the social section, always came first; systematic research, sometimes conducted by research assistants and carrying Lewis himself into "the field" like any cultural anthropologist, followed; the story came last, devised to carry home and usually limping under the burden of data. If the result in some ways filled the Norris prescription for a novel of the contemporary social character, it was still by no means a naturalistic product; at the same time, precisely what was "new" in it was what D. H. Lawrence called "dead," and he would have howled in outrage at the complacency with which Lewis asserted that his stories described "the adventure of the soul in religion and patriotism." For in the world of Sinclair Lewis there is no soul, and if a soul were introduced into it, it would die on the instant.

The world of Sinclair Lewis rests upon two observations: the standardization of manners in a business culture, and the stultification of morals under middle-class convention. All his critical observations are marshalled in support of these propositions, and his portrait of the middle class rests entirely upon them. The proliferation of detail within these observations gives them an apparent breadth, and his easy familiarity with the manners—in Robert Cantwell's catalogue—of "the small towns and square cities, the real-estate developments and restricted residential areas, the small business men, the country doctors, the religious fakers, the clubwomen, the country officeholders, the village atheists and single-taxers, the schoolteachers, librarians, the windbags of the lower income groups, the crazy professors and the maddened, hyperthyroid, high-pressure salesmen—the main types of middle-class and lower-middle-class provincial society, conspicuous now because he has identified them so thoroughly"[6]—all this gives his observations an apparent richness and variety; yet in fact it is all there in support of the extremely limited program. Similarly, his world is broken into many social sections—the small town, business ethics, medical science, evangelical religion, marriage, the career woman, professional philanthropy—and this is to name only those that come most immediately to mind; but every section rests, again, on one or both of the two primary principles. This is an extremely narrow and intellectually feeble perspective, but given the particular character of Lewis's achievement, its force paradoxically rests upon its narrowness.

For its narrowness projects a very sharply defined image. "Life dehumanized by indifference or enmity to all human values—that is the keynote of both Gopher Prairie and Zenith," wrote T. K. Whipple nearly thirty years ago in what remains one of the very few critical essays on Lewis.

> ... nowhere does this animosity show itself more plainly than in hostility to truth and art. The creed of both towns is the philosophy of boosting, a hollow optimism and false cheeriness which leads directly to hypocrisy, as in making believe that business knavery is social service. Toward ideas likely to break this bubble of pretense the people are bitterly opposed; toward new ideas they are lazily contemptuous; toward other ideas they are apathetic. ... intellectually both are cities of the dead, and in both, the dead are resolved that no one shall live.[7]

Dead in the senses as they are in intellect and the affections, these people are horrible ciphers, empty of personality or individual consciousness, rigidly controlled by set social responses; and yet, being dead, together they do not form a society in any real sense, but only a group, a group which at once controls them and protects them from the horrors of their own emptiness. Their group activities, whether as families, as clubs, as friends, are travesties of that human interchange that makes for meaningful social activities: conversation is buffoonery, affection is noise, gaiety is pretense, business is brutal rush, religion is blasphemy. The end result is vacant social types in a nonsocial world. Quite brilliantly T. K. Whipple made and Maxwell Geismar developed the observation that *Babbitt* is set in Hell: "it is almost a perfectly conceived poetic vision of a perfectly ... standardized hinterland."[8]

Poetic, that is to say, in a sense that it *is* visionary, *not* documentary, so that nothing is either a lie or the truth. These are categories that have no relevance. Collecting his massive accumulations of social data with the naturalist's compulsiveness, Lewis creates a visual world and a world of manners that appear to be absolutely solid, absolutely concrete; but all that accumulation of data has from the outset been made to submit so severely to the selective strictures of two highly limited and limiting observations that what emerges in fact is an image and a criticism of middle-class society and not in the least a representation of it. A fragment blown into the proportions of the whole, it is a fantastic world dominated by monstrous parodies of human nature. Elmer Gantry, in his hypocrisy and self-deception, his brutal cruelty and fearful faith, his shallow optimism and wretched betrayals, his almost automatic identification of salvation and economic success, his loathing of all thought, his hatred of all human difference, his incapacity for any feelings but lust and fear and self-interest: in all this he carries to its extreme Sinclair Lewis's conception of the middle-class character. Both the paradox and the secret of such a creation lie in the fact that, except for the power of observation, the sensibility of the creator has few resources beyond those of the thing created, that Lewis's own intellectual and moral framework, and the framework of feeling, is extremely narrow, hardly wider than the material it contains. And the power of the creation, I would insist, lies in these limitations.

The limitations are so apparent that we need do little more than name them. As his conception of middle-class society is fragmentary, so his sense of history is vestigial. The characteristic widening of his shutter over social space does not qualify or alter the narrow social conception:

> Eight thousand radio-owners listening to Elmer Gantry—
> A bootlegger in his flat, coat off, exposing his pink silk shirt, his feet up on the table. . . . The house of a small-town doctor, with the neighbors come in to listen—the drugstore man, his fat wife, the bearded superintendent of schools. . . . Mrs. Sherman Reeves of Royal Ridge, wife of one of the richest young men in Zenith, listening in a black-and-gold dressing-gown, while she smoked a cigarette. . . . The captain of a schooner, out on Lake Michigan, hundreds of miles away, listening in his cabin. . . . The wife of a farmer in an Indian valley, listening while her husband read the Sears-Roebuck catalogue and sniffed. . . . A retired railway conductor, very feeble, very religious. . . . A Catholic priest, in a hospital, chuckling a little. . . . A spinster school-teacher, mad with loneliness, worshiping Dr. Gantry's virile voice. . . . Forty people gathered in a country church too poor to have a pastor. . . . A stock actor in his dressing-room, fagged with an all-night rehearsal.
> All of them listening to the Rev. Dr. Elmer Gantry as he shouted. . . . (pp. 399–400)

Similarly, the characteristic extensions into time do not enrich the sense of history but merely provide broadly ironic contrasts that are analogically meaningless, both in the drama and in the intellectual framework:

> So Elmer came, though tardily, to the Great Idea which was to revolutionize his life and bring him eternal and splendid fame.
> That shabby Corsican artillery lieutenant and author, Bonaparte, first conceiving that he might be the ruler of Europe—Darwin seeing dimly the scheme of evolution—Paolo realizing that all of life was nothing but an irradiation of Francesca—Newton pondering on the falling apple—Paul of Tarsus comprehending that a certain small Jewish sect might be the new religion of the doubting Greeks and Romans—Keats beginning to write "The Eve of St. Agnes"—none of these men, transformed by a Great Idea from mediocrity to genius, was more remarkable than Elmer Gantry of Paris, Kansas, when he beheld the purpose for which the heavenly powers had been training him. (p. 409)

The characters of this world are aware of no tradition within which their lives are located; behind them lies no history except for the faintly heroic figure of a pioneer whose sacrifice their lives have made meaningless. And if the seat of this deficiency is in the imagination of the author, its result is the captive blankness of their existence, which is a large element in the egregious parody.

From an early if not very forcibly held socialist position, Sinclair Lewis, in his best novels, swung round to the antidemocratic views of H. L. Mencken; yet paradoxically, he had no values of his own (not even Mencken's vague Nietzscheanism) except those of the middle-class that both were lampooning. The ambition to find in the East what is not available in the Midwest is always exposed as false; and when "the East" is pushed on to mean Europe, the same evaluation is made. The Midwest is shown as hopelessly narrow, yet somehow it is shown finally as the only sensible place to choose. Aristocrats are suspect if not phoney; workmen tend to become shiftless mongrels; intellectuals and artists are irresponsible bohemians. The picture of middle-class provincialism is framed by a middle-class provincial view. "Russian Jews in London clothes," Lewis writes in *Dodsworth*, "going to Italian restaurants with Greek waiters and African music." And again, if the deficiency in a sense of tradition and of history is the author's own, it contributes to the force of his image, for it permits his characters no escape. Always excepting the figures of Doctors Gottlieb and Arrowsmith, with their dedication to pure science, the dissident figures in Lewis's novels, the critics of this society, are permitted no realizable values toward which they or that society may aspire.

The feeblest characters in *Main Street*, and those most quickly routed, are the discontented. Carol Kennicott's vaporous values are the equivalent of that deeply sentimental strain in the author that led him as a young man to write in imitation of the early Tennyson and, as a man of over fifty, to say that "he, who has been labeled a 'satirist' and a 'realist,' is actually a romantic medievalist of the most incurable sort." Thus Carol:

> ...a volume of Yeats on her knees.... Instantly she was released from the homely comfort of a prairie town. She was in the world of lonely things—the flutter of twilight linnets, the aching call of gulls along a shore to which the netted foam crept out of darkness, the island of Aengus and the elder gods and the eternal glories that never were, tall kings and women girdled with crusted gold, the woeful incessant chanting.... (p. 120)

Thus the Babbitt who momentarily challenges Zenith does not so much present us with a scale of humane values that we can oppose to the inhumanity of the environment, as he presents us with all the insecurity on which Babbittry, or the environment, rests. The fact that there is never any real opposition of substantial values to "convention," or false values (as there is never any truly individual character to resist the social types), is what makes Lewis's world so blank and limits so drastically his social realism. In *Elmer Gantry* we do not have these fitful glimmerings in the realm of reverie. This is a world of total death, of social monsters without shadow. It is, in my view and on re-reading, the purest Lewis.

The publication of *Elmer Gantry* early in 1927 was not so much a literary event as it was a public scandal, and from the beginning, therefore, excitement took the place of criticism. Preceded by the well-publicized "Strike me dead" episode, it called forth remarks like this from William Allen White: "Sinclair Lewis stood in the pulpit of a Kansas City church last spring and defied God to strike him dead. So far as Sinclair Lewis, the artist, is concerned in the book 'Elmer Gantry,' God took him at his word." Municipal bans extended from Kansas City to Camden; from Boston to Glasgow. Its initial printing of 140,000 copies was probably the largest to that date of any book in history, and the whole emphasis of the promotion campaign was on the *size* of the enterprise: the book was advertised on billboards; a publicity release from the publishers was headed "What it Means to Manufacture the First Edition of *Elmer Gantry*," and provided statistics on amounts of paper, thread, glue, board, cloth, and ink, both black and orange—black for the text, orange for the cover. (But then, as Lewis tells us in the novel, "Elmer was ever a lover of quantity.") In April of 1927, in a resolution supporting the Anti-Saloon League of New York State, the Rev. Dr. Otho F. Bartholow declared at the annual session of the New York East Conference, "The Methodist Church is cordially hated, not only by the class represented by Mr. Sinclair Lewis and the rum organizations, but also by every evil organization of every kind whatsoever," while, two weeks later, the graduating class of New York University voted Sinclair Lewis its favorite author. A news item in an Ohio newspaper ran as follows:

> Trouble in the home of Leo Roberts, general manager of the Roberts Coal and Supply Company, began when his wife brought home a copy of "Elmer Gantry" and he burned it as undesirable reading matter, according to Mrs. Roberts at a hearing Wednesday before Judge Bostwick of Probate Court, when Roberts was ordered to a private sanitarium for a short rest, after his wife, Mrs. Margaret Roberts, 1671 Franklin Park South, charged him with lunacy.

Literary appraisal seems to have been a quite secondary matter. Yet, if only because the images that Lewis projected came to play such a powerful role in the imagination both of America and of Europe, it is worth our time to analyze the method or lack of method that established them. Leslie Fiedler recently wrote as follows:

> . . . no one has succeeded since the age of Sinclair Lewis and Sherwood Anderson in seeing an actual American small town or a living member of the Kiwanis club. The gross pathos of Anderson or the journalistic thinness of Lewis is beside the point; for all of us, the real facts of experience have been replaced by Winesburg, Ohio and by Babbitt; myth or platitude, we have invented nothing to replace them.[9]

How, then, did *he* invent them? What props up and holds in place that terrifying buffoon, Elmer Gantry—that "gladiator laughing at the comic distortion of his wounded opponent," as he sees himself; that "barytone solo turned into portly flesh," as Lewis shows him to us?

The primary fact in Lewis's method is the absence of conflict between genuine orders of value, and in *Elmer Gantry* this fact emerges most starkly.

In *Elmer Gantry*, any drama exists in the immediate victory of the worst over the weakest (who are the best), or in the conflict of the bad to survive among the worst: all is corrupt. In this extraordinarily full account of every form of religious decay, nothing is missing except all religion and all humanity. As there are no impediments to Elmer's barbarous rise from country boob to influential preacher, so there are no qualifications of the image of barbarity. On the very fringes of the narrative, among his scores of characters, Lewis permits a few shadowy figures of good to appear—Bruno Zechlin and Jim Lefferts, the amiable skeptics who are routed before they are permitted to enter the action; Andrew Pengilly, a humane preacher who asks the most striking question in the novel ("Mr. Gantry, why don't you believe in God?") but who himself no more enters the conflict than his question enters the intellectual context; and finally, Frank Shallard, who does come and go in the story, an honest human being, but one so weak that he presents no challenge to Elmer, serves only to illustrate the ruthlessness of Elmer's power.

In the novel, values can be realized only in action, and the action of *Elmer Gantry* is an entirely one-way affair. This is the inevitable consequence in structure of Lewis's method. Like most of Lewis's novels, *Elmer Gantry* is a loosely episodic chronicle, which suggests at once that there will be no sustained pressure of plot, no primary conflict about which all the action is organized and in which value will achieve a complex definition or in which that dramatization of at least two orders of value that conflict implies will be brought about. The chronicle breaks down into three large parts, each pretty nearly independent of the others. In each event Elmer's progress is colored and in two of them threatened by his relation with a woman, but from each Elmer emerges triumphant. The first part takes us through his Baptist education, his ordination, his first pulpit, and his escape from Lulu; the second takes us through his career as an evangelist with the fantastic Sharon Falconer; the third takes us through his experience of New Thought and his rise in Methodism, together with the decline of his marriage to Cleo and his escape from Hettie, who threatens to bring him to public ruin but who is herself routed as, in the final sentence, Elmer promises that "We shall yet make these United States a moral nation."

It should not be supposed that the frank prominence in *Elmer Gantry* of sexual appetite—a rare enough element in a Lewis novel—or the fact that it several times seems to threaten Elmer's otherwise unimpeded success, in any way provides the kind of dramatized counterpoint on the absence of which we are remarking, or that it in any way serves to introduce an element of human tenderness that qualifies Elmer's brutal nakedness. On the contrary, it is an integral part of his inhumanity and an integral part of the inhumanity of the religious environment within which he exists. Indeed, of all the forms of relationship that the novel presents, the sexual relation is most undilutedly brutish, and it is perhaps the chief element in that animus of revulsion that motivates the creation of this cloacal world and upon which I shall presently comment. Finally, its identification with the quality of Elmer's religious activity is made explicit in the climactically phantasmagoric scene in which Sharon capitulates to Elmer before an altar where she associates herself, in a ritual invocation, with all goddesses of fertility.

> It is the hour! Blessed Virgin, Mother Hera, Mother Frigga, Mother Ishtar, Mother Isis, dread Mother Astarte of the weaving arms, it is thy priestess, it is she who after the blind centuries and the groping years shall make it known to the world that ye are one,

and that in me are ye all revealed, and that in this revelation shall come peace and wisdom universal, the secret of the spheres and the pit of understanding. Ye who have leaned over me and on my lips pressed your immortal fingers, take this my brother to your bosoms, open his eyes, release his pinioned spirit, make him as the gods, that with me he may carry the revelation for which a thousand thousand grievous years the world has panted. . . .

Ye veiled ones and ye bright ones—from caves forgotten, the peaks of the future, the clanging today—join in me, lift up, receive him, dread nameless ones; yea, lift us then, mystery on mystery, sphere above sphere, dominion on dominion, to the very throne!

. . . O mystical rose, O lily most admirable, O wondrous union; O St. Anna, Mother Immaculate, Demeter, Mother Beneficient, Lakshmi, Mother Most Shining; behold, I am his and he is yours and ye are mine! (pp. 186–87)

The extravagant absurdity of this scene is underlined by the absence in it of any candid recognition of human need or of human fulfillment. The travesty that it makes of both the sexual and the religious experience is of course to be associated with the temper of orgiastic evangelism with which the book is full. Dramatically, however, it must be associated with such an earlier scene, as homely as this one is horrendous, in which a deaf old retired preacher and his wife are going to bed after twenty-seven years of marriage, and the whole of that experience of twenty-seven years is equated with an "old hoss."

They were nodding on either side of a radiator unheated for months.

"All right, Emmy," piped the ancient.

"Say, Papa—Tell me: I've been thinking: If you were just a young man today would you go into the ministry?"

"Course I would! What an idea! Most glorious vocation young man could have. Idea! G'night, Emmy!"

But as his ancient wife sighingly removed her corsets, she complained, "Don't know as you would or not—if I was married to you—which ain't any too certain, a second time—and if I had anything to say about it!"

"Which is certain! Don't be foolish. Course I would."

"I don't know. Fifty years I had of it, and I never did get so I wa'n't just mad clear through when the ladies of the church came poking around, criticizing me for every little tidy I put on the chairs, and talking something terrible if I had a bonnet or a shawl that was the least mite tasty. ' 'Twant suitable for a minister's wife.' Drat 'em! And I always did like a bonnet with some nice bright colors. Oh, I've done a right smart of thinking about it. You always were a powerful preacher, but's I've told you—"

"You have!"

"—I never could make out how, if when you were in the pulpit

you really knew so much about all these high and mighty and mysterious things, how it was when you got home you never knew enough,
and you never could learn enough, to find the hammer or make a
nice piece of cornbread or add up a column of figures twice alike or
find Oberammergau on the map of Austria!"

"Germany, woman! I'm sleepy!"

"And all these years of having to pretend to be so good when
we were just common folks all the time! Ain't you glad you can just
be simple folks now?"

"Maybe it is restful. But that's not saying I wouldn't do it over
again." The old man ruminated a long while. "I think I would.
Anyway, no use discouraging these young people from entering the
ministry. Somebody got to preach the gospel truth, ain't they?"

"I suppose so. Oh, dear. Fifty years since I married a preacher!
And if I could still only be sure about the virgin birth! Now don't
you go explaining! Laws, the number of times you've explained! I
know it's true—it's in the Bible. If I could only *believe* it! But—

"I would of liked to had you try your hand at politics. If I could
of been, just once, to a senator's house, to a banquet or something,
just once, in a nice bright red dress with gold slippers, I'd of been
willing to go back to alpaca and scrubbing floors and listening to
you rehearsing your sermons, out in the stable, to that old mare we
had for so many years—oh, laws, how long is it she's been dead now?
Must be—yes, it's twenty-seven years—

"Why is it that it's only in religion that the things you got to
believe are agin all experience? Now drat it, don't you go and quote
that 'I believe because it *is* impossible' thing at me again! Believe
because it's impossible! Huh! Just like a minister!

"Oh, dear, I hope I don't live long enough to lose my faith.
Seems like the older I get, the less I'm excited over all these preachers
that talk about hell only they never saw it.

"Twenty-seven years! And we had that old hoss so long before
that. My how she could kick—Busted that buggy—"

They were both asleep. (pp. 70–71)

The two scenes, the extravagantly repulsive and the devastatingly barren,
supplement one another; they represent the extremes of the nightmare
image of a world that, totally empty of human value, monstrously, and
without relief, parodies the reality.

If the narrative method of loose chronicle, without sustained dramatic
conflict, is the primary means to this end, certain orders of technical
detail contribute no less and seem to me entirely consistent with the
imagination that is working through the narrative method. It has been
complained, for example, that there is a coarsening of Lewis's style in
this novel, and that his view of the hinterland threatens to fall into a
kind of cracker-barrel stereotype. Both charges are true, but it can be
argued that both qualities make possible the kind of effect we are trying

to describe. *Elmer Gantry* is the noisiest novel in American literature, the most *braying, guffawing, belching* novel that we have, and it is its prose that sets this uproar going; if we are to have a novel filled with jackasses and jackals, let them, by all means, bray and guffaw. On the same grounds, I would defend the "By crackee, by jiminy" crudities of the physical environment within which this noise goes on, this imbecilic articulateness, only pointing out in addition that Lewis's old ability to invoke a concrete world—the smell of Pullman car dust, the food at a church picnic, the contents of the library of a small Methodist bishop— is still sufficiently in force to cram full the outlines of his stereotypes. One can go further. At each of his three climaxes, Lewis abdicates such sense of the dramatic scene as he may have had and retreats into melodrama: once to an inversion of the farmer's daughter situation, once to a catastrophic fire, finally to a cops-and-robbers treatment of some petty criminals who have attempted to play the badger game on old Elmer. In each situation, through bad timing, through a refusal to develop even a suggestion of suspense, any potential human elements in the situation are sacrificed to the melodramatic stereotype. And yet, out of this very weakness, cumulatively, arises again the whole impression of bare brutality which is, after all, the essential social observation. As the drama is only half realized, so the social observation is only half true, but in its partiality resides such force of which it is capable.

Most novels operate through a conflict, dramatized in a plot, of social and individual interest, and the more sustained the pressures of the plot, the more likely is the individual to be forced into a position of new self-awareness, which prominently contains an awareness of his relation to his society. A certain dynamic interchange has been at work, and the result is that the historical forces which contain the individual's experience have been personalized in his awareness. What is most characteristic of the novels of Sinclair Lewis, and above all of *Elmer Gantry*, is the fact that there are no such dynamics of social action, that we are presented with a static, unpersonalized image—and that *there* lies its horror.

Elmer Gantry has perhaps one brief moment of honesty. He has come to Sharon's fantastic home, he is looking out upon the river, he fancies himself in love:

> "Shen-an-doah!" he crooned.
> Suddenly he was kneeling at the window, and for the first time since he had forsaken Jim Lefferts and football and joyous ribaldry, his soul was free of all the wickedness which had daubed it—oratorical ambitions, emotional orgasm, dead sayings of dull seers, dogmas, and piety. The golden winding river drew him, the sky uplifted him, and with outflung arms he prayed for deliverance from prayer.
> "I've found her. Sharon. Oh, I'm not going on with this evange-

listic bunk. Trapping idiots into holy monkey-shines! No, by God, I'll be honest! I'll tuck her under my arm and go out and fight. Business. Put it over. Build something big. And laugh, not snivel and shake hands with church-members! I'll do it!" (pp. 180–81)

Then and there his rebellion against himself ends, and after that he knows nothing of self-recognition. This is about as close to it as he can come:

"I'll have a good time with those folks," he reflected, in the luxury of a taxicab. "Only, better be careful with old Rigg. He's a shrewd bird, and he's onto me. . . . Now what do you mean?" indignantly. "What do you mean by 'onto me'? There's nothing to be onto! I refused a drink and a cigar, didn't I? I never cuss except when I lose my temper, do I? I'm leading an absolutely Christian life. And I'm bringing a whale of a lot more souls into churches than any of these pussy-footing tin saints that're afraid to laugh and jolly people. 'Onto me' nothing!" (p. 315)

A character so open to self-deception is not in a position to estimate the forces that have made him so: to him, society is given, accepted, used. Elmer Gantry was raised in an important if stultifying American tradition: the protestantism of the hinterland; and Sinclair Lewis gives us a complete and devastating account of it that extends over four pages and from which I now draw fragments, reluctantly omitting Lewis's substantiating body of detail:

The church and Sunday School at Elmer's village . . . had nurtured in him a fear of religious machinery which he could never lose. . . . That small pasty-white Baptist church had been the center of all his emotions, aside from hellraising, hunger, sleepiness, and love. And even these emotions were represented in the House of the Lord. . . . the arts and the sentiments and the sentimentalities—they were for Elmer perpetually associated only with the church. . . . all the music which the boy Elmer had ever heard was in church. . . . it provided all his painting and sculpture. . . . From the church came all his profounder philosophy . . . literary inspiration . . . here too the church had guided him. In Bible stories, in the words of the great hymns, in the anecdotes which the various preachers quoted, he had his only knowledge of literature. . . . The church, the Sunday School, the evangelistic orgy, choir-practise, raising the mortgage, the delights of funerals, the snickers in back pews or in the other room at weddings—they were . . . a mold of manners to Elmer. . . . Sunday School text cards . . . they gave him a taste for gaudy robes, for marble columns and the purple-broidered palaces of kings, which was later to be of value in quickly habituating himself to the more decorative homes of vice. . . . And always the three chairs that stood behind the pulpit, the intimidating stiff chairs of yellow plush and carved oak borders, which, he was uneasily sure, were waiting for the Father, the Son, and the Holy Ghost.

He had, in fact, got everything from the church and Sunday School, except, perhaps any longing whatever for decency and kindness and reason. (pp. 25–28)

And having neither decency nor kindness nor reason (as the novel contains no animated examples of these humane virtues), Elmer is necessarily unaware of the history in which he is involved.

That history, perhaps no larger than it is beautiful in our tradition, is nevertheless considerable, and Sinclair Lewis was aware of it even if, because he had no alternatives, he could not let his characters become so. (The tradition survives, of course: a Madison Avenue patina, extending from Washington, D.C., to Whittier, California, does not alter the motives of cynically opportunistic politicians; it merely moves boorish Elmer into gray flannel and the seat of power.) The whole brutally accurate conception of R. H. Tawney, which coupled business success and salvation, and then, in popular culture, began to pay dividends on the "saved" soul; the obvious connection between the Puritan repressions (I use Lewis's terms, not mine) and the orgiastic outbursts of middle-border evangelism; the Gospel of Service (made in Zenith) becoming the equivalent of the Gospels—all this is in the author's mind as he creates his characters, but the very nature of his creation prohibits it from in any way sharing his knowledge. The result is that the Lewis character cannot separate itself from the Lewis society; and this, in the dynamics of fiction, means that the Lewis character *has* no character apart from the society in which it is embedded, and that therefore the Lewis society is not a society at all, but a machine. And this is the moral, for criticism as for life today, of Lewis's novels, and especially of this one.

"All vital truth," said D. H. Lawrence, "contains the memory of all for which it is not true." And Frank Norris, that infinitely simpler man, said, "You must be something more than a novelist if you can, something more than just a writer. There must be that nameless sixth sense or sensibility. . . . the thing that does not enter into the work, but that is back of it. . . ." Here these two unlikely companions become companionable: both are asking for a certain reverberating largeness behind any concretely conceived situation if that situation is to echo back into the great caverns of the human condition. This quality, I think, even a partisan could not claim that Sinclair Lewis had. Quite justly, Robert Cantwell described him as one "who thought of his writing, not in terms of its momentary inspirations and the . . . pressure of living that played through him and upon him, but in terms of the accomplishment of a foreknown task";[10] and quite plausibly, Maxwell Geismar wrote that "Just as there is really no sense of vice in Lewis's literary world, there is no true sense of virtue. Just as there is practically no sense of human love in the whole range of Lewis's psychological values, and no sense of real hatred—there is no genuine sense of human freedom."[11] Most of this indictment one may allow, but if we are speaking specifically of *Elmer Gantry*, we would wish to insist on two of the items that these descriptions deny him: "the pressure of living that played through him and upon him," and the "hatred."

Elmer Gantry is a work of almost pure revulsion. It seems to shudder and to shake with loathing of that which it describes. The very fact that the novelist must create the image of the thing he loathes, in order to express his loathing, points to the peculiar imaginative animus that motivates this novel. We can speculate about its sources: Lewis's own early evangelistic impulse, his dedication to the missionary field now turning in upon itself; the lonely, goofy boy at Oberlin, himself pushing the handles of a handcar (as Elmer Gantry does) to get to a rural Sunday School where, without conspicuous success, he doled out Bible stories; the poor fool of the hinterland at New Haven, who had never been given more by the hinterland than the dubious gift of deriding it, and therefore of having to love it. Perhaps such speculations are not much to the point. The point is only that in no novel does Sinclair Lewis more clearly announce his loathing of the social environment with which he is concerned, and in no novel does he make it more mandatory that we remain within the terrifying limits of that environment.

Sinclair Lewis is not unlike Elmer Gantry. The vicious circle in this picture exists, of course, in the fact that Elmer remakes society in precisely the terms that society has already made him. No one can break out; everyone, including the novelist, spins more madly in the mechanical orbit.

The novelist trapped in his own hallucination of the world as a trap: this seems to be the final observation that we can make. But it is not quite final. Finally, we are left with the hallucination of the novels themselves, with their monstrous images of what we both are and are not, their nearly fabulous counter-icons in our culture. They stand somewhere between the two conceptions of the novel with which we began: they tell us too much of why we are dead and not enough of how we can live to satisfy the prescription either of Lawrence or of Norris, deprived as they are of all that psychic affirmation that would meet the demands of the first, and of most of that social realism that would meet those of the second. But they have—for this very reason—their *own* quality. If that quality is of the half-truth, and the half-truth has moved back into our way of estimating our society, the judgment falls on us, on our own failure of observation and imagination. If we accept the half-truth for the fact, then the novel is indeed the most important literary instrument in and for our world; and we can only lament the inability, not of our novelists to provide the stimulus, but of ourselves to repel it, of our failure, in the sympathetic consciousness, to recoil from it. *Elmer Gantry* reminds us that we continue to embrace as fervently as we deny this horror that at least in part we are.

Notes

1. *Lady Chatterley's Lover* (Florence, 1928), p. 118.

2. *"The Responsibilities of the Novelist" and Other Literary Essays* (New York, 1903,) pp. 5–11.

3. "The Novel with a Purpose," *Ibid.*, pp. 25–32.

4. From an unpublished "self-portrait," perhaps intended as a publicity release, apparently written in about 1935, among the Lewis papers, Yale University. All quotations from Sinclair Lewis's writings are used here with the permission of Melville H. Cane and Pincus Berner as Executors under the will of Sinclair Lewis, and the quotations from *Dodsworth, Main Street,* and *Elmer Gantry* are used with the further permission of the publishers, Harcourt, Brace and Company.

5. From an unpublished letter, printed here by permission of August Mencken, literary executor of the late H. L. Mencken.

6. "Sinclair Lewis," *After the Genteel Tradition*, ed. Malcolm Cowley (New York, 1937), p. 115.

7. "Sinclair Lewis," *Spokesmen* (New York, 1928), pp. 210–11.

8. Geismar, *The Last of the Provincials: The American Novel, 1915–1925* (Boston, 1947), p. 96.

9. "The Ant on the Grasshopper," *Partisan Review* (Summer, 1955), p. 414.

10. Cantwell, *Genteel Tradition*, 117.

11. Geismar, *Last of the Provincials*, p. 108.

Sinclair Lewis's Unwritten Novel   Sheldon Grebstein*

Sinclair Lewis and his books had been headline news all through the 1920's, but in the decade that followed Lewis was to yield the eminent place in America's literary consciousness that he had established with *Main Street, Babbitt, Arrowsmith, Elmer Gantry,* and *Dodsworth,* a place he was never to regain despite the wide critical and popular success of such later books as *It Can't Happen Here* and *Kingsblood Royal.* Perhaps Lewis had been exhausted by the labor it had taken to write five important books in nine years. Perhaps, as some critics have said, Lewis lost touch with the temper of the time. Perhaps his ego had in some way been damaged by the award of the Nobel Prize. However,

*Reprinted, with permission of the author and publisher, from *Philological Quarterly* 37 (October 1958):400–409.

it is more likely that the change in Lewis which was reflected in his work after 1930 had its roots in more subtle and complex causes than exhaustion, loss of vision, or the assurance of a permanent literary niche. Consequently, it is the purpose of this study to investigate one of the underlying factors in Lewis's fall from the heights: specifically, the novel that Lewis did not write.

Of course, Sinclair Lewis did not stop writing after 1930 nor did he run out of things to say, for in the years from 1930 to 1940 alone, Lewis produced six novels,[1] published a volume of short stories,[2] delivered more than twenty speeches,[3] wrote many essays,[4] and was increasingly active in the theater as a playwright, producer, director, and actor,[5] to mention only his major activities. However, as soon as the furor surrounding the award of the Nobel Prize to Lewis had died down, he seemed to retire quietly from the view of the national and international reading public, except for a brief flurry of publicity from time to time. In only one novel written in the 1930's, *It Can't Happen Here*, did Lewis provoke a stir even faintly reminiscent of that caused by earlier books, and although it was one of the most significant and timely books of the decade, it was not enough to alter the growing conviction of both critics and readers that something had happened to Sinclair Lewis, "America's Angry Man." It is true that in other of Lewis's novels of the thirties, notably *Ann Vickers* and *The Prodigal Parents*, there still flashed occasional sparks of his satiric fire, but they were not the hot flames of old. In fact, his entire literary production from 1930 to 1940 was characterized much more by indecision and by an increasing amount of nostalgia, sentiment, and a new and surprising conservatism than by any other elements.[6]

Yet, even the most astute student of Lewis's career could not have predicted in the early years of the decade the new direction in which the writer would turn, for immediately before and after the award of the Nobel Prize to Lewis in 1930 and in the following year, he continued to be a one man show and the subject of considerable notoriety. For example, almost as soon as Lewis learned that he had been chosen by the Nobel Committee, he took the opportunity in a series of interviews and lectures to issue various pronouncements regarding American life, society, and literature. In one interview he stated that while Main Street had changed but little since 1920, he still had hopes the industrial age would pass and America would finally realize its great potential.[7] In a speech in New York City, November 25, 1930, Lewis made the charge (already familiar to his readers) that the nation does not take its literature seriously enough, although in this case he blamed the writers for not asserting the importance of their social role.[8] After he received the prize, Lewis declared from Berlin that he was not a reformer but a critic, and that if he had his way, all the reformers would be exiled from America

(Lewis's whole career stands in contradiction to these statements).[9] In another interview in Berlin Lewis asserted that America had improved since the writing of *Main Street* and *Babbitt,* and went on to voice his affection for his country.[10] Shortly after this Lewis charged that our colleges were not truly democratic and suggested a complete renovation of American higher education.[11] In the same spirit of reform he maintained, in a speech given a few months later in New York, that the new danger confronting America was not the "Red menace" but the conservative menace, and concluded that we must find some means of restoring our lost greatness.[12]

But these episodes and others, like the occasion when Lewis was refused the use of Washington's Constitution Hall by the Daughters of the American Revolution,[13] and the affair in which Lewis was slapped by Dreiser after he had accused Dreiser of plagiarism,[14] have little ultimate significance in the total view of Lewis's career, nor do they explain why his writing in the 1930's should suddenly have lost the distinctive energy and genius that had resulted in his being the first American to be honored with the Nobel Prize for Literature. The explanation for this change, however, may lie in the project that had fascinated Lewis for several years, one he earnestly attempted again and again. This absorbing project was the writing of a massive novel about American labor, and Lewis's inability to complete it may indeed have marked a pivotal point in his career.

Lewis had long been thinking about a novel on American labor, apparently for almost ten years. On December 13, 1921, even before the publication of *Babbitt,* Lewis had written to his friend and publisher Alfred Harcourt of his intention to make his next book different from the two satiric masterpieces he had already done. In this letter Lewis wrote:

> I think I shall make my next novel after Babbitt not satiric at all; rebellious as ever, perhaps, but the central character heroic. I'm already getting gleams for it. I see it as the biggest thing I've tackled.[15]

Lewis was a better prophet than he realized, for the book he actually wrote next was *Arrowsmith,* whose central character was heroic but rebellious, and which Lewis later thought was his best novel. However, the topic he had in mind when he wrote this letter was something entirely different from medicine. It was American labor, and the hero of the book, although Lewis's concept of him was often to be altered, was to be an outstanding and controversial labor leader like Eugene Debs.[16]

As it happened Lewis put this idea aside for the first time to write *Arrowsmith,* although it is somewhat ironic that one version of the genesis of *Arrowsmith* states that Lewis first got the inspiration for it while he was doing research on the labor book.[17] This source has it that Lewis had gone to Chicago early in 1923 to gather material for his labor novel and there met Dr. Paul de Kruif, who was to become his technical advisor in the writing of *Arrowsmith*. They are supposed to have met in the office of Dr. Morris Fishbein, then editor of *Hygeia*, and become friendly at once. Soon after this meeting, Lewis, de Kruif, and Fishbein went to Elmhurst to see Eugene Debs, who was in a sanatorium there, and the idea for *Arrowsmith* grew out of the conversation on the long ride back. In this way Lewis decided to do a medical novel instead of a labor book, and with the promise of de Kruif's help, immediately made plans to go abroad to get the background for his new book.

Despite this lapse in his plans necessitated by *Arrowsmith*, Lewis's enthusiasm for the labor novel remained keen all through the rest of the decade. The book was tentatively titled "Neighbor," and Lewis continued to be convinced it would be his finest work. He makes references to it in several of his letters to Harcourt during the 1920's, references that reveal his burning ambition to write the novel and his high hopes for it. But always some other, more immediate, project would distract him, and he turned away from his preparation of the book to write, successively, *Elmer Gantry* and *Dodsworth* just as he had first put it aside for *Arrowsmith*.

One thing remains clear, however; as often as he was to change his concept of the book, Lewis never gave up the idea of eventually writing it, no matter what he was working on. For example, by the spring of 1927 he had formulated a definite plan for the theme of the novel which was based on the life of Debs, and which was to have the title "The Man Who Sought God." At the same time Lewis was stimulated in his planning for the book by the Sacco-Vanzetti case because it seemed to point up some of the very conflicts Lewis intended to handle. A few months later the novel took even more definite shape on a walking trip through Alsace which Lewis took with Ramon Guthrie, and on this occasion Lewis proposed to build the story around the theme "Blessed are they which are persecuted for righteousness' sake." A character was evolved who symbolized cynicism. He was to be called "the international waiter," but Lewis later decided that this character deserved a novel all his own. The hero of the book was to be a worker who awakens to political awareness in his search for God and then runs afoul of both church and state in his quest for truth. The crisis of the story was to revolve on this man's inner struggle against a messiah complex that threatens to destroy his humility and integrity.

But Lewis gave up this particular idea soon after because he somehow believed that he was not yet artistically ready to write it (after *Main Street*, *Babbitt*, and *Arrowsmith*!) and he wanted the experience of doing one more book before attempting the labor novel.

Thus, he still had it in mind while he wrote *Dodsworth*, and in 1929, after *Dodsworth* was finished, he finally made his first actual attempt to write it at the Vermont farm where he had settled with his second wife, Dorothy Thompson. However, Lewis found it difficult to make any headway in his work because he was disturbed by the crowd of experts and celebrities who were always to be found in Mrs. Lewis's presence. They not only disturbed him in his writing but also discouraged him in every possible way about Debs as the hero of the book, convinced him of the enormous complexity of the labor situation, and pointed out to him his lack of background for such a demanding task. With these deterrents and with his own doubt in his ability to tackle the project, it is not surprising that Lewis once more put the plan aside.[18]

Two years later Lewis again tried to begin the book at his Vermont farm. In the interim his enthusiasm had been sustained and his background strengthened by extensive reading so that he once more had become serious enough about the labor book to ask Louis Adamic to help him prepare for it. Lewis wanted Adamic to go with him through the industrial midwest to gather material and then to Europe to help in the writing. They corresponded for some time about this plan and then, with the indecision that was becoming typical of the whole project, Lewis again dropped it, probably to write *Ann Vickers*.[19]

Now, it might be well to point out here that Lewis's indecision was above all not the result of a lack of interest or sympathy, for his feeling for the working man had already been made very clear. For example, Lewis had displayed almost from the beginning of his career a sympathy for the masses and a belief in a coming "new order" that had resulted in his joining the socialist party just after he left college.[20] This same sympathy crept into Lewis's books. It can be seen in his five novels before *Main Street*, where the hero or heroine in each case is a perfect representative of the proletariat. Moreover, in *Main Street* one of Carol Kennicott's greatest antipathies toward Gopher Prairie had been its reactionary attitude toward labor and the farmer, while Babbitt in his brief revolt had stepped closest to the edge of disaster in his world by defending the workers of Zenith in their strike for better conditions.

Nor was Lewis's sympathy with labor confined only to fiction, as is evidenced by his series of articles from Marion, North Carolina, in 1929, where Lewis had gone to report for the Scripps-Howard newspapers a textile workers' strike, the clashes between strikers and peace officers, and the deplorable conditions in the Southern textile mills. These articles of Lewis's were not only brilliantly written but as openly pro-labor and as savage an attack on "the bosses" as anything in the annals of contemporary journalism.[21] To put it succinctly, a labor novel would have been the logical outcome of opinions and sympathies which Sinclair Lewis had long held.

After the unsuccessful attempt in 1931 to write the labor novel, Lewis seems to have let the project lapse for several years. But in 1936, heartened by the reception of *It Can't Happen Here*, Lewis was again ready to work on his long-deferred book. Its plot was still basically similar to that of the earlier plan and in June, 1936, again in collaboration with Ramon Guthrie, who had been influential in helping Lewis work out one of the original conceptions of the book, Lewis started practical research for what was to be his last attempt at the labor novel. With his usual care for detail he traveled all over New England, interviewing people in different occupations and on all social levels. From this research the idea emerged for a new hero, to be called "Roy," a man from a New England village whom Lewis somehow visualized as a reflection of himself. But once more, and this time for no apparent reason, the plans for the book were suddenly and completely dropped. It was as though Lewis had either wearied of the whole thing or finally and irrevocably convinced himself that he would never write his labor novel. By the end of that summer of 1936 Lewis was working on another book, and it might be added, it turned out to be one of his worst (*The Prodigal Parents*, which critics and readers joined in rejecting).

In only one novel, his next-to-last, the mediocre *The God-Seeker* (New York, 1949), did Lewis's projected labor book ever come to life, and then it was but a fragment of the original idea. To be more specific, only the last twenty pages of *The God-Seeker* are concerned with labor in that they deal with the supposed founding of a labor union in frontier Minnesota, although there seems to be a certain residue all through the book of parts of Lewis's great project. For example, Aaron Gadd, the hero of *The God-Seeker*, was also the name of the hero in one of the early outlines of the labor novel. In that particular plan the labor book was to trace three generations of American radicals, beginning with a frontiersman (in *The God-Seeker* Aaron Gadd is a kind of frontiersman since he goes to mid-nineteenth-century Minnesota as a missionary to the Indians). It is also significant that Gadd's nickname is "Neighbor," one of the earliest proposed titles for the unwritten labor novel which Lewis mentioned several times in his letters to Harcourt. Finally, the title of the later novel, *The God-Seeker*, is obviously a rephrasing of another of the projected titles for the labor book, "The Man Who Sought God." In any case, *The God-Seeker* was a far cry from the kind of book Lewis had wanted to write in his plans for the labor novel, and one gets the feeling that it was a poor book for other reasons than Lewis's waning artistic and physical powers.

Why did Sinclair Lewis never write his labor novel? There have been several answers. Louis Adamic, who met Lewis when the idea was strong in his mind, believed that Lewis was afraid to risk doing a book on labor and idealism that might be unpopular. Despite his success Lewis was bothered by a feeling of insecurity about himself and, according to Adamic, his relationship with his new publisher, Doubleday Doran (Lewis had broken with Harcourt-Brace soon after he received the Nobel Prize). Also, Lewis's financial obligations were heavy: they included the payment of alimony to his first wife, the expense of his ceaseless traveling, and the maintenance of his recently acquired Vermont estate. Moreover, Adamic said, Lewis's wife Dorothy was a rising literary figure in her own right and her success challenged both his masculine and literary pride. For all these reasons, Adamic concluded, Lewis feared to do a book on such a dangerously volatile subject as labor in a time when depression gripped the land.[22]

Another writer, Ben Stolberg, long a close friend, asserted that Lewis dropped the labor novel because he was intellectually and temperamentally unfitted for writing it, since he discovered that a labor leader is inextricably connected with social movements and he discovered that he had no flair for dealing with involved social and economic theories. A labor leader, Stolberg believed, unlike a Babbitt, has to be judged with reference to an entire movement and its place in society. Stolberg summed it up this way:

> In short, a labor novel is an ideological as well as a literary enterprise, and Lewis is not an intellectual; his pet aversions are "highbrows". . . .
> He knows as no one else the details of American life, but he cannot tell you what it all adds up to.[23]

Both Adamic's and Stolberg's explanations are reasonable, but by far the most perceptive comments and deepest insights (which also must be critically considered) have been provided by Ramon Guthrie, who probably had a greater share than anyone else in helping Lewis prepare for the labor book. Guthrie concluded that it was Lewis's attitude toward his father, which was a "mixture of awed reverence and rankling resentment," that was the determining factor in his inability to do the book. According to Guthrie, Lewis's relationship with his father was vital in his entire literary career, or, as Guthrie himself put it:

> All of his best books were an affirmation of his hard-won emancipation from being Harry Lewis of Main Street. Yet throughout his life whenever Red stood on the verge of giving the true measure of himself and the forces that were in him, the shade of Dr. E. J., as Red always called him, snorted the phrase that never lost its power to bring him to heel: "Harry, why can't you do like any other boy ought to do!"[24]

In Guthrie's view of Lewis's career, Lewis hated to be called Harry, yet was sometimes compelled to *be* Harry. Thus, his worst books, like *Work of Art* and *Prodigal Parents*, were written to please his father's spirit, although they were actually at odds with his own. The labor novel would have been the most direct attack that the son had ever made on everything old Dr. Lewis represented. Lewis had won his success with books he felt he ought *not* to write. He had started his career with no intention of becoming "the bad boy of American letters," as Parrington called him, but he was a natural rebel who revolted even against his own inclinations. Perhaps it was this rebellion, this refusal to be coerced, that resulted in Lewis's revolt against his own compulsion to do the labor novel, a revolt that never let him write the book he most wanted to write. All this, according to Guthrie, was at the root of Sinclair Lewis's failure to create the work that might have been his best.

In the final analysis it is probably not possible to determine exactly why Lewis's labor novel was never written. As has been demonstrated, three men, all literary men and Lewis's friends, have recorded three entirely different versions of the matter. Guthrie suggested the psychological cause of Lewis's feelings toward his father, feelings which might be extended to include Lewis's boyhood in Minnesota and his self-identification with the very people and nation he satirized, yet all this did not keep Lewis from writing *Main Street*.[25] Stolberg concluded that Lewis's intellectual equipment was inadequate to the task, yet this same intellectual equipment was enough to enable Lewis to probe into the complexity of the medical research field in *Arrowsmith*. Adamic reasoned that Lewis was afraid to write an unpopular book, but that fear hadn't stopped him from writing his enormously controversial attack on America's religion and clergy, *Elmer Gantry*, or from predicting that America could succumb to fascism in *It Can't Happen Here*. Above all, if Lewis's career indicates any one thing, it is that he never ran from a fight.

If a single factor must be chosen, it is that labor in America has been in such a state of flux and is so gigantic and far-reaching a topic that it defies the definitive treatment Lewis wanted to give it, although novels such as Ernest Poole's *The Harbor*, Steinbeck's *In Dubious Battle*, and Dos Passos' *USA* have more or less successfully handled various aspects of it. Moreover, Sinclair Lewis was a writer who, in his major works, was unable to confine himself to particular movements, but wrote in terms of the universal and the general; for example: the small town, the businessman, science, religion, the American abroad, native fascism, philanthropy, marriage, racial prejudice. To write such a book about labor in America was a task too great even for Lewis. However, the creative impulse that inspired Lewis to attempt the great American labor novel in the 1930's did not go completely to waste, for it was channeled into other books. But no matter what fame or fortune his later books brought, and there was much of both, Sinclair Lewis was never again to reach the literary heights he had already scaled, and it is very likely that the novel he left unwritten marked the crossroads in his career.[26]

Notes

1. These novels were *Ann Vickers* (1933), *Work of Art* (1934), *It Can't Happen Here* (1935), *The Prodigal Parents* (1938), and *Bethel Merriday* (1940).

2. *Selected Short Stories* (New York, 1935).

3. The *New York Times* has reports of twenty-four speeches that Lewis made between 1930 and 1940. It is safe to assume that he made a good many others not reported.

4. Lewis wrote at least twelve essays which appeared in books and periodicals in this decade, not including those he wrote over a period of several months in 1937–38 as book reviewer for *Newsweek*.

5. Lewis collaborated with Sidney Howard in adapting *Dodsworth* for the stage (produced in New York in the fall of 1934); with Lloyd Lewis in writing *Jayhawker* (also produced in New York in the fall of 1934); adapted, directed, and starred in the New York production of *It Can't Happen Here* in 1936; and wrote and played the lead in a touring company in *Angela Is Twenty-Two*. Lewis was also active in summer stock in the late 1930's. His novel *Bethel Merriday* was the result of his theatrical experiences.

6. The change in Lewis can perhaps best be seen in the fact that he became in the 1930's a member of both the National Institute of Arts and Letters and the American Academy of Arts and Letters, organizations he had savagely attacked in his Nobel speech.

7. S. J. Woolf, "Back On Main Street With Mr. Lewis," *New York Times Book Review*, LXXX (November 16, 1930), 3.

8. Anon., "Lewis Finds Irony In 'Serious' America," *New York Times*, LXXX (November 26, 1930), 3.

9. Anon., "Lewis Would Exile All Our Reformers," *New York Times*, LXXX (December 23, 1930), 3.

10. Anon., "Lewis Holds Books Do Not Prevent War," *New York Times*, LXXX (December 30, 1930), 3.

11. Anon., "Lewis Questions Keeping Colleges," *New York Times*, LXXX (April 22, 1931), 30.

12. Anon., "A Conservative Menace," *New York Times*, LXXI (November 1, 1931), sec. ix, p. 2.

13. Cf. the *New York Times*, LXXX (March 13, 1931), 1, for a report of this incident. Lewis revenged himself on the D.A.R. in *It Can't Happen Here* (New York, 1935), pp. 5–6, where he called it as ridiculous an organization as the Ku Klux Klan.

14. This event had taken place at a dinner for a visiting Russian novelist in March, 1931, which was attended by many literary notables. Lewis, one of the scheduled speakers, arose and said that he declined to speak in Dreiser's presence because Dreiser had plagiarized three thousand words from Dorothy Thompson's book on Russia in his own *Dreiser Looks At Russia*. The two men continued the argument after dinner and in the course of it Dreiser struck Lewis. Dreiser later explained that he and Mrs. Lewis had had access to the same material and that any similarity was accidental. For further details on the matter cf. the *New York Times*, LXXX (March 21, 1931), 11; *Literary Digest*, CIX (April 11, 1931), 15–16; and Allen and Irene Cleaton, *Books and Battles* (Boston, 1937), p. 252.

15. Harrison Smith, editor, *From Main Street To Stockholm: The Letters of Sinclair Lewis, 1920–1930* (New York, 1952), p. 90.

16. For much of the account of the genesis of Lewis's labor novel and some of the discussion about why Lewis did not write it I am indebted to material in Ramon Guthrie's valuable essay, "The Labor Novel Sinclair Lewis Never Wrote," *New York Herald Tribune Book Review*, XXVIII (February 10, 1952), 1, 6.

17. The source for this version of the genesis of *Arrowsmith* is Barbara Grace Spayd's introduction to a reprint edition (New York and Chicago, 1945), p. xxii.

18. The best account of Lewis's life on his Vermont farm at this time is Jack Alexander's article, "Rover Girl in Europe," *Saturday Evening Post*, CCXII (May 25, 1940), 20–21, *passim*.

19. Cf. Louis Adamic, *My America, 1928–38* (New York, 1938), pp. 96–104. This is another excellent source for information about Lewis's labor novel.

20. The Yale collection of Lewis material has his membership card in the Socialist party of New York, showing Lewis was a member from January, 1911 to April, 1912. For other information bearing on Lewis's youthful radicalism, see the present writer's "The Education of a Rebel: Sinclair Lewis at Yale," *New England Quarterly*, XXVII (September, 1955), 372–382. Lewis's socialism, it should be noted, was never of the active variety. In his case it seemed to be a way of expressing his rebellion, non-conformity, and romantic idealism, all combined.

21. These articles were reprinted as a pamphlet by the United Textile Workers of America. Its title is *Cheap and Contented Labor: The Picture of a Southern Mill Town in 1929* (New York, 1929).

22. *My America*, p. 53.

23. Benjamin Stolberg, "Sinclair Lewis," *American Mercury*, LIII (October, 1941), 455–456. This essay is also a valuable general reference.

24. "The Labor Novel Sinclair Lewis Never Wrote," p. 6.

25. Cf. the present writer's "Sinclair Lewis' Minnesota Boyhood," *Minnesota History*, XXXIV (Fall, 1954), 85–89.

26. Grace Hegger Lewis's recent book, *With Love From Gracie* (New York, 1956), pp. 209–216, offers further comment on Lewis's labor novel. She quotes letters by Lewis written to her from Chicago in late August, 1922, which indicate that Lewis met Debs in 1922 and that Lewis was discouraged about his projected labor novel from the beginning. The book also notes Lewis's supposed inability to visualize a representative central character and his consistent lack of sympathy with the labor movement because of its sectarian quarrels and its predominant membership of "plain boobs."

Aspiration and Enslavement   D. J. Dooley[*]

The systematic nature of Lewis's assault on American life is obvious enough to have been often commented on.[1] Having examined the life

[*]From D. J. Dooley, "Aspiration and Enslavement," *The Art of Sinclair Lewis* (Lincoln: University of Nebraska Press, 1967), 97–117. © 1967 by the University of Nebraska Press. Reprinted by permission of the publisher.

of the village and the city, Lewis went on to explore the world of medicine in _Arrowsmith_, of religion in _Elmer Gantry_, of business leadership in _Dodsworth_, and of social work in _Ann Vickers_. Arthur B. Coleman shows that he employed the same social generalizations and the same pattern of plot in the later novels as he had used in the earlier: in each a character standing for a constructive way of life is pitted against representatives of everything restrictive, narrow, hypocritical, wasteful, and stupid in society. But the later protagonists differ from the earlier in being clearer in their ideas, stronger in their beliefs, and more uncompromising in their positions. Employing a term which Lewis used for the title of a late novel, Coleman describes these heroes as "god-seekers."[2] But did their creator believe that there were any gods to be found? At the end of his pamphlet on Lewis, published by Harcourt, Brace at about the same time as _Babbitt_, Stuart Sherman wrote that the one serious objection heard against Lewis's writings was that his standards were not sufficiently in evidence. As if in reply to the criticism, Lewis's next two important novels after _Babbitt_ gave indications, first, of what he did believe in, and, second, of what he did not. Yet, in spite of their considerable degree of success as novels and as satires, they left his standards still in question.

Sherman had said that _Babbitt_ would have been improved by the introduction of one or more characters "capable of reflecting upon the Babbitts oblique rays from a social and personal felicity, more genuine, more inward than any of the summoned witnesses possesses"; he had also declared that eventually, if Lewis did not wish to pass for a hardened pessimist, he would have to produce a hero registering his notion of the desirable.[3] Even before he had seen the pamphlet, Lewis had written Harcourt from Italy to say, "I think I shall make my next novel after _Babbitt_ not satiric at all; rebellious as ever, perhaps, but the central character _heroic_. I'm already getting gleams for it; I see it as the biggest thing I've tackled."[4] During the summer of 1922, when he had finished _Babbitt_ and was waiting for its publication, he was a novelist in search of a hero. He still had only vague gleams until the day in August when, at Carl Sandburg's home in Chicago, he met Eugene Victor Debs, former railway fireman, labor leader, and Socialist candidate for President, who had been sentenced to prison in 1918 for advocating pacifism and had recently had his sentence commuted by President Harding. Lewis wrote enthusiastically to his wife that he had found his hero; Gene was "really a Christ spirit. He is infinitely wise, kind, forgiving. . . ."[5] He was also, apparently, a good listener: he gave close and sympathetic attention while Lewis quickly sketched a plan for a labor novel, to be entitled _Neighbor_ and to contain "something of himself—tho vastly different in details. . . ."[6] Three days later, however, Lewis's enthusiasm for the subject—but not the hero—had waned; he wrote that he was melancholy and felt rather lost because he did not believe that he would be able to write the novel:

> For an hour or a day I can work up a complete conformist sympathy with the union men; then the sight of a group of lolling & ignorant rough necks, addressed by an agitator who is going immediately to supplant the capitalists—& who couldn't run a fruit stand—gets my goat & I compare him with doctors, bankers, editors we know. A Debs lasts; he is pure spirit; he would walk to his crucifixion with firm & quiet joy. But there's so few Debses![7]

Meanwhile, another subject had caught his fancy. A year previously, he had met Dr. Morris Fishbein, who in the course of a long career as spokesman for the American Medical Association and editor of its journal was to acquire a fame comparable to Lewis's own and an influence far greater. Now Fishbein introduced him to Paul de Kruif, a bacteriologist who had recently had to leave the Rockefeller Institute after writing a book entitled *Our Medicine Men* in which he had mocked the so-called experimental rigor of some Rockefeller scientists testing a new type of serum. Since the occasion on which Lewis met de Kruif turned into a prolonged, alcoholic, and confusing evening. Lewis's recollections of it are not entirely trustworthy; yet it seems likely that, as the other two talked about how difficult it was for a young man in America to devote himself to pure research, Lewis realized that he had found the theme for his next book. In an account which appeared in *The Designer and the Woman's Magazine* in June, 1924, he recalled that as he listened to the others he meditated, "Here's my next novel. . . . What protagonist of fiction could be more interesting, more dramatic, and less hackneyed than a doctor who, starting out as a competent general practitioner, emerges as a real scientist, despising ordinary 'success'?"[8] But if Lewis was capable of grasping the significance of this subject, de Kruif's memoir *The Sweeping Wind* indicates that he was also capable of forgetting it. Lewis proposed that they collaborate on the projected novel; he thought that he had found the ideal scientific informant in de Kruif, and de Kruif, jobless and striving to gain a foothold in the literary world, considered this a heaven-sent opportunity. But later on when they met in New York, de Kruif found to his dismay that the novel seemed to have evaporated from Lewis's memory. Instead, Lewis rapidly outlined a plan for a series of short stories, "stories with a new type of hero, a character—bacteriologist, doctor, public health detective—all in one. A kind of scientific Clarence Budington Kelland production." It took the diplomatic intervention of Harcourt, Brace, de Kruif recalls, to keep Lewis from dragging "me with him on a relapse into the George Horace Lorimer school of literature."[9]

While Lewis had been in Chicago, his wife and son had been enjoying a resort life at Fishers Island, New York. For the winter the family took what Grace referred to as an "amusing" house in Hartford, but their cordial welcome in that city was soon outlived. The Lewises were appalled at the smug commercialism of Hartford, which Lewis called only another Gopher Prairie or Zenith, and Hartford in turn was shocked by the Lewises' social indiscretions. Lewis escaped to New York, then went on a six-week lecture tour, traveled to Quebec with his wife, and finally left on a ship with de Kruif. In December de Kruif and he signed a contract providing for their collaboration on a novel dealing with medicine; Lewis was to receive 75 per cent of the royalties and de Kruif 25. With a very substantial advance to his credit, de Kruif returned to Michigan to marry a former student of his at the University, before rejoining Lewis for an alcoholic leave-taking of America's shores on January 4.

His publishers apparently hoped that Lewis's growing dependence on alcohol would be restrained by de Kruif, who had promised "to keep our genius, Red, this side of delirium tremens."[10] On their voyage to the Virgin Islands and the Barbados aboard the British ship *Guiana* and during their cruise of the Spanish Main aboard the Dutch ship *Crynssen*, there were ample opportunities for conviviality. But despite "ruinous rum swizzles" and other concoctions, they did a great deal of hard work. Much of it consisted of talking and arguing; out of such discussions Lewis got the material for "hundreds of notes, schedules, maps. . . ." De Kruif had known some great men of science, in particular Jacques Loeb at the Rockefeller Institute and Dr. Frederick George Novy at the University of Michigan, and he was able to convey to Lewis exactly what dedication to scientific research really meant. His theoretical instruction was supplemented with practical when they visited research laboratories, first in Panama and later in Paris and London. As the voyage continued, the skeleton of the book became more and more clearly outlined. De Kruif recalled how a large square on Santa Lucia, deserted on a lazy Sunday afternoon, suggested to their minds the tropical city smitten by bubonic plague which was to be an important setting in the novel. Lewis was enthusiastic about his collaborator; he wrote that de Kruif was perfection—he had an astonishing grasp of scientific detail and yet the imagination of a fiction writer. De Kruif, on his part, was equally admiring. In an account of the experience entitled "An Intimate Glimpse of a Great American Novel in the Making," he described his wonder at Lewis's ability to pick his brains and to assimilate scientific information.[11]

On February 18 Lewis wrote his father that the book was going superbly and that he had written twenty-five thousand words of plan. He had already decided that he would not return to New York but would go to England to do the actual writing; and by early March he was established in London once again, working at the manuscript of a novel provisionally entitled *The Barbarian*. Lewis and Harcourt carried on a lengthy correspondence about other possible choices; when he announced "the plan all finished" in early May, he still had a list of ten titles to be considered. Eventually he decided on *Dr. Martin Arrowsmith* for the serialized version and simply *Arrowsmith* for the American edition of the book, noting that *"it's his personal and scientific career that counts much more than his medical career...."*[12]

When his wife arrived in mid-May, Lewis put his work aside and attempted to make up for some months of neglect by taking her on a walking tour of Devon and engaging her in a gay round of social life in London. For the summer they rented a house near Fontainebleau, just outside of Paris; there Lewis got back in stride, and after three months of the most concentrated effort he was able to show de Kruif, whose response was enthusiastic, a mammoth first draft of 748 pages, or 245,000 words. This accomplished, Lewis and his wife went on a holiday in Switzerland and Italy, depositing Wells in a boarding school in Lausanne on the way. While they were rambling through the towns of northern Italy, Harcourt was doing his best to contact them, and, when he was unable to do so, deciding on his own to sell the first serial rights of *Arrowsmith* to the *Designer* for fifty thousand dollars—"the highest bona fide price for magazine serialization that I've every heard of."[13]

When the family returned to London, Lewis rented an office in a lawyer's sanctuary, the Inner Temple, and resolutely began the five months' work of rewriting his novel. He had enough spare time, however, to make what the *Daily Express* termed a "strange irruption into British politics"—he canvassed in Chelsea for the Labour candidate in the general election, Bertrand Russell. When the election was over and Labour had won its first victory, Lewis wrote a letter to the *Express*, not so much to defend himself as to praise his friend Brigadier-General C. B. Thompson, who was soon to be given a peerage and put in charge of the Air Ministry. Between his literary friends and his new political acquaintances, Lewis was now, as he reported, seeing "millions of people." He took to the mad round zestfully, but his wife found the English winter very trying. She tried to escape from a succession of colds by going for a holiday to Torquay, and in March she and Lewis went to Spain in search of the sun. According to her account, it had not been a successful year for their marriage; whatever his side of the story may have been, she felt pained by "his ruthless and quite public abasing of me before others...."[14] Meditating long afterward on what had happened and where she had failed, she stressed the irreconcilable tendencies—her need for roots and security, his restlessness and desire to escape. The winter over, Lewis escaped again without her; he announced that he and his brother Claude were going on a trip to the Canadian north, and pointed out that it would hardly be worth while for her to return to the United States with him.

Claude and he had arranged to leave in early June on a Canadian Government Treaty Trip—an annual expedition made by agents of the Department of Indian Affairs to pay the Indians the bounty due them in exchange for the loss of their lands. Lewis expected to be in complete wilderness in northern Saskatchewan for two months or more, "which will be just the thing to set me up after a year and a half or more of much too sedentary life."[15] His enthusiasm lasted throughout the alcoholic preliminaries—"twelve days of carousal," according to Schorer. When he dispatched a last note to his publishers, "before vanishing quite beyond post-boxes until I emerge at The Pas, Manitoba, some time between Aug. 15 & Sept. 5," he stated that he had not had a drink for eleven days and that the trip was going beautifully. Eleven days later, however, he decided to quit; in spite of Claude's pleadings he had made up his mind to leave the party at the first opportunity. When his wife heard that he was back in civilization, she commented sardonically, "Enough is enough apparently. The wilderness is all right in its place but not too much of the same place."[16] Schorer reveals that before the "prodigal Thoreau" returned to "the thin parental bosom" in Sauk Centre at the end of July, there had been enough alcoholic indulgence to undo any good which the period of hearty open-air life may have done him.

Out of the experience came the "shorter and more adventurous" novel Lewis had mentioned to Harcourt in a letter of December 3, 1923, as an interlude between *Arrowsmith* and the next long work; but this shorter work, *Mantrap*, was not to be written until about a year after the trip. Meanwhile, Mrs. Lewis, who had not followed her husband's suggestion that she should spend the summer in France, was staying on Nantucket Island, and he joined her there. The proofs of *Arrowsmith* kept him busy, though the *Nation* got him to report, in a series of articles, how Main Street viewed the forthcoming presidential election; curiously, in one article he had a surprisingly mature and sensible Will Kennicott explain why people like him were going to vote for Coolidge, while he only very perfunctorily allowed Guy Pollock to say why people should vote for LaFollette. Election time found him far from America's shores; almost before she knew it, Mrs. Lewis relates, they were back in London, though not to stay. They enrolled Wells in a school in Switzerland, tramped in the Alps, and settled down—for a whole month and a half—in Paris. Then Philip Goodman, a heavy drinker of the Menckenite persuasion, appeared on the scene and convinced Lewis that Munich at carnival time would be an ideal place for the two of them to try writing a play. After two weeks in Munich, however, Lewis declared that the idea would not work—if they ever completed the play, it would be cheap and sensational. He wrote Harcourt and Brace to this effect on March 4, the day before *Arrowsmith* was published.

As in the preceding novels, Lewis has two intentions in *Arrowsmith*: to tell a story and to expose a situation. Here the two aims are closely linked, and the result is a much better plot than either *Main Street* or *Babbitt* possesses. The analysis of American medicine is just as interesting as the anatomy of the village or the city, and the conflict in which Martin Arrowsmith is engaged is far more gripping than the marital difficulties of Carol Kennicott or the rebellion of George F. Babbitt. The story gains enormously by having a central character who is clearly sympathetic to the author, instead of only doubtfully so; the reader can assume the normalcy of his point of view and laugh, weep, or deplore with him when he encounters examples of irrational or vicious behavior.

What way of life does Martin Arrowsmith seek to follow? There is no chance of his becoming an aesthete; Lewis makes him a man of action, suspicious of whatever may be effete and decadent, and clinches matters by giving the spokesman for literature the contemptible name of Brumfit and describing him as a literary playboy. When Martin examines religion as a guiding principle, Lewis's treatment is cavalier. Martin found himself viewing the cadaver he worked on "as a machine, fascinating, complex, beautiful, but a machine. It damaged his already feeble belief in man's divinity and immortality." The model of Christian behavior whom Martin meets at the University of Winnemac is a grotesque figure, the Reverend Ira Hinkley:

> He never ceased trying to stop their profanity. After three years on a backwoods football team he still believed that he could sterilize young men by administering reproofs, with the nickering of a lady Sunday School teacher and the delicacy of a charging elephant. [18][17]

Having rejected the principles of this moral pest, Martin puts his faith in the scientism of Max Gottlieb, his instructor in bacteriology. There is nothing certain in life, says Gottlieb, except the quantitative method; employing it, he seeks to discover general laws governing natural phenomena in order to extend man's knowledge and develop new concepts of life. Following him, Arrowsmith embarks on "the search for the fundamental laws which the scientist . . . exalts above temporary healing as the religious exalts the nature and terrible glory of God above pleasant daily virtues" (120). Here is a good example of Lewis's prime rule for the handling of ideas: be brisk with them and count on the flow of words to sweep the reader right past their implications. Who could be so callous as to submit such a high-minded statement to analysis, to ask whether contemplatives really consider that the glory of God makes the practice of the virtues of little account, to question the validity of a scientist's belief that the cure of the sick is of small consequence in comparison with the search for the fundamental laws of nature? Lewis gives the impression of having gone deeply into the problem of the rational foundation for devotion to science, but there is more appearance than reality. He gives Martin's position no metaphysical basis, in fact, no sanction outside itself; furthermore, it seems to be undermined by a radical skepticism, not a mere withholding of judgment:

> She had called Martin a "lie-hunter," a "truth-seeker." They decided now, talking it over in their tight little two-and-a-quarter room flat, that most people who call themselves "truth-seekers"—persons who scurry about chattering of Truth as though it were a tangible separable thing, like houses or salt or bread—did not so much desire to find Truth as to cure their mental itch. In novels, these truth-seekers quested the "secret of life" in laboratories which did not seem to be provided with Bunsen flames or reagents; or they went, at great expense and much discomfort from hot trains and undesirable snakes, to Himalayan monasteries, to learn from unaseptic sages that the Mind can do all sorts of edifying things if one will but spend thirty or forty years in eating rice and gazing on one's navel.
>
> To these high matters Martin responded, "Rot!" He insisted that there is no Truth but only many truths; that Truth is not a colored bird to be chased among the rocks and captured by its tail, but a skeptical attitude toward life. He insisted that no one could expect more than, by stubbornness or luck, to have the kind of work he enjoyed and an ability to become better acquainted with the facts of work than the average job-holder. [271]

Does this leave Martin with any better reason for acting than the "mental itch" he derides? If truth is nothing more than a skeptical attitude towards life, why not be skeptical about the value of scientific research?

It is interesting to observe that Lewis gains support for Martin's position partly by caricaturing alternatives to it, partly by associating with it moral and intellectual attitudes which the reader is likely to favor (honesty, open-mindedness, a disposition to question received opinions, and so on), and partly by attaching religious overtones to it. He gives prestige, if not an intellectual defense. The comparison of the scientist to the religious occurs many times. Science is the new religion to supplant outmoded creeds, and Gottlieb is its prophet; Arrowsmith says, "You think Gottlieb isn't religious, Hinkley. Why, his just being in a lab is a prayer" (30). Like the Messiah, Gottlieb has to endure scorn and ignominy:

> Not once did he fail to be hated by his colleagues, who were respectful to his face, uncomfortable in feeling his ironic power, but privily joyous to call him Mephisto, Diabolist, Killjoy, Pessimist, Destructive Critic, Flippant Cynic, Scientific Bounder Lacking in Dignity and Seriousness, Intellectual Snob, Pacifist, Anarchist, Atheist, Jew. [124]

Gottlieb himself refers to great scientists as though they were members of a priesthood or a religious order: "Father Koch and Father Pasteur and Brother Jacques Loeb and Brother Arrhenius." In a moment of spiritual rapture, Martin composes a scientist's prayer which concludes with the paradox "Give me strength not to trust to God!" In the manner of Comte, Lewis tries to ennoble science by referring to it in religious terms and to present it as a worthy successor to religion as an object of mankind's devotion.

The novel might be described as an anatomy of the obstacles in the scientist's way. They are put there by the medical profession, by the character of the scientist himself, by various social groups, and by the general outlook of the American people. Almost all the possible attitudes toward research are presented, and each one is supported or illustrated by an impressive amount of detail. The Main Street view is shown when Martin goes to Wheatsylvania, North Dakota; here the doctor is a medicine man and conformity to the tribal code is much more important than medical skill. The view of Babbitt's friends is shown when Martin gets a job in Nautilus, Iowa, another Zenith: "The only difference between Nautilus and Zenith is that in both cases all the streets look alike but in Nautilus they do not look alike for so many miles." Here the Public Health Director must be a Booster and not a conscientious pursuer of germs; in fact, the worst mistake he can make is to try to clean up dirty houses or dirty restaurants owned by influential citizens. Everywhere, it seems, the Boosters overcome the Truth-seekers. Pharmaceutical houses are so unscrupulous that they market preparations even before they have been tested and continue to sell them after they have been proved useless; clinics are mere medical factories which will tolerate no research nonsense; and even genuine research organizations are only the playthings of so-called philanthropists.

All these are valid subjects for satire. But the last great obstacle to scientific asceticism, humanity, is not. Should the quest for scientific knowledge override every other human consideration? In Gottlieb's life, it does. Martin decides in favor of humanitarianism when he abandons his controlled experiment on St. Hubert during an epidemic and administers his serum to everyone, but he regards himself as a traitor to science. At the end, he casts everything else aside for the sake of research. The pursuit of truth to the exclusion of error is clearly something desirable; the pursuit of scientific truth to the exclusion of all human values is something else again. We have moved, therefore, from an area in which satire attacks deviations from a reasonable, normal position to an area in which there is a dramatic tension between two kinds of value. But the transition is not awkward; the central character this time does not make an unpredictable change, and the book does not break in two like *Main Street* and *Babbitt*.

But it does have two types of characters—the realistic and the unrealistic. The latter can be identified by their comic-strip names. Martin works under Dr. Benjamin Holabird in a research institute headed by Dr. A. De Witt Tubbs and financed by Capitola McGurk, the Great White Uplifter. Earlier he has served under Dr. Almus Picker-baugh, dynamic Director of Public Health in Zenith, Booster extraordinary, and father of the Healthette Octette—eight strapping girls floridly ranging from Orchid to Gladiola. Through this brilliant caricature, Lewis shows that the archetypal qualities of the Booster—brashness, vulgarity, hatred of nonconformity, worship of success—are as conspicuous in the world of medicine as they are in real estate and advertising. Yet Lewis's use of such comic-strip characters would seem to give the lie to those who consider the primary quality of his work its documentary veracity or photographic realism. For the moment, it is perhaps sufficient to observe that Lewis's use of characters with extravagant names and personalities is not necessarily an error in artistic judgment: these parodies or travesties of human beings illustrate his contention that America, in seeking to develop a new kind of person, has only turned out new specimens of the grotesque.

If Lewis's central theme in *Arrowsmith* was the difficulty of avoiding the prostitution of standards in medical science, the theme had wider implications. T. K. Whipple, in an excellent review in the *New Republic*, pointed out that the novel really showed how the American environment affects the creative spirit. In the United States, he said, art and religion are made bondslaves to practical success—and he took Lewis himself as an example. Lewis made greater use of irony as a defensive weapon than any other writer Whipple knew; he always wrote as if he were conscious of a hostile audience, and he took endless pains to make clear that he was more sophisticated than his characters, to ridicule their naive enthusiasms. In other words, he exemplified the morbid self-consciousness and insecurity of his own creations, who were always suspicious that they were the objects of comment and who had no inner standards of their own because they had no integral personalities. Like them, Whipple said, Lewis was a man of multiple personality, though his many attitudes could be resolved into two—the romantic and the philistine. Besides the conventional Tennyson-and-water romanticism, there was also, as in Arnold Bennett, the romance of the commonplace; allied to it was a philistinism which was homey and folksy and strongly opposed to anything "arty" or "superior." Even *Arrowsmith*, Whipple wrote, was the work of a mangled artist. But he conceded that Lewis's romanticism and philistinism and vulgarity of style made him powerful because they made him popular; the attack on practicality needed its shock troops, and perhaps it was worth spoiling an artist to have him take so salutary a revenge. "Lewis is the most successful critic of American society," he concluded, "because he is himself the best proof that his charges are just."[18]

In showing what had happened in one field of endeavor, Lewis was describing the failure of the epic dream: America had aspired to be a nation of free individuals, but the worship of material success by the many had forced the few independent spirits to turn their backs on their fellow men. Carl Van Doren said that readers found in the story a familiar American pattern of behavior. Despairing of medical practice because of its confusions and compromises, Arrowsmith forsook it to do his true work in a wilderness, "almost exactly as Leather-Stocking and Daniel Boone had in the eighteenth century turned away from the corrupted settlements to be themselves beyond the tumult of mankind."[19] Arrowsmith is aware of his resemblance to other types of pioneer; when he explains to Joyce, his wealthy wife, that he is going to escape from the captivity which her way of life imposes on him, he refers to "those of us that are pioneers." In fact, the pioneering theme is established in the opening scene of the novel, which depicts the intrepid determination of Arrowsmith's great-grandmother in the Ohio wilderness.

Arrowsmith's mental make-up is derived from the pioneer ethos at least as much as from Max Gottlieb. Maxwell Geismar is dubious about the scientific skepticism of the novel and would prefer to call it a fashionable cynicism,[20] but actually Martin holds to the tradition of dissent which Geismar describes in his *American Moderns* as perhaps the most vital element in American democracy:[21]

> Gradually Martin's contemplation moved beyond Almus Pickerbaugh to all leaders, of armies or empires, of universities or churches, and he saw that most of them were Pickerbaughs. He preached to himself, as Max Gottlieb had once preached to him, the loyalty of dissent, the faith of being very doubtful, the gospel of not bawling gospels, the wisdom of admitting the probable ignorance of one's self and of everybody else, and the energetic acceleration of a movement for going very slow. [228]

We have seen that Lewis is so much of Geismar's mind regarding the tradition of dissent that near the end of *Main Street* he makes institutions rather than individuals responsible for everything he has satirized. The truest American, in his view, is the aloof, independent, egocentric, suspicious pioneer. So strong is his emphasis on isolation that—as Geismar stresses, though Raymond H. Palmer said it long before him[22]—he nowhere gives a picture of a true home or a true church or a true corporate life of any kind; he has taken the tradition of dissent to its logical and ultimate conclusion. As Raymond Williams states in a discussion of Dickens, there is always a system of some kind, and the argument against system per se is usually either fretful or ignorant. This type of anti-institutionalism seems to be the retained position of the adolescent, the innocence which essentially rejects the adult world.[23] On the evidence of Lewis's life and writings, Palmer is justified in calling him "the great undisciplined American, the apotheosis of American individuality and irresponsibility."[24] *Arrowsmith* is thus a paradoxical combination of an attack on conditions which inhibit scientific progress and a flight from maturity, a plea for a return to a simpler and more uncomplicated way of life than the modern world can offer.[25]

There were, of course, two versions of *Arrowsmith*. In his reply to Harcourt's news about the sale of the serial rights, Lewis paid less attention to the amount of money involved than to the possibility of editorial interference; he expressed the hope (in capital letters) that the magazine publisher understood that he would not "change the thing into a sunny sweet tale." When the same magazine made overtures for his next novel, he rejected them, fearing to be deprived of "the freedom without which very few decent novels are written." In a comparison of the two versions of *Arrowsmith*, however, Lyon N. Richardson has shown that the greater freedom which Lewis could employ in the book version was not really helpful to him. "Indeed, it can well be argued," Richardson declares, "that the story really lost little in the serial form and in many ways was improved by deletions of words and sentences which merely belabored the ideas or were blatant Lewisian expletives and obtrusive, derisive remarks."[26] The *Designer* could not tolerate some of his "mere buzzing and stinging" at moral smugness; the changes sometimes indicated squeamishness on the part of the magazine's editors, but on the other hand they imposed a wholesome restraint on such things as Lewis's heavy-handed overworking of references to the Wassermann test. It checked what Richardson calls "the more angular characteristics of his satire"—seeking emphasis by expletives; satirizing hypocrisy, selfishness, mediocrity, and so on "with the petulant impatience of a zealot unarmed by humor"; and manipulating characters too obviously to prove a point. Richardson concludes that most of the many deletions made for serial publication removed irritating blemishes: "Lewis and the editor of the *Designer* improved the story, though the author, in his eagerness to challenge hypocrisy and mediocrity, would not believe it."

Couch notes that *Arrowsmith* has been one of the most highly praised—some would say overpraised—of Lewis's works. To many reviewers it was either a genuine step forward by its author or conclusive proof of his excellence as a novelist.[27] Its weaknesses, however, have become more apparent with the passing of years. Many male readers seem to have fallen in love with Leora: Harcourt called her "just about the best woman character in American fiction that I know of."[28] But Martin Light thinks her quite incredible—chiefly a convenience who does all the right things, especially in never interfering with her husband's plans, and who tops it all off by becoming a martyr to science. He is equally unimpressed by the character of Arrowsmith; although Lewis says that he matures, he doesn't show it, and his tone throughout remains that of an exuberant schoolboy.[29] A similar criticism was made by Warren Beck in a notable attack on Lewis's reputation. He grudgingly allowed that Arrowsmith was one of the two consistent characters Lewis had created—Babbitt was the other—but maintained that Lewis had failed to control him: "He has run off not only with many a reader but with his author, for in glorifying Arrowsmith as scientist Lewis seems unaware of what a crude and lopsided human being he had made of him."[30] Arrowsmith as doctor has been both criticized and defended; perhaps the most famous criticism is that by Hans Zinsser, in *Rats, Lice and History*, to the effect that if an epidemiologist on a plague study behaved in the manner of Arrowsmith he would be regarded by his associates as a yellow ass and a nuisance.[31]

De Kruif, giving a verdict "aged in the wood of my head over many years," does not criticize Arrowsmith so much as Gottlieb, whom he considers a muddied mélange of his own scientific mentor and of Jacques Loeb, "who was my master in a philosophy of the mechanistic conception of life, of God a mathematician, of God a Univac, of God a superstition, of God a childish concept, of God nonexistent."[32] This conception, he writes, accorded with Lewis's own philosophy. For Loeb, it was undoubtedly the product of considerable reflection about causality, creation, the existence of matter, and related topics. But when Lewis writes, "Like all ardent agnostics, Martin was a religious man," it is obvious that there is not very much deep reflection behind the remark; it is merely a glib paradox designed to give an appearance of profundity. Light finds the heroic pretensions of the novel embarrassing, in view of the slick-magazine language of many of its passages;[33] when Lewis writes that Martin "was homesick for the laboratory, for the thrill of uncharted discoveries, the quest below the surface and beyond the moment," we feel, as we did about Babbitt's dreams of his fairy child, that the whole thing is overwritten and slickly contrived. In spite of the excellence of much of the satire and the author's success in fusing satire and novel, the book shows that Lewis could not do what Sherman asked him to do—give a satisfactory exposition of values.

Notes

1. See especially Robert Cantwell, "Sinclair Lewis," *New Republic*, LXXXVIII (1936), 298–301, and Leo and Miriam Gurko, "The Two Main Streets of Sinclair Lewis," *College English*, LV (1943), 288–292.

2. Arthur B. Coleman, "The Genesis of Social Ideas in Sinclair Lewis" (Ph.D. dissertation, New York University, 1954), p. 80. Martin Light discusses the same

point in his "A Study of Characterization in Sinclair Lewis's Fiction" (Ph.D. dissertation, University of Illinois, 1960), p. 80.

3. Stuart Sherman, *The Significance of Sinclair Lewis* (New York: Harcourt, Brace, 1922), p. 20.

4. Letter to Harcourt, December 13, 1921, *From Main Street to Stockholm: Letters of Sinclair Lewis 1919–1930*, ed. with an intro. by Harrison Smith (New York: Harcourt, Brace, 1952), p. 90.

5. Grace Hegger Lewis, *With Love from Gracie: Sinclair Lewis: 1912–1925* (New York: Harcourt, Brace, 1955), p. 210.

6. *Ibid.*, p. 211.

7. *Ibid.*, p. 212.

8. *The Designer and the Woman's Magazine*, LX (June 1924), 2.

9. Paul de Kruif, *The Sweeping Wind* (New York: Harcourt, Brace, 1962), p. 76.

10. *Ibid.*, p. 103.

11. *The Designer and the Woman's Magazine*, LX (June 1924), 64.

12. Letter to Harcourt, December 3, 1923, *From Main Street to Stockholm*, p. 147.

13. Letter to Lewis, October 30, 1923, *ibid.*, p. 144.

14. *With Love from Gracie*, p. 274.

15. Letter to Harcourt, March 26, 1924, *From Main Street to Stockholm*, p. 156.

16. Letter to Donald Brace, July 29, 1924, *ibid.*, p. 162.

17. *Arrowsmith* (New York: Harcourt, Brace, 1925).

18. T. K. Whipple, "Sinclair Lewis," *New Republic*, XLII (April 15, 1925), 3.

19. Carl Van Doren, *Sinclair Lewis: A Biographical Sketch* (Garden City: Doubleday, Doran, 1933), p. 45.

20. *The Last of the Provincials: The American Novel, 1915–1925* (Boston: Houghton Mifflin, 1949), p. 101.

21. *American Moderns: From Rebellion to Conformity* (London: W. H. Allen, 1958), p. 26.

22. Raymond H. Palmer, "The Nobel Jury Judges America," *Christian Century*, XLVII (1930), 1448. Geismar develops the point in detail in both *The Last of the Provincials* and *American Moderns*.

23. Raymond Williams, *Culture and Society, 1780–1950* (London: Chatto and Windus, 1958), pp. 59, 95–96.

24. "The Nobel Jury Judges America," p. 1448.

25. William Couch, Jr., in "The Emergence, Rise and Decline of the Reputation of Sinclair Lewis" (Ph.D. dissertation, University of Chicago, 1954), points out that Alfred North Whitehead contended in his *Science and the Modern World*, published in the same year as *Babbitt*, that the concept of the self-sufficing, independent man, with his peculiar advantages which concerned no one else, possessed no validity for modern civilization. The same point of view was taken by John Dewey in his *Individualism Old and New* (1930). As Couch says, Dewey would have regarded Arrowsmith as an example of the tragedy of the lost individual, unable to accept modern corporate society and mistakenly viewing science as an isolated and independent activity, a refuge from the modern world.

26. Lyon N. Richardson, "Arrowsmith: Genesis, Development, Versions," *American Literature*, XXVII (1955–1956), 230.

27. See Couch "Reputation," pp. 110 ff. Two examples he cites are Henry Seidel Canby in the *Saturday Review of Literature* and Henry Longan Stuart in the New York *Times*, both of whom said in effect that it was time to stop prating of the limitations of Sinclair Lewis and give him credit for his brilliant studies of his society.

28. Letter to Lewis, March 11, 1925, *From Main Street to Stockholm*, p. 179. See also Canby's and other rhapsodic eulogies of Leora quoted by Couch, "Reputation," pp. 111–112.

29. Light, "Characterization," pp. 252, 263. Sheldon Grebstein, in his *Sinclair Lewis*, "United States Authors Series" (New York: Twayne, 1962), p. 87, argues that in each of the novel's situations Martin learns from his mistakes.

30. Warren Beck, "How Good is Sinclair Lewis?" *College English*, IX (1947–1948), 177.

31. Hans Zinsser, *Rats, Lice and History* (Boston: Little, Brown, 1935), p. 13. The medical correspondent of the Chicago *Tribune*, Dr. Evans, examined in detail Arrowsmith's performance as a doctor and concluded that there were a number of improbable things. Fishbein replied to this, in an article signed with his initials, "Dr. Evans and Arrowsmith," *Hygeia*, October, 1925, pp. 588–589. See Couch, "Reputation," p. 113.

32. De Kruif, *The Sweeping Wing*, p. 109.

33. Light, "Characterization," p. 253.

The Serialized Novels
of Sinclair Lewis
Martin Bucco*

Contrary Sinclair Lewis owed much of his phenomenal literary success and failure to popular American magazine fiction. As far back as 1910, while hacking in the dream factories of the East, this raw Middle Westerner brooded over his hometown and his alma mater—Sauk Centre, Minnesota, and Yale University—and yearned for fame and fortune. Restless and tormented, he seemed always out of tune with people and places. When not playing the role of medieval lyricist or prairie euphuist, he contributed to the slow displacement of good fiction in magazines by cynically turning out, as he once confessed, "a swell piece of cheese to grab off some easy gravy."[1] But what editors of the big slicks balked at, many literary critics admired; and what the critics denounced, magazine editors praised.

Nowhere is Sinclair Lewis' split sensibility more visible than in a collation of his serials and books.[2] In addition to casting into the Dead Sea of literary mercantilism more than a hundred short stories. Lewis also

*Reprinted, with permission, from *Western American Literature* 4 (Spring 1969): 29–37.

tossed in seven serial novels, later revised and published in book form. For $1000 and *Woman's Home Companion* ("Service to the Modern Home"), he potboiled in two installments the Pickwickian travels of "The Innocents" (February-March, 1917), his fourth novel (*The Innocents: A Story for Lovers*, 1917). When *Saturday Evening Post*, which earlier had rejected "The Innocents" as too bathetic, bid for stories of American romance and adventure—of Horatio Alger types scurrying up the ladder of material success—Lewis rehashed three articles ("Adventures in Autobumming") based on his four-month tour of the American West in a Model T Ford and sold his four-part serial, "Free-Air" (May 31-June 21, 1919), and its two-part sequel, "Danger—Run Slow" (October 18-25, 1919); both constituted the frame for his fifth novel (*Free Air*, 1919) and the inspiration for his unserialized *Main Street* (1920). To *Designer and the Woman's Magazine* the now famous writer sold for $50,000 his shorter version of the modern pioneer spirit in eleven installments of "Dr. Martin Arrowsmith" (June, 1924-April, 1925), afterwards published as Lewis' eighth novel (*Arrowsmith*, 1925). In 1926, for $42,500, the die-hard magazinist answered the call of *Collier's Weekly* for more action and more obvious motivation with twelve installments of his shoddy Western Canadian melodrama, "Mantrap" (February 13-May 8), his ninth novel (*Mantrap*, 1926). After Sinclair Lewis accepted the Nobel Prize in 1930, he resolved to create in the Great Tradition; but, still composing with one eye on the serial market, he granted first publication and bowdlerization rights to affluent *Redbook Magazine* (August, 1932-January, 1933), *Cosmopolitan Magazine* (May-October, 1945), and—the wheel comes full circle—*Woman's Home Companion* (January-February, 1951) for, respectively: his thirteenth novel (*Ann Vickers*, 1933), nineteenth novel (*Cass Timberlane*, 1945), and twenty-second and last novel (*World So Wide*, 1951).

Since their readers craved uncomplicated narratives, magazine editors consistently objected to the best thing in Lewis—his social satire. Nimble in the calling of pleasing the flesh-and-blood counterparts of Mrs. Babbitt, serial editors and author expunged the gargantuan sniping, lashing, carping, smearing, grumbling, and general denouncing. The trick: to alienate or to insult no one, especially middle-class Americans who admired middle-class Americans. For example, in Lewis' weary "World So Wide," with its soporific irony (American hero travels to strange land, meets strange woman, but in the end marries familiar girl next door), the *Companion* editors removed the criticism of America from the Italian point of view, the biting remarks from the expatriot point of view, and even censored the touring heroine's mild observation, for instance, that Americans in Italy are richer in their hearts than Americans back home who take themselves "so seriously selling whisky or lawsuits or college-alumni enthusiasm" (p. 249).

From the earlier *Redbook* version of Lewis' "Ann Vickers," the editors deleted nearly a thousand paragraphs and thousands of phrases and single words, most dealing with politics, religion, and education. The serial heroine is Wordsworthian, the book heroine Marxian. Ann's girlhood rebellion against Sunday School is not in the serial—not even so tepid a sarcasm as her listening to "a lovely elocutionist gentleman with black wavy hair recite Kipling at the entertainment of the Order of the Eastern Star" (p. 19). Little of Lewis' anti-academicism taints the serial; *Redbook* readers never learn, for instance, that schools like Smith and Vassar are excellent because scholarship there is *equal* in rank to tennis. And since the literary taste of serial readers is above suspicion, perhaps editors felt obligated to blue pencil the suggestion that there are better American writers than Zane Grey and Harold Bell Wright—a pair who were outselling even such popular Western authors as Frank Norris and the writer to whom Lewis in 1910 had sold story plots—Jack London..

Since magazine publishers envisioned their readers as belonging to the "better off" middle class, an optimistic and cheery group that by income or interest typified American ambitions, editors automatically eliminated objectionable Lewisian details. When characters drank, swore, gambled, disrobed, confronted crudity or cruelty, discussed sex, or did anything contrary to the prevailing dictates of middle-class public morality, Lewis expected—in fact, made or suggested—alterations. Editors regarded the statements of Lewis' unreconstructed lady radicals much as editors today of, say, *Good Housekeeping* might regard the stream of consciousness of Joyce's Molly Bloom. Thus Lewis' serial heroes and heroines were conventionalized, especially their libidos. The sense of propriety of *Saturday Evening Post* fans in 1919 seems as quaint today as some of Lewis' dated satire. Not only did the *Post* not permit a comic figure in "Free Air" to dance around "in the costume of Adam" (p. 343), but it did not admit that the drenched heroine, Claire Boltwood, "stripped off her stockings and pumps" (p. 368) and that both she and the hero, Milt Daggett, "rubbed their legs with their stockings" (p. 369). Naturally, the serial Ann Vickers is forbidden unholy sexual alliances. And Jenny Marshland, who sports a lynx jacket in *Cass Timberlane*, is decidedly more aggressive and flirtatious than is her serial counterpart, who wears a Persian lamb coat. The student of American popular art understands what monologist Lowell Schmaltz (*The Man Who Knew Coolidge*, 1928) means when he pronounces *Cosmo* a repository of the "best literature" (p. 105).

But what editors of *Designer* and *Redbook* excinded from "Dr. Martin Arrowsmith" and "Ann Vickers" in the way of violence, cruelty, squalor, and sex reflects how Lewis often wrote in opposition to a large segment of the magazine-buying public—and then how, after heavy editing, he reaped from that same golden harvest. From "Dr. Martin Arrowsmith" editors and author cut out the grotesque medical school scenes—for example, corpses hanging from hooks. Although Lewis was opposed to literary obscenity, he used a liberal supply of "damn," "hell," and "God" omitted from the serial.[3] In "Ann Vickers," hardly recognizable as a muckraking novel of penal reform, the serial reader is oblivious to the book's solitary confinements, whippings, bloody razors, foaming mouths, skull-crackings, lynchings, foul odors, flies, rats, roaches, slop, vomit, and other naturalistic tidbits. Nor does Ann ever ponder accident, exile, kidnapping, assassination, starvation, poisoning, and rape. The hero, Judge Barney Dolphin, is not even involved in the "Queens sewer case" (p. 531)—just in "a certain case" (January, p. 115). The serial eliminates all allusions to bawdy, pornography, seduction, sexual intercourse, abortion, and childbirth. Indeed, any critical reader can point a just finger at the book's morbid sensationalism; but the serial does not even admit phrases like "the stirring of puberty" (p. 29) or words like "adultery" (p. 145), "precautions" (p. 179), "Wasserman" (p. 311), "prostitute" (p. 314), and "morning sickness" (p. 489). Thus Edwin Balmer, *Redbook* editor, confidently proclaimed Sinclair Lewis' latest serial as "the best of our time as long as literary records of America are preserved."[4]

Yet whatever gaucheries the editors of popular fiction deleted from Lewis's serials, many thematic clichés remain—to inform even the great debunker's unserialized work. Almost automatically, Lewis champions the humble against the powerful, the poor against the rich, the adventurous against the timid, the idealist against the materialist, the romantic against the realist, the maker against the intellectual, and the country against the city. These "commercial" attitudes appear, often ambivalently, in all Lewis' books—from the second rate *Our Mister Wrenn* (1914), to the first-rate *Babbitt* (1922), to the third-rate *World So Wide* (1952). Especially conspicuous is the East-West theme, perhaps the central tension in Lewis' life and work. In pitting the elegant, class-conscious, confined East against the drab, egalitarian, free West, Lewis shrilly defended the West sometimes, but without conviction. Try as he might to love the virgin land, he never succeeded. None of his books evokes the sense of what, thanks to Max Westbrook, has become a critical truism when discussing Western literature: "sacrality."[5] Lewis' view of the West is essentially simplistic, sentimental, and exterior. He renders humor, speech, and manner, but not soul, deity, or sublimity—not even in *The God-Seeker* (1949), his unserialized historical novel set in the Minnesota wilderness. If the hero of *Work of Art* (1934) happily manages a little Kansas hotel, and if the battle against tyranny in *It Can't Happen Here* (1935) begins out West, there is still, among other things to beset Lewis, the spectre of Grand Republic racism in *Kingsblood*

Royal (1947). Ultimately Lewis' ambivalence means: if the idyllic West is antidote to the cramped East, then the cultivated East, in turn, is antidote to the blank West—and remedy for both is the open road— anywhere!

A new or revisited place, Lewis half believed, would make a new person. The old Cape Cod couple in "The Innocents" end up in Delaware, but in the book version they head West in the mythic manner, optimistically seeking self-reliance and the joys of village life. Beginning in the serial "Free Air" and intensifying in the book version, a raw Western mechanic learns the social graces as part of his cross-country courtship of an Eastern socialite, while she apparently learns the meaning of democracy. The shorter "Dr. Martin Arrowsmith" sets the tone for the full development of the pioneer spirit when the hero's great grandmother declares at the start: "We're going on jus' as long as we can. Going West!" In "Mantrap" Lewis, waxing ebullient over the Great Outdoors, drops his citified Ralph Prescott smack into the tradition of Raw Meat survival. And in his Nobel Prize Speech Lewis spoke of Theodore Dreiser's *Sister Carrie* as having come to airless America as "a great free Western wind" and Lewis then called for a literature of America "worthy of her vastness."[6] Thus in "Ann Vickers" the Middle West town, unlike *Main Street*'s Gopher Prairie, receives Lewis' nostalgic approbation, but only in the book version does frustrated Ann declare: "I would be glad if some ranchman out of an idiotic 'Western novel' came along and married me off ..." (p. 409). Also, in his novel of modern marriage, "Cass Timberlane," Lewis re-identified himself with the West—Grand Republic opposes New York City. So in "World So Wide" Hayden and Roxanna Chart return home to Newlife, Colorado, with new perspectives. In all these novels, however, the author's capricious overtones suggest private dubiety—as if he half believed that a new or revisited place would not really make a new person.

While magazinists, then, objected to Sinclair Lewis' social satire and to his naturalistic details, they welcomed not only his commercial romanticism, but also his electric improvisation. Originally Lewis wrote his contemporary Western novel, "Free Air," for example, as a four-installment Open Road serial for *Saturday Evening Post*. But as he enlarged the tale for book publication, he advised his publisher, Alfred Harcourt, to advertise the book as "romance with dignity and realism."[7] Meanwhile, so popular was the serial version that *Post* editor George Lorimer pleaded with Lewis for a sequel—an unprecedented request. Having already revised the original four installments for book publication, Lewis seized an extra $2,500 and the inspiration of the moment, made an about-face, and revised his extended book episodes as a two-installment sequel. The *Post* then published "Danger—Run Slow" four months after "Free Air," in appearance and in effect, had ended. How Lewis exploited the commercial possibilities of "Free Air"—how he *bridged* the sixteen issues between the serial's last installment and the sequel's first—is a classic of improvised swagger.

In a thousand words Lewis re-established the last scene on the train, his hero and heroine traveling West to marital bliss. In the process, he re-identified Milt Daggett and Claire Boltwood, summarized the earlier four installments, and then made a strenuous effort to convince readers with moderate recall that the story of Milt and Claire, after all, is not really over: Just now she is "violently engaged in falling out of love"—for how can she introduce this poor mechanic to her wealthy Seattle relatives? The serialist speaks:

> She saw no way out—except cruelty.
> And so her story, which had seemed ended, was begun.
> The end of every comedy is the commencement of a tragedy. When the wedding bells have sounded their pink gayety and the author with considerable weariness and an interested thought in royalties leaves the happy couple surrounded by kisses and presents, and indicates that this is The End—then it is time for another author to creep in and reveal the actual story, with the tragedies of dull evenings and social slights and sickness and the loss of bachelor friends, with the drama of enduring loyalty and of pride in children that is so much more alive than courtship's tepid experiments, with the abrupt disaster or the glorious endurance of the effort, and all the deep sweet humanness of the trudging years.
> So now, when Claire Boltwood and Milt Daggett believed that their real story was the motor flight in which they had found the easy and romantic companionship of outdoors, this typical prelude of the unengaged young man meeting a disengaged young woman was over, and their real struggle with life was beginning. (October 18, p. 3)

To be sure, Lewis gave the book version of *Free Air* more "dignity" by purging it of slapdash serial absurdities, but this rediscovered bridge exhibits to a sad degree the cynical banality of our first Nobel Prize Winner.

Serial and slick-story engineering was so natural to Sinclair Lewis that even after he committed himself to writing masterworks in the 1920s he consciously or subconsciously appropriated the serial form. Thus both the serialized and the unserialized Lewis novel—that is, every book in his choppy social canon—displays a more or less compelling series of contracted flights, each flight concluding with a teasing, installment-esque climax or cliff-hanger. Like the picaresque novel, the serial's loose, episodic, linear structure encouraged Lewis to extemporize with aplomb. While this narrative method enabled him to preserve or to insert both germane and gratuitous blocks of social criticism in his book versions, it also enabled serial editors and Lewis to liquidate blocks of social commentary without impairing the story line. In the serial, "Cass Timberlane," for example, the book's brilliant intercalary "Assemblages" disappear; in "World So Wide" both social critique and the sense of place are gone. This method of composition—of "doing up a subject"—naturally plays havoc with structural and tonal unity. Because of his awesome reputation, however, Sinclair Lewis could defy a few stock serial formulas. In *Collier's* "Mantrap," for example, he introduces his heroine not in the conventional first or second installment, but in the fifth; he sets his story in a familiar America, but then shifts to the Canadian woods; and he writes a downbeat ending. But all too often the free-swinging Lewis overcompensated for serial straitjacketing by pouring forth in fantastic language embarrassing melodrama and sentimentality. In the padded book version of *The Innocents*, for example, Mother Appleby acts even more improbably than in the serial—her change is revolutionary; and, ironically, it is in the world of commercial fiction where precipitant change is counted a blessing. Besides being more robust than the serial "Mantrap," the book version also is more sentimental. And although in serials good people love horses and dogs, the book *Cass Timberlane* has too many saccharin comments on Cleo, the family cat. On the positive side, early serial publication (besides gaining Lewis money and limelight) taught him to re-see his characters and to develop them for the more critical book reader. The Eastern shop owner in "The Innocents," for instance, sells only shoes; but the shop owner in the book version, a Middle Westerner, also sells Lipsittsville—five years before George F. Babbitt sells Zenith:

> "Aside from any future business dicker between you and me personally, I'd like to show you just why Lipsittsville is going to be a bigger town than Freiburg or Taormina or Hongkong or Bryan or any of the other towns in the country, let 'em say what they like!" (p. 190)

Drab Western scenes which Lewis added to *Free Air* for Claire Boltwood's edification prefigure similar scenes which Carol Kennicott views in *Main Street*. Thus, even if censorious, American popular fiction encouraged Lewis to direct his blazing camera-eyes on the contemporary American scene. Also, between serial and book publication, Lewis always tidied up or energized his style. Since decorous homemakers liked his swift, nervous, bold language in its lower and middle registers, the serials display fewer verbal acrobatics. For example, "traveling men" in the serial "Free Air" (May 31, p. 123) becomes in the book version "pioneers in spats" (p. 87). Although Lewis' lucid, flexible prose yields a range of feeling from the maudlin to the savage, his coarse diction and brazen phrase (like frontier inflation) never adequately renders interior nuance.

The man of letters and the historian of ideas, fascinated by the struggle of opposing forces in the human soul, must indeed wonder about this sentimental realist or satiric romantic. Like Charles Dickens, Lewis improbably managed at times to transcend his education in the conventions of popular magazine fiction. But was ever a major writer in hot pursuit of the American Dream quite so divided as Sinclair Lewis? In 1946 Frederick Manfred described his fellow Minnesotan: "The face I saw was a face to haunt one in dreams. It was a face that looked as if it were being slowly ravaged by a fire, by an emotional fire, by a fire that was already fading a little and that was leaving a slowly contracting lump of gray-red cinder."[8] Was ever a novelist out of the American West quite so parsimonious and prodigal as Lewis? Were he alive today, shuttling between the Establishment and the Movement, Sinclair Lewis would give to these rhetorical questions a pair of fabulously contradictory answers.

Notes

1. *The Intimate Notebooks of George Jean Nathan* (New York, 1932), p. 16.

2. I have treated the subject comprehensively in *The Serialized Novels of Sinclair Lewis: A Comparative Analysis of Serial and Book* (unpublished doctoral dissertation, University of Missouri, 1963). Also, I have examined intermediate manuscripts among the Sinclair Lewis Papers, Yale University Library. For early suggestions I am indebted to Mark Schorer and, of course, to his monumental *Sinclair Lewis: An American Life* (New York, 1961); useful in its compactness is Sheldon Norman Grebstein's *Sinclair Lewis*, TUSAS (New York, 1962).

3. Lyon N. Richardson, "*Arrowsmith:* Genesis, Development, Versions," *American Literature*, XXVII (May, 1955), 225–44.

4. Schorer includes in his biography, p. 578, a letter from an irate gentleman who read *only* the November installment: "Why you dirty low down smelly nasty disgusting, obscene, maggot filled manure minded, skunkassociating sap, of just what value do you think a story of that kind would be to the world or to the readers." Lewis sent the man a complimentary copy of the *book!*

5. See, for example, "The Practical Spirit: Sacrality and the American West," *Western American Literature*, III (Fall, 1968), 193–205.

6. *The Man From Main Street: A Sinclair Lewis Reader*, edited by Harry E. Maule and Melville H. Cane (New York, 1953), p. 8.

7. *From Main Street to Stockholm: Letters of Sinclair Lewis, 1919–1930* (New York, 1952), p. 15.

8. "Sinclair Lewis: A Portrait," *American Scholar*, XIII (Spring, 1954), 166.

Sinclair Lewis and Western Humor   James C. Austin*

There are two contradictory sides to the work of Sinclair Lewis. He has been called a realist, a satirist, a social critic on the one hand; a romantic, a sentimentalist, and a Babbitt on the other. He lastingly branded American smugness and hypocrisy, yet defended American warmth and integrity. Some commentators have recognized his inconsistencies and have more or less succeeded in explaining them. Perhaps the most successful and the most recent critic is D. J. Dooley in *The Art of Sinclair Lewis* (1967).

> Many critics have pointed out that his middle-class world was a nightmare world; at times his vision resembles that in *The Waste Land* of people walking meaninglessly around in a ring, or the Orwellian image of drawn and cowed people in an Airstrip One. But his florid, loud-mouthed representatives of the class which spins not and toils chiefly at salesmanship proved to be richly varied and full of life and gusto. Lewis was never happier than when a Marduc or a Pickerbaugh, a Windrip or a Blausser, had sprung full-blown into existence in the world of his imagination and begun to wax eloquent. These were characters to be treated with satiric humor; some of them were menaces, some of them were conspiring to destroy all freedom and all individuality, but except in his gloomier moments, Lewis never believed that they would succeed. He kept his faith in the American Dream. (pp. xv–xvi)

The conflict within Sinclair Lewis was not unique. He expressed a dilemma which, as Charles L. Sanford suggested in *The Quest for Paradise* (1961), was a part of the culture of the Middle West. Further, he drew upon the humor of that region for his mode of expression. Lewis was not only a product of his region but the outstanding representative of the tradition of American humor as it developed in the Northern states west of Ohio.

In Sauk Centre, Minnesota, around the turn of the century, Lewis could read George Ade, Finley Peter Dunne (Mr. Dooley), and Henry M. Hyde (One-Forty-Two) in copyrighted columns in the Minneapolis *Tribune*.[1] He could also read the witty Ralph W. Wheelock, who wrote a daily column, "Thoughts on Things: Material and Immaterial," for the same paper. He certainly read the comic filler, which sometimes made up a third of the copy, aside from advertising, in F. E. Barnum's Sauk Centre *Avalanche*, a newspaper for which young Lewis worked for at least a few days. The point is not that he was specifically influ-

*From *American Dreams, American Nightmares*, ed. David Madden (Carbondale and Edwardsville: Southern Illinois University Press, 1970), 94–105. Reprinted by permission of the author and publisher.

enced by any one of these writers, but that a journalistically-minded boy could not have escaped an awareness of the humor that was a lively part of Western newspapers.

The Western humor that Lewis knew as a boy derived from the old Yankee humor. Constance Rourke, in *American Humor* (1931), clearly distinguished the two main streams of native humor. Although the comic Yankee was a close relative of his Southern counterpart with the coonskin cap, he favored certain forms, techniques, and subjects that distinguished him from the Davy Crocketts and Sut Lovingoods. In brief, the Northern humorist preferred the loosely connected anecdotal essay—often in the form of a letter to the editor. He relied on wordplay for most of his comic effects, frequently employing a highbrow style to mock highbrow pretensions. He delicately avoided sex and scatology; and violence was minimized or dehumanized. His wit generally had a satiric edge; he ridiculed, however mildly, politics and society. All these traits contrast with the boasting, boisterous, sadistic, colorful humor of the Old Southwest. And they are all represented in the opening paragraph of one of the first books of Yankee humor, Seba Smith's *The Life and Writings of Major Jack Downing* (1834):

> I now take my pen in hand to let you know that I am well, hoping these few lines will find you enjoying the same blessing. When I come down to Portland I didn't think o' staying more than three or four days, if I could sell my load of ax handles, and mother's cheese, and cousin Nabby's bundle of footings; but when I got here I found Uncle Nat was gone a freighting down to Quoddy, and Aunt Sally said as how I shouldn't stir a step home till he came back agin, which won't be this month. So here I am, loitering about this great town, as lazy as an ox. . . . I've been here now a whole fortnight, and if I could tell ye one half I've seen, I guess you'd stare worse than if you'd seen a catamount. I've been to meeting, and to the museum, and to both Legislaters, the one they call the House, and the one they call the Sinnet. I spose Uncle Joshua is in a great hurry to hear something about these Legislaters; for you know he's always reading newspapers, and talking politics, when he can get anybody to talk with him. I've seen him when he had five tons of hay in the field well made, and a heavy shower coming up, stand two hours disputing with Squire W. about Adams and Jackson—one calling Adams a tory and a fed, and the other saying Jackson was a murderer and a fool; so they kept it up, till the rain began to pour down, and about spoilt all his hay.

There is a similarity between that paragraph and the opening paragraphs of Sinclair Lewis' *The Man Who Knew Coolidge* (1928), which is the purest example of native American humor that Lewis composed:

> And I certainly do enjoy listening to you gentlemen and getting your views. That's one of the nice things about being on a Pullman

like this: you can guarantee that you'll meet a lot of regular he-Americans with sound opinions and ideas.

And now let me tell you: the way I look at these things—

I don't mean to suggest for one second that I've got any better bean than the plain ordinary average citizen, but I've given a whole lot of attention to politics and such matters and—In fact, strikes me that it's the duty of all the better-educated citizens to take an interest in the affairs of the State, for what, after all, as a fellow was saying to us at the Kiwanis Club the other day—what is the Government but the union of all of us put together for mutual advantage and protection?

And me—why say, I read the political editorials in the *Advocate*—that's the leading paper in my town—Zenith—I read 'em like most folks read the sporting page. And as a result of all this and certain personal information that I can't disclose the sources of, I've come to the firm conclusion—

Here's something maybe you gentlemen never thought of. . . .

And the monolog rambles on to Calvin Coolidge, the speaker's daughter and son, Prohibition, labor relations, and so on and on.

It is more than coincidence that both Lewis' narrator, Lowell Schmaltz, and Smith's Jack Downing are traveling peddlers with little sense of humor. Both speak in the first person and wander from subject to subject without any seeming connection. Both make the most of incongruous juxtaposition of words. Jack's reference to the meeting house, the museum, and the state legislature in one series is no accident. Nor is Schmaltz's "And me—why say, I read the political editorials in the *Advocate* . . . like most folks read the sporting page." Jack's first sentence, "I now take my pen in hand, . . ." mocks genteel epistolary style, while Schmaltz's assertion that "it's the duty of all the better-educated citizens to take an interest in the affairs of the State" mocks the pretensions of the bourgeois gentleman. As for taboos, in all their loquacity neither Jack Downing nor Lowell Schmaltz ever mentions anything more shocking than the latter's "I *have* got a lady friend in New York, simply a little darling and at least twelve years younger than Mame, too—but I don't believe in divorce, and then there's the children to think of." Finally, both Seba Smith and Sinclair Lewis satirize politics and society. While Smith leads gently into ridicule of the Maine legislature and later of the social and political implications of Andrew Jackson's administration, Lewis dryly exposes the complacency of the middle-class supporters of Calvin Coolidge.

As Yankee humor moved west with the pioneers, it did not merge with Southern humor to form a single Western humor, as has often been implied. It occasionally showed the influence of the Southern tradition, of course. Mark Twain, the greatest Southern yarn spinner, left his mark on virtually all American prose writers who succeeded him, not least of all the humorists. But just as the humor of Texas and Oklahoma is simply an extension of that of the Old Southwest, so the humor of Minnesota is basically the same as that of New England.

Still the humor of the northern West and Midwest developed a certain emphasis that gave it a new complexion. That emphasis was an ambivalence, a reaction against itself, even in the end a kind of self-torture. There was a jarring note of skepticism in some of its most cocksure assertions. There was a defensiveness in its tolerance, an uneasiness in its smugness, a neurosis in its common sense, a deviousness in its prudery, an irony in its boasting. Such contradictions can be seen in the writing of the Midwestern humorists Finley Peter Dunne and George Ade, in the witticisms of numerous Midwestern newspaper writers, in the novels of Sinclair Lewis, and in much of the comedy in the *New Yorker*, which was influenced by Midwestern humor despite its Eastern protestations. They are an essential part of the character of the Little Man, whom Norris Yates, in *The American Humorist*, has shown to be the chief character type in twentieth-century humor, and a reflection of the American self-image.

One example of the ambivalence of the Midwestern mind was in its attitude toward moral "decency." On the whole, Northern humorists retained the prudishness of their puritan and genteel forebears. Harold Ross's strict standards of morality in the *New Yorker* are well known. The outright bawdiness in the Sut Lovingood yarns of the Southern writer George Washington Harris is nowhere to be found in the work of James Thurber, for example, or of Sinclair Lewis. But Northern "morality" had its obverse side—its contradictory reaction against its puritan background—which showed itself most often in the "dirty story." It was notably furtive and puerile. Wilford H. Fawcett, a Minnesota acquaintance of Sinclair Lewis', established a fortune with his *Captain Billy's Whiz Bang*, a humor magazine catering to that taste. The following joke from the December 1920 issue (page 17) will illustrate:

LEAD ME NOT INTO DEEP WATER

The teacher had requested that each pupil bring an original short poem to school next day. After two hours of earnest effort, little Johnny produced this one:

> Poor little Mary a-fishing for bass,
> Waded in water up to her knees
> And dried herself on the cool, green grass.

"Why, Johnny," said the teacher. "That doesn't rhyme very good, does it?"

"No," replied Johnny, "the water was too shallow for bass fishing."

The "smuttiness" of the *Whiz Bang* is implied in the characters of Lowell Schmaltz, Tub Pearson, and Clif Clawson, though Lewis correctly left it to implication.

A more attractive aspect of Western humor was its tough egalitarianism, which was closely related to regional pride, though there was a negative side to this characteristic too. The following item from the Minneapolis *Journal* for December 21, 1898 (page 4, reprinted from the Omaha *Herald*), reflects the positive aspect.

> A Boston girl, who witnessed an Indian sham battle in the west, thought she would try to talk to a young Indian brave sitting next to her. "Heap much fight," she said. Lo [?] smiled a stoical smile, drew his blanket closer about his stalwart form and replied: "Yes; this is indeed a great exposition, and we flatter ourselves that our portion of the entertainment is by no means the least attractive here. May I ask who it is that I have the honor of addressing?" The dear girl from Boston was thunderstruck. She blushed a rosy red—even Boston girls can blush when they thaw out—and hastily fled. She had been addressing one of the Carlisle Indian school graduates.

Not all Western humor was so kind to the Indian, but a disdain for class distinctions and for the superior airs of Easterners was pervasive. Another item in the same paper for December 18, 1899 (page 4), reads: "After mature deliberation the editor of *L'Autorite*, a Paris daily, has come to the conclusion that America is It and the Americans They, and he gives some figures that go to show he isn't so very far off, either. This may be news to the Paris editor's subscribers, but it is a matter of common knowledge on this side of the pond."

Examples of the same kind of boosting are lavishly abundant in Lewis' novels. The following lines, spoken by Alec Kynance in *Dodsworth* (1929), are typical: "Europe? Rats! Dead's a doornail! Place for women and long-haired artists. Dead! Only American loans that keep 'em from burying the corpse! All this art! More art in a good shiny spark-plug than in all the fat Venus de Mylos they ever turned out."

Yet social and regional pride had its obverse side. The boosting spirit was common in all Western humor; more so, in fact, in the South than in the North. Pride in fertility of the soil, the abundance of game, the healthiness of the climate, the growth of towns and of business was perhaps the outstanding trait of Texas humor. Newspaper humor was especially given to boosting, for advertising the locality was considered to be the duty of the press to its subscribers and its advertisers. But even in the newspapers and probably more often in folk humor, local pride was often a mock pride. And in the North, where the geography gets more and more inhospitable the farther west one goes, the humor often turns upon itself. The South Dakota saying, "There will always be another year," is at least as much a grim recognition of crop failure as it is an expression of hope.

The following quip from Ralph Wheelock's Minneapolis *Tribune* column for January 18, 1902, is expressed in a light tone of mockery. It was written while Minneapolis was enjoying an unusually warm winter: "It is no longer proper to say from 'hades to breakfast,' in describing any great range of expression. According to the data furnished by the weather bureau in Eagle, Alaska, the mercury dropped to 68 below last winter, and in Phoenix, Arizona, it went to 119 above in June last. From Eagle to Phoenix is the proper expression. About midway you will find the delightfully temperate climate of Minnesota all year around." Or more directly satirical is the same columnist's comment on water pollution, a problem that was beginning to arise in the growing towns and cities of Minnesota. It refers to St. Cloud, the principal town in Sinclair Lewis' home county, lying some seventy-five miles up the Mississippi from Minneapolis. "St. Cloud is in the midst of a boil-the-water agitation," wrote Wheelock (January 14, 1902). "Can't be that our supply has taken to running up hill."

Other Western journalists were of a more sarcastic turn than Wheelock. A brief item in the Sauk Centre *Avalanche*, written while United States troops were putting down the Philippine attempt to achieve independence (February 23, 1899), is in direct contrast to the chauvinism expressed in "America is It and the Americans They": "In a recent speech Cashman K. Davis is reported as saying, 'the United States is the great and consecrated evangelist of humanity.' Certainly we are. Didn't we declare war with Spain in the name of humanity—to see Cuba free. Now, haven't we given Spain $20,000,000 to purchase the Philippines, and are we not pushing our 'evangelist of humanity' in the shape of rapid fire guns and 13 inch cannon promiscuously among the Filipinos so that they, too, may become humane, and bend to the iron will of the dominant party in this great and glorious land of liberty loving people."

Or, to choose an example from B. A. Botkin's *A Treasury of Western Folklore* (1944), there is deliberate mockery of the boosting spirit in the following account of a Western tornado: "On the 18th of May in 1916, a man near Scotland, South Dakota, had just put the finishing touches on a garage in preparation for a new Ford that he intended purchasing when one of the typical midwest cyclones appeared on the horizon. After the passage of the storm he emerged from his cyclone cellar and was surprised to find in his garage a brand new Buick bearing a Kansas license tag." The underlying grimness, the even masochistic enjoyment of hardship and failure, is perhaps the outstanding characteristic that distinguishes the humor of the Midwest and Northwest. It contrasts with the boasting and the sadism of Southern humor. It is an expression of disillusionment with the boosters' dreams. The land of milk and honey, the Beulah Land, turned out often to be the heartbreaking and backbreaking land of Ole Rölvaag's *Giants in the Earth* (1927) or of some of Willa Cather's novels. It is the basic ingredient of all of Sinclair Lewis' most effective satire. Humor was, perhaps, a way of making life more bearable, but it was not a happy humor.

The so-called "revolt from the village"—which was simply an extension of the revolt from the farm—was an expression of the same discontent, the same self-torture, that is expressed in Western humor. But Sinclair Lewis, Sherwood Anderson, and Edgar Lee Masters vehemently denied that they were revolting against the village. In fact, Carl Van Doren's theory of the revolt was a half-truth. Though perhaps illogical, there was a sort of love-hate syndrome in Western and Midwestern character. The evils of the village and the farm were very real, but there were also values and pleasant memories. Indeed, there was an ingrained loyalty to the region and a kind of exasperated humility in the face of its evils.

Walter Blair, in an article entitled "The Urbanization of Humor," pointed out that the "crackerbox" tradition in American humor had become citified and sophisticated in the twentieth century.[2] By way of illustration, he cited Harold Ross's often-quoted statement that the *New Yorker* was not written for the old lady in Dubuque. But Blair failed to say that it was read in Dubuque. What is more, Ross himself came from Aspen, Colorado, James Thurber from Columbus, Ohio, and Ring Lardner from Niles, Michigan. Preceding them in the urbanization of American humor were the Chicago journalists George Ade and Finley Peter Dunne.

In *The American Humorist: Conscience of the Twentieth Century* (1964) Norris W. Yates argues that the Little Man of Ade, Thurber, and other twentieth-century humorists was in part a result of the urbanization of the humor of the Midwest. The Little Man was overwhelmed by nature, women, and machines. In a sense, he was the opposite of the giants in the earth and the rip-roaring Davy Crocketts and Mike Finks. He was a glorification of the urban middle-class American with some education, yet he was an anti-hero. He was neurotic, but at bottom he was sane in the midst of an insane and at least partly malignant world. He was the comic symbol of the lost generation, and his more tragic or pathetic side was shown in the work of F. Scott Fitzgerald, another Minnesotan. He was a reaction against the noble frontiersman, the indomitable pioneer, and the mythical cowboy—dreams which still persist and which have their spiritual truth as the Little Man has his realistic truth. Dreams which Walter Mitty dreamed. Dreams which were vulgarized anud commercialized in the mind of George F. Babbitt.

As everyone knows, Babbitt was something of a self-portrait of

Sinclair Lewis. Lewis was forever torn between the dreams and the reality. His later work was often almost sentimentally nostalgic about the simplicity and morality of Midwestern small-town life. "It is twenty-nine years since I left Sauk Centre," he wrote in 1931 in "The Long Arm of the Small Town." "Yet it is as vivid to my mind as though I had left there yesterday. . . . It was a good time, a good place, and a good preparation for life" (*The Man from Main Street*, pp. 271–72). On the other hand, his exposure of the smugness, materialism, and anti-intellectualism of the small town hardly needs illustration. The irony of the opening paragraphs of *Main Street* (1920) is apparent as the book proceeds: "The days of pioneering, of lassies in sunbonnets, and bears killed with axes in piney clearings, are deader now than Camelot; and a rebellious girl is the spirit of that bewildered empire called the American Middle-west." And the prologue to the same novel is a gem of satiric exaggeration: "Main Street is the climax of civilization. That this Ford car might stand in front of the Bon Ton Store, Hannibal invaded Rome and Erasmus wrote in Oxford cloisters. What Ole Jenson the grocer says to Ezra Stowbody the banker is the law for London, Prague, and the unprofitable isles of the sea; whatsoever Ezra does not know and sanction, that thing is heresy, worthless for knowing and wicked to consider."

In ridiculing the Midwest, Lewis was ridiculing himself, and it is that masochistic twist which sometimes makes his humor painful. In his nonfiction—frequently more fictitious than his fiction—Lewis often ridiculed himself directly. In "I'm an Old Newspaperman Myself," he pictured himself in Sauk Centre as "a skinny, perpetually complaining small boy named 'Ole Doc Lewis's youngest boy, Harry,' or, more intimately, 'Claude Lewis's red-headed kid brother,'" and he deliberately exaggerated his ineptitude as a journalist (*The Man from Main Street*, p. 76). Note that even in his youth he was complaining, and his most successful work might be viewed as a long series of complaints sublimated by humor. The innocent pose had developed from the bumptious wisdom of Major Jack Downing in the 1830's to the self-torture of the Little Man in the 1920's.

Furthermore, the masochism extended to the Midwestern readers of Lewis' work, at least according to Lewis himself: "*Main Street . . .* was my first novel to rouse the embattled peasantry and, as I have already hinted, it had really a success of scandal. One of the most treasured American myths had been that all American villages were peculiarly noble and happy, and here an American had attacked that myth. Scandalous! Some hundreds of thousands read the book with the same masochistic pleasure that one has in sucking an aching tooth" ("Self-Portrait [Nobel Foundation]," *The Man from Main Street*, p. 54). And the number of readers who identified themselves with Carol Kennicott was surprising.

Lewis' early novels may be seen as an experimentation with his native humoristic elements before reaching his stride as an American humorist in *Main Street*. *Our Mr. Wrenn* (1914), for example, was a sentimental picture of what Lewis himself called "a very little Little Man" ("Breaking into Print," *The Man from Main Street*, p. 73). *Free Air* (1919), on the other hand, reverted to the Western hero type, in the person of the mechanic Milt Daggett, who melodramatically rescues and marries the sophisticated Eastern belle Claire Boltwood. Meanwhile, the author was polishing his already natural "journalistic manner," to quote Alexander Cowie in *The Rise of the American Novel* (1948), a manner that "relied in part on vivacity of tone and on the apt use of the vernacular." His unflattering depiction of Western geography is also evident in *Free Air*, where he described Minnesota mud, or gumbo, as "mud mixed with tar, flypaper, fish glue, and well-chewed, chocolate covered caramels"; and in the same novel he described sardonically the towns of "Gopher Prairie" and "Schoenstrom."

The continuing debate over Lewis' ambivalence—his savage ridicule as against his "happy endings," his deadly effects as against his protestations of sympathy—is perhaps due to the fact that Lewis was a humorist first and a satirist only secondarily. Furthermore, he was attempting to transform the brief hit-and-run method of newspaper humor into the sustained form of the novel—a feat at which no one but Mark Twain had really succeeded before him. Critics have pointed out that the latter part of *Main Street* is no longer social satire, but restricts itself to the personal relationship between Will and Carol Kennicott, and concludes with their reconciliation. The same criticism can be leveled at most of the novels that followed *Main Street*. The apparently happy ending is, of course, a convention in the comic novel. Whether this is an aesthetic flaw, a slavish bowing to tradition, is largely a matter of individual taste. The farcical ending of *Huckleberry Finn* has likewise been debated. Twain too was a humorist—though he became a straight satirist in his old age, with "The Man That Corrupted Hadleyburg" and *The Mysterious Stranger*. Actually, the endings of *Main Street* and *Huckleberry Finn* are only partly happy. Carol Kennicott achieves submission, not victory: "She looked across the silent fields to the west. She was conscious of an unbroken sweep of land to the Rockies, to Alaska; a dominion which will rise to unexampled greatness when other empires have grown senile. Before that time, she knew, a hundred generations of Carols will aspire and go down in tragedy devoid of palls and solemn chanting, the humdrum inevitable tragedy of struggle against inertia." And Huck concludes: "But I reckon I got to light out for the territory ahead of the rest, because Aunt Sally she's going to adopt me and sivilize me, and I can't stand it. I been there before."

It is not necessary to exclude other views in order to view Sinclair Lewis as a humorist. But it helps to clarify our conception of his total achievement to see him as a novelist working with the journalistic and folk materials of native American humor to arrive at a culminating expression of that humor as it had developed in the upper West. Like much of the humor of that region, Lewis' humor reflects the contradictory pulls of regional loyalty and realistic clear-sightedness, of pride and complaint, of a dream and a disillusionment with that dream.

Notes

1. Lewis acknowledged his early reading of Dunne and Ade in "My First Day in New York," *The Man from Main Street* (New York, 1953), p. 58. My use of Minnesota newspapers in this essay was made possible through the assistance of the Minnesota Historical Society and especially of Mr. Edward Swanson, Head, Newspaper Division, and through the support of the Research and Projects Committee of Southern Illinois University, Edwardsville.

2. In *A Time of Harvest: American Literature, 1910–1960*, ed. Robert E. Spiller (New York, 1962), pp. 54–64.

Dodsworth and the Question of Art   Robert L. Coard*

"That poor, driven, drunken, greedy Sinclair Lewis had an art is certain. We understand this much, but not a great deal more." In these words Sheldon Grebstein in a review of D. J. Dooley's *The Art of Sinclair Lewis* (*American Literature*, March, 1968) phrases the question largely evaded by Dooley: How have Sinclair Lewis's novels acquired millions of readers though they are, critics tell us, shallow in thought, careless in diction, shaky in plot, and superficial in characterization? In brief, how can a writer who can't write attract and hold millions of readers, win both the Pulitzer and Nobel prizes, and, today, two decades after his death, have ten titles in paperback?

By analyzing *Dodsworth* (1929), composed at the height of Lewis's power and coming close after such successes as *Main Street, Babbitt, Arrowsmith,* and *Elmer Gantry,* I hope to suggest an answer to this mystery. *Dodsworth,* a best seller at the time of publication and still in print, is the story of Sam Dodsworth, a Midwestern automobile manufacturer, who after his retirement at age fifty, travels in Europe with his wife Fran, who is nine years younger. There he gets to know himself and his snobbish and flirtatious wife better, so much better in fact, that

*Reprinted, with permission, from *Sinclair Lewis Newsletter* 3 (1971):16–18.

at the novel's end he will divorce his unfaithful wife and marry a woman who encourages, rather than stifles, his creative business projects.

CONTROVERSY

One reason for choosing *Dodsworth* for analysis is its comparative absence of controversy, a familiar Lewis ingredient for attracting readers. In *Arrowsmith* Lewis was already showing signs of putting down the prod of controversy and the whip of satire, but in *Dodsworth* the break is sharper. Since Lewis is forced to draw on his full artistic resources to sustain his story, the analyst of Lewis's art is given a neat focus for study. The formula of gaining an audience by being contemporary and controversial is so widely employed today in books, magazines, movies, TV talk shows, and college classes, that we can now better understand how Lewis acquired many of the readers for his preceding novels by a timely lambasting of villagers, businessmen, and clergy.

Though relying less on controversy and satire, Lewis remains contemporary in *Dodsworth* as he does in all his novels except the inconsequential *The Godseeker*. The action proper of *Dodsworth* begins in 1925 (15) and continues through 1927. [All page references to *Dodsworth* are to the Signet paperback edition.] In *The Cavalcade of the American Novel* Edward Wagenknecht remarks on the extent of contemporary references in Lewis's fiction, but I am still startled by their easy availability in *Dodsworth*: to golfer Bobby Jones (43); to prizefighter Jack Dempsey (132); to authors Hugh Walpole (16) and Mrs. Edith Wharton (233); to author Sinclair Lewis's character Babbitt (18, 276); to Sinclair Lewis's Main Streeters and H. L. Mencken's Booboisie (83); to "President Coolidge and Secretary Hoover and Governor Smith" (232). The 1929 reader caught the same leap of life he got from his movie newsreel or the latest *Literary Digest*. In a period too when the average reader of *Dodsworth* had no experience of foreign travel (except for the doughboys and they didn't see any of Dodsworth's Europe), there was fascination in vicariously getting a glimpse of life aboard a luxury liner (Chapters 5 and 6); in experiencing the first landfall; in seeing something of London, Paris, and Berlin; in collecting the names of foreign foods; in riding a new-fangled passenger plane (Chapter 28); and in residing in a villa on the Bay of Naples.

CLEAR PLOT

Besides the many contemporary references and numerous bits of travelog, Sinclair Lewis also presents his reader with a clearly definable main plot centering on the common and perennially interesting topic of

marital discord. The selfishness and snobbery of the attractive Fran
Dodsworth comes out in her flirtations and affairs with a series of men
ending with the best of the lot, the poor young Austrian count Kurt von
Obersdorf who actually wants to marry her until his mother disapproves
of the match. In a litany of damns Dodsworth calls the roll of Fran's
men, beginning with a "Damn Lockert!" and ending with "Oh, damn
Kurt!" (213). Fran's affairs had been foreshadowed in "the complimentary teasing of half a dozen admirers" (10) in the opening chapter and
echoed in "Fran made much of tea with half a dozen men" (349) in the
concluding chapter.

That Lewis underplayed the full conflict inherent in these affairs is
evident when one compares the novel with its successful 1934 dramatization by Sidney Howard with some assistance from Lewis. Howard's
play not only brings Sam and Fran together for a climactic showdown
over Kurt as the novel had done but also precedes it with a big triangular
scene with the lover Arnold Israel actually participating. In the novel
the Israel affair is reported in Fran's letters to Sam. He reads between
the lines and then confronts only her. For good measure, Howard even
dramatizes another reported scene in which the old Austrian countess
forbids the marriage of Kurt and Fran.

FLAWED PLOT

That Lewis intentionally weakened the conflict in the novel is apparent enough. Rather than violent action, he wanted to emphasize the
brooding changes in Dodsworth as he comes to realize he must seek a
meaning to life without the supports of a fixed occupation or true marriage. A real flaw in the plot though comes in the casual introduction
and hurried development of Mrs. Edith Cortright, the amazingly sym
pathetic lady who befriends Dodsworth and acts as such an obvious foil
to the poisonous Fran. In the interests of verisimilitude, Howard forces
Mrs. Cortright onto the stage at an earlier point in the plot. Among other
changes Howard excises many of the long speeches of the novel: the
remarks of the salesmen on British-American differences at the Hurd
stag dinner; the lecturing of Herr Braut on American-European differences at the Berlin party; the outpourings of the journalist Ross Ireland
on similar subjects. Although difference between genres explain some
of the changes, many of the dramatic alterations point to Lewis's occasional rambling from the plot of the novel in pursuit of congenial topics.
The talk about comparative cultures in the novel in itself, however, is
not a digression, for the basic plot and theme of the novel center on a
distinction between true culture and false by Dodsworth. Laboriously
he distinguishes between the sterile, acquisitive, pretentious way of life

of his wife Fran and his own groping, responsible, creative outlook. Foreign travel with its cultural contrasts affords a good background for Sam's seeking, but Lewis can't always subordinate the facts gathered from his own travels to the requirements of plot and character.

COMPARISON AND CONTRAST

Like the plotting, the characterization of *Dodsworth* has a certain schematic quality about it, with one character often set against another to form a checkerboard pattern of comparison and contrast. First come the central figures: Sam and Fran, husband and wife, altruist and egotist, mature person and child. Perhaps it's no accident that they have names that seem to rhyme but actually don't. Contrast as well seems to split Dodsworth himself into two not entirely reconcilable personalities, a split that may represent a flaw in conception rather than meaningful ambiguity. There is the commanding Dodsworth, doer and corporation executive; and, much different, the timid Dodsworth in whom his wife plants an inferiority complex. Logical or not, the depiction of the timid Dodsworth's aimless drifting in a world of hotel lobbies, bars, and trains after "the incredible jar of being dismissed by Fran" (303) is the most moving part of the novel.

At least three of the other women in the novel serve as foils to Fran Dodsworth: Mrs. Cortright, the quiet healer undoes the work of Fran, the nagging irritant; Matey Pearson, the overweight wife with the big heart, advises Dodsworth to abandon Fran, the slender wife with the sliver of a heart; coarse and vital alley cat Nande Azeredo contrasts with the cold and elegant Fran. Other female contrasts exist. Though not placed in immediate juxtaposition, Madame de Pénable represents the slick but corrupt Europe; Princess Drachenthal and Baroness Ercole, the unpretentious but sound Europe.

Male characters are also set against each other: the uneasy restlessness of Sam against the fat complacency of his friend Tub; the honest creativity of Sam, the auto magnate, against the ruthless materialism of Alec Kynance, the auto magnate; the sincere American abroad like Ross Ireland the journalist against pretentious Americans abroad like Lycurgus "Jerry" Watts, the art dabbler, and Endicott Everett Atkins, the ponderous critic. Even Kurt, the worthiest of Fran's lovers, contrasts with his lightweight predecessors. Less mechanical than it sounds, this checkerboard pattern of characterization is relieved by some variation and qualification. For example, Fran Dodsworth at the beginning of Chapter 11 springs to Sam Dodsworth's defense in an acrimonious discussion.

AMERICA AND EUROPE

If more qualification gets into *Dodsworth* than into its predecessors, Lewis still works up a pattern of sharp contrast in large matters and small. Bringing Sam Dodsworth back to America in the middle of the book sets off a whole series of American-European comparisons beginning at dockside with a comparison of New York and Parisian taxi-drivers. Walter Fuller Taylor in *The Story of American Letters* makes this point: "The foreignness of Paris is portrayed through the eyes of the newly arrived Dodsworth; the chaotic uproar of New York, through the eyes of the same Dodsworth, after he has gained a cosmopolitan viewpoint." And there are other contrasts in this middle section of the book. An effective passage describes Dodsworth's visit to his closed Zenith home with its rolled-up rugs and drawn blinds (173–174), a passage prepared for by Dodsworth's earlier horror at Fran's remark about selling the house (34). With its detail about the dismantled bedroom the scene clearly points ahead to the dissolution of their marriage.

Contrast is employed less successfully in those passages of "instant irony" in which Lewis overindulged himself even in *Dodsworth*, the most sophisticated of his novels. One example will suffice. Lady Ouston, wife of Sir Francis Ouston, "had been born—and her father and mother before her—in Nashville, Tennessee" (81). With this information plainly commented on, the reader is not surprised to find her delivering an anti-American diatribe on the next page.

DOG AND CAT

Sharp contrast gets into the smallest units. Several images, for example, present Sam as a dog and Fran as a kitten or cat: "The sight of her made Sam Dodsworth feel clumsy as a St. Bernard looking at a white kitten" (10), and Sam again is "apparently as dependable as an old Newfoundland" (19), but "He soon felt like a lost dog" (58). Fran after being an aesthetic object in her sleek coat "like a snow-sprinkled cat pouncing on flying leaves" (28) gets nastier "and faced him, like a snarling white cat" (138). Paradox and oxymoron with their sharp contrast and contradiction are employed freely. One illustration will have to suffice for the many paradoxes: "Thomas J. Pearson and Samuel Dodsworth had always been too well acquainted to know each other" (178). Because of their brevity more oxymorons can be cited: "the steamer's scanty seven meals a day" (39), "unhappy young-old women" (40), "the professional amateur of Zenith" (123), and "this saint of unmorality" (273).

ILLUSION OF REALITY

Such sharp contrasts of ideas and character with plenty of paradox and oxymoron are needed to organize and enliven the mass of details that Lewis depends on to convey the illusion of reality. The flippant reference to "the steamer's scanty seven meals a day" comes in the middle of a litter catalog, commencing "a litter of shaken-out frocks, heaps of shoes, dressing gowns, Coty powder, three gift copies of 'The Perennial Bachelor,' binoculars, steamer letters, steamer telegrams, the candy and the Charles & Company baskets of overgrown fruit and tiny conserves. . . ." To keep the reader from nodding, Lewis also snaps him to attention with numerous eye-breaks or white spaces between paragraph blocks. Though he no longer numbers them as in previous best sellers, Lewis freely uses these sub-chapters or reading blocks in Dodsworth. These sub-chapters may run from a few of six pages in my paperback edition to a good many of less than a page, with an average, I'd guess, of under two pages. The jerky movement they give the prose may be partly responsible for the frequent contemporary comparison of Lewis's fiction to the movies. Perhaps a better analogy might be furnished by the telegram or the night letter: for, after all, their substance is words and sometimes they aren't much longer than a telegram. Reproducing one of the shortest reading blocks may be instructive. Dodsworth is visiting his son:

> Brent was bright with compliments about Sam's knowledge of Europe; he remarked that Sam's football glories were still remembered at Yale. And Sam sighed to himself that he had lost the boy forever. (166)

Besides the general brevity, one also notices the brevity of the two paragraphs, the shortness of the last sentence, and its strong sense of climax, all recurring devices in Lewis's fiction.

The telegram analogy likewise has some validity because of the many sentence fragments in Lewis's fiction. An extreme example of fragments more broken than a telegram occurs in a description of Paris: "Fish. Breads. Beards. Brandy. Artichokes. Apples. Etchings. Fish. A stinking-looking alley. A splendid sweeping boulevard" (110). In addition to these strategies, Lewis relieves his details with dashes of talk, brisk bits of conversation usually on contemporary topics and phrased in current slang and colloquialisms like "pos-o-lutely" (26), "icky" (32), "comfy" (63), "fat head" (65), "hang-outs" (168), "highty-tighty" (271), and "hell's big bells on a mountain" (292). But the number of foreign speakers in Dodsworth reduced Lewis's opportunities for displaying his knowledge of American speech.

Lewis's ear for slang and colloquialisms did not extend to the wider vocabulary of English prose. To impart a sense of speed, vividness, and novelty, he consistently overwrote, a result perhaps of his long fictional apprenticeship in popular magazines. In a single paragraph (21) I notice six elegant variations for "said": "rumbled," "chirped," "indicated," "caroled," "shouted," and "condescended." When Lewis's characters move, they don't go quietly: "Sam clumped up-stairs" (18), "he clumped up to join Fran" (104), "he clumped after the porter" (193), "he clumped toward the Bauer-Grünwald" (319). Also overwrought is the vomit-metaphor, "Now a tourist steamer vomited a rush of excited novices. . ." (307).

THE POPULAR NOVELIST

By now it is probably apparent that the Lewis art Sheldon Grebstein speaks of in the book review of Dooley's *The Art of Sinclair Lewis* is nothing more mysterious than the art of the popular novelist of the early twentieth century, a period in which the Average American reader, lacking omnipresent television, wanted its entertainment equivalent in fiction in magazines and even newspapers. Having served a long apprenticeship in this field, Lewis, always a painstaking worker, had mastered his craft. With uncanny shrewdness, he had guessed that this mass audience, increasingly educated to high school and even college level, was ready for the stronger meat of controversy if enlivened with satire and presented through brisk fictional techniques. Lewis knew the ingredients for writing for this new popular audience of the 1920's: a controversial topic; a contemporary setting; lots of accurately observed details; a clear plot; broad contrasts of characters, ideas, and language; plenty of eye breaks in chapters and paragraphs and sentences; plenty of sentences strongly phrased and climactically located. When this popular art met a popular topic and found a popular character type to embody it, Lewis could set down the results with blunt vigor. He had a real talent for lovingly recording the nasty fact. These gifts still attract their share of readers today when the fleeting relevance that appealed to the Now Generation of the 1920's (and the Nobel Prize Committee) have faded. As long as the American heritage lasts, the dust will blow on Main Street; the businessman Babbitt will babble of service; and the preacher Elmer Gantry will commit adultery and grow rich.

But when Lewis takes up more complex subjects, he has only the fictional techniques of the popular novelist to sustain him and though he tries manfully to qualify and refine them, they aren't enough. He can give his hero Arrowsmith a great thirst for the bottle, but he can't make that fault conceal the fact that Arrowsmith is a glamorous knight of scientific research rather than a human being. He can attempt a realistic story of the dissolution of a marriage; but Sam Dodsworth emerges as a split between a masterful executive and a hurt adolescent, and Fran Dodsworth emerges as an uncomplicated bitch. Strain as Lewis might, and he must be credited with a prodigious striving, the popular art he had mastered was not capable in *Dodsworth* or elsewhere of recording niceties of characterization or nuances of thought and feeling.

The Quixotic Motifs of *Main Street*   Martin Light*

In his studies of the influence of Cervantes on European and American literature, Professor Harry Levin mentions the resemblance Carol Kennicott bears to Emma Bovary, who is the archetype of the "female quixote."[1] But neither Carol nor *Main Street* has been analyzed thoroughly as an expression of quixotism, though such an analysis can uncover sources of the novel's vitality and appeal by placing the book in a significant literary context.[2] Approaching *Main Street* from the perspective of its quixotic elements aids our understanding of Carol's ambitions, illusions, doubts, and persistence. Furthermore, such an approach allows us to account for the book's episodic movement, in which Carol's impractical idealism challenges the complacency of small town America and is in turn rejected time and again.

Looking at Sinclair Lewis's work through the perspective of quixotism is entirely consistent both with his analysis of himself and with the events of his life. Though a self-publicist and gamesman who baited those critics who harrassed him, Lewis was not merely being perverse in announcing that he was neither a satirist nor a realist but a "romantic medievalist of the most incurable sort."[3] In fact, the backward pull of romance was strong in him and fought against the new imperatives of realism, as it did in society and literature as a whole during the transition years from 1880 to 1920. The romantic bent of Lewis's mind developed early. As a youth he was an avid reader of Scott, Kipling, and tales of King Arthur. Though we must not forget the pleasure he took in Balzac, Dickens, and Wells, whose work he considered models of the realistic method, we hear him praise, even well into his twenties, not only poetry by Tennyson and Swinburne, but Stedman's "Aucassin and Nicolette" ("as fine a lyric as we Americans have had"[4]), Major's *When Knighthood Was in Flower*, and LeGallienne's *The Quest of the Golden Girl*. Indeed, Lewis's career began with the writing of pastel poems of knights and ladies. The protagonists of the novels of his apprentice years are

*From *Arizona Quarterly* 29 (Autumn 1973):[221]–34. Reprinted by permission of the publisher and author.

whimsical and playful, while those of his maturity are, usually, fantasists and idealists, throwing themselves against a disillusioning society.

The first image Lewis projected of himself was of a young knight setting out from Minnesota to conquer the East ("conquer" is the word he used in his reminiscences[5]). Later he saw himself as a troubadour or jester, adventuring with or serving his lady. It was with the vocabulary of medieval romance that he courted his first wife, the "Lady Grace."[6] At the same time, Lewis's work in publishing houses in New York brought the realities of the city before him. Soon he would face the realities of marriage as well, and later those of fame. The tensions between romance and reality embodied in *Don Quixote* lived within Lewis himself throughout his life, becoming the subject of his fiction and the source of his misery.

Imagination helps all of us to move into the future. At our most sane, we prepare for the future with the help of a model of the life we would lead, and, if necessary, we adjust our imagined model as our confrontation with reality requires. The quixote imagines a model also, but draws the pattern from romances and is seduced so completely by them that he cannot adjust to reality, but instead re-creates reality to suit his fancy. In the Cervantine formulation, the quixotic hero has been maddened by books. With his head full of illusions and idealism, he goes forth to try to set injustices aright, to honor his beloved lady, and to cultivate fame. Impelled by idealism to aid the weak and to combat injustice, the quixotic hero becomes a challenge to the conventional community. The peculiarity of his challenge disconcerts the community and can cause it to expose its own folly and corruption. The quixote's madness can induce a kind of maddened response in others, or at least unsettle them enough to reveal their hypocrisies. Thus the targets of the quixotic novel can become both the hero and society; satiric and ironic tension may arise from this conflict between the quixote and his community.

The quixote's problem is one of vision; his reading and his will to believe what he reads have left his vision fogged. He transforms what he sees into what his reading has led him to see, and indeed into what he now wishes to see. Windmills are perceived as giants. If he is told that the windmills are but windmills and nothing more (and if for a passing second he recognizes them to be so) he quickly declares that they appear to be windmills only because they are enchanted, but that they are giants nonetheless.

Professor Richard Predmore lists three elements of the quixotic world: "literature, which is an all-pervasive presence and source of illusions; adventures, which arise from the clash between illusions and reality; and enchantment, which serves to defend illusions against inhospitable reality."[7] Applying a modification of this formula to Carol

Kennicott, we will study her in terms of her "literary" imagination, her missionary venture to redress wrongs in her community, and her need to romanticize reality. We will also consider the conflict between the quixote and society—the conflict that occasions both psychological insight and satire.

The quixote's career begins in the library. Of Emma, Professor Levin writes: "From the drab milieu she has known as a farmer's daughter, her extracurricular reading conjures up the allurements of escape: steeds and guitars, balconies and fountains, medieval and Oriental vistas."[8] We may say much the same thing about Carol, for she can conjure up a bower of roses, a château, a Chinese entertainment, an exotic Frenchman, a poet-lover. She brings to Gopher Prairie a romantic model of what a village should be and a fantasy of her role in life. However, as she settles into her plain and frigid Gopher Prairie home, so different from the one she has imagined, she cries, "Why do these stories lie so?"[9]

The opening chapters of *Main Street* give only fragmentary information about Carol's childhood, but they suggest an environment that encouraged romanticizing. She recalls that her father was "the tenderest man in the world" (p. 173). He created "Christmas fantasies" from "the sacred old rag doll at the top of the tree" (p. 195), and he would transform the terrors of the night into a "hearth-mythology" of "beneficent and bright-eyed creatures." There were the "tam htab, who is woolly and blue and lives in the bathroom" and "the ferruginous oil stove, who purrs and knows stories" (pp. 6–7). Her father let her read anything she wished, and she is said to have "absorbed" Balzac, Rabelais, Thoreau, and Max Müller at an early age. But what Carol saw in Thoreau, one suspects, was woodsy escapism and inaction, for at one point she recalls, "I used to sit there on the cliffs above Mankato for hours at a time, my chin in my hand, looking way down the valley, wanting to write poems" (pp. 173–74).

At college she announces that she hopes to "conquer the world" (p. 3). Vaporous images from her further reading point to the reformist mission that she must undertake. "She wanted, just now, to have a cell in a settlement-house, like a nun without the bother of a black robe"; from the cell she will "improve a horde of grateful poor." The icon of her dormitory room is "a miniature of the Dancing Bacchante" (p. 5). Having glanced at a book on village-improvement, she plans to convert a village to the greens and garden-walls of France. Or she wishes to "turn a prairie town into Georgian houses and Japanese bungalows" (p. 10). She declares, "I don't understand myself but I want—everything in the world! Maybe I can't sing or write, but I know I can be an influence in library work. Just suppose I encouraged some boy and he became a great artist!" (p. 9).

Meanwhile she is learning to transmute reality. For instance, as she climbs along the banks of the Mississippi, she sees the river as her fanciful mind dictates. She listens to the fables of the river

> about the wide land of yellow waters and bleached buffalo bones to the West; the Southern levees and singing darkies and palm trees toward which it was forever mysteriously gliding; and she heard again the startled bells and thick puffing of high-stacked river steamers wrecked on sand-reefs sixty years ago. Along the decks she saw missionaries, gamblers in tall pot hats, and Dakota chiefs with scarlet blankets. . . . (p. 6)

She has created a tableau and placed within it the figures of her own imagining—dreams, Lewis says later, "governed by the fiction she had read, drawn from the pictures she had envied" (p. 234). To give another illustration of her fancy, at the commencement exercises at Blodgett College "she saw the palms as a jungle, the pink-shaded electric globes as an opaline haze, and the eye-glassed faculty as Olympians" (p. 8).

During a year in Chicago after graduation, these impulses are strengthened. Carol spends an evening at a bohemian Studio Party, where she hears talk of "Freud, Romain Rolland, syndicalism, the Confédération Générale du Travail, feminism vs. haremism, Chinese lyrics, nationalization of mines, Christian Science, and fishing in Ontario" (p. 10). Significantly, her first job is at the library in St. Paul, where, while she works, she reads "scores of books." The subject list is especially suited for the development of her fancy: "volumes of anthropology . . . Parisian imagistes, Hindu recipes for curry, voyages to the Solomon Isles, theosophy with modern American improvements" (p. 10). At dances, "in dread of life's slipping past, she turned into a bacchanal" (p. 11). Her sense of mission returns; she will transform and redesign a prairie town.

At this point, Dr. Will Kennicott enters her life. He woos her by exploiting her desire to find a purpose for herself, declaring that his village needs her. Dr. Kennicott provides a notable occasion for us to apprehend the way in which the vision of the quixote converts reality to illusion. He shows Carol some photographs, and, though they are streaked and vague, she perceives them as (in her need for adventure) she must. She sees his amateurish snapshots of lakes as "etchings" that delineate "snow in crevices of a boggy bank, the mound of a muskrat house, reeds in thin black lines." Intuiting Carol's nature, Kennicott uses one picture especially well. It shows a forest clearing and a log cabin. In front of the cabin is "a sagging woman with tight-drawn hair, and a baby bedraggled, smeary, glorious-eyed." Kennicott tempts Carol by saying, "Look at that scared baby! Needs some woman with hands like yours. Waiting for you! Just look at that baby's eyes, look how he's begging—" Carol succumbs (pp. 18–19). Such photographs will return later, once at the end of the book when Kennicott is courting Carol again after her flight from Gopher Prairie, and once at the middle of the book when she visits the home of this baby in the snapshot and, perceiving that he is an idiot, turns away.

After Carol and the doctor marry, they ride the train into Gopher Prairie, the town she will "conquer" and reform. She has her first view of the reality she must work with. When she sees their house and her room, the shock is great. She blames her reading. "She glanced at the houses; tried not to see what she saw; gave way in: 'Why do these stories lie so? They always make the bride's home-coming a bower of roses. Complete trust in the noble spouse. Lies about marriage.... And this town—O my God! I can't go through with it. This junk-heap!' " (p. 29). She has read "too many books." She goes to the bedroom window "with a purely literary thought of village charm—hollyhocks and lanes and apple-cheeked cottagers." What she sees is "the side of the Seventh-Day Adventist Church—a plain clapboard wall of a sour liver color." This was "the terraced garden below her boudoir"—"How these stories lie!" Muttering, "I'm mildly insane" (p. 32), she goes out to see the village, the "empire" she is going to "conquer." She takes one of the most memorable promenades in our literature. She finds a Main Street characterized by the reek of blood from the meat market, by yellow buildings, by a cat sleeping on the lettuce in the grocery window. But Carol is not broken by that view of Main Street. For a long time she survives and returns to the fray. Her resiliency originates in her transmuting imagination; she is like Don Quixote with bandaged head taking to the road once more. Her enthusiasm, at least at first and in one so young ("plastic" and "innocent," as Lewis says), is even engaging.

Her adventures test not only Carol's notions but also the beliefs and actions of society. In the face of the challenge that she brings, members of the community reveal themselves as corrupt and hypocritical—or at least foolish in their own way. For instance, when Carol attends her first party in Gopher Prairie, she carries to it the image of herself as "a smart young married woman in a drawing room, fencing with clever men" (p. 48). She expects good talk, and she believes that she can enter into conversation as an equal to the men. But they have been arguing all evening about the kind of dog an old-timer had owned years ago. When Carol confronts them with a question about labor relations, she draws from them comments that are the hallmark of Lewis's satire. Jackson Elder asserts that he is for freedom and constitutional rights: "If any man don't like my shop, he can get up and git. Same way, if I don't like him, he gits. And that's all there is to it." He mumbles on about such "poppycock" as profit-sharing, welfare work, insurance, old-age pensions. It "enfeebles a workman's independence—and wastes a lot of honest profit" (pp. 49–50).

By such a pattern of challenge and reaction throughout the novel, each satiric monologue achieves its organic place. At every thrust from Carol, a villager exposes his own foolishness or hypocrisy about education, economics, politics, religion. Each encounter provides Lewis with the opportunity to exhibit his virtuosity in creating the grotesque rantings of gossips, churchwomen, preachers, journalists, boosters. Carol induces the community mind to expose itself. Her own response to these encounters remains unchanging, nonetheless. Even as she drags herself homeward from them, past a "hulking house," "a streaky yellow pool," or "a morass," she tells herself that "her beautiful town" still exists—in her mind (p. 139). She believes in the village she has imagined. What she is now seeking is a person to share it with.

Several secondary figures in *Main Street* reinforce Carol's quixotism. Guy Pollock, whom Lewis declared to have been the protagonist of the book in its earliest conception (though no draft of that version exists and Lewis's biographer doubts whether such a version ever got on paper[10]) —Pollock too is maddened by reading. He "hints his love" for Sir Thomas Browne, Thoreau, Agnes Reppelier, Arthur Symons, Claude Washburne, and Charles Flandrau, authors who can nourish the fancy (p. 67). Carol visits Pollock at his rooms, where he reveals the content of his imagination. Here, he says, are his "office, town-house, and château in Picardy, . . . but you can't see the château and town-house (next to the Duke of Sutherland's)" (p. 154). Of course Carol *can* see them, quite as well as he can. Carol and Pollock discuss the possibility of reforming the town, but Pollock is by now incapable of rebellion. Like Prufrock, he wishes only to be an attendant, "the confidant of the old French plays, the tiring-maid with the mirror and the loyal ears" (p. 159). Carol wonders whether Pollock might be her Prince Charming, but she later realizes that he was only a frame on which she hung "shining garments" (p. 203).

Toward her husband, Carol feels a genuinely painful conflict. Kennicott is a capable doctor, but his very competence is paradoxically a problem for Carol, who finds that capable people are often shallow and bigoted. At their best, without what Lewis would two years later call "babbittry," these figures are heroes, "doers." Kennicott shows admirable courage and ability as a physician and surgeon in several crises. But even at such moments Carol must re-create him in romanticized and literary terms: "She . . . saw the drama of his riding by night to the frightened household on the distant farm; pictured children standing at a window, waiting for him. He suddenly had in her eyes the heroism of a wireless operator on a ship in a collision; of an explorer, fever-clawed, deserted by his bearers, but going on" (p. 177). She tells Pollock that he and she are "a pair of hyper-critical loafers,... while [Will] quietly goes on and does things" (p. 180). She restates the dichotomy: Kennicott "speaks a vulgar, common, incorrect German of life and death and birth and the soil," while she reads "the French and German of sentimental lovers and Christmas garlands" (p. 192). Such a division lies at the heart of the book, as when Will calls Carol neurotic, and she labels him stupid. But Carol, the doctor, and the novel itself are considerably more complex than this formulation suggests, and Carol knows it upon reflection. This complexity is creditable in ways that have been forgotten by Lewis's detractors. Carol knows that Kennicott is not simply a quiet doer. He is noisy, opinionated, narrow, prejudiced, quarrelsome, and wanton, and the novel takes pains to display him as such. Carol's neurosis, meanwhile, is compounded of idealism, enthusiasm, doubt, disillusionment, and alienation.

In the midst of her despair, Carol inquires into books once more in an effort to understand herself and her village. Formerly, in reading popular stories and plays, Carol had found only two traditions about the American town. The first tradition, she reports, is that the American village remains the one sure abode of friendship, honesty, and clean sweet marriageable girls.... The other tradition is that the significant features of all villages are whiskers, iron dogs upon lawns, gold bricks, checkers, jars of gilded cat-tails, and shrewd comic old men who are known as 'hicks' and who ejaculate 'Waal I swan' " (p. 264). Her experience of Gopher Prairie, however, tells her that the town thinks "in cheap motor cars, telephones, ready-made clothes, silos, alfalfa, kodaks, phonographs, leather-upholstered Morris chairs, bridge-prizes, oil-stocks, motion-pictures, land-deals, unread sets of Mark Twain, and a chaste version of national politics" (p. 264). With this small town, Carol—along with hundreds of thousands of young people like her—is not content. She believes that she has derived insight and other "convictions" from her recent reading. She has "driven" her way through books of a somewhat different kind from those she read as a girl. These books were written by the "young American sociologists, young English realists, Russian horrorists; Anatole France, Rolland, Nexo, Wells, Shaw, Key, Edgar Lee Masters, Theodore Dreiser, Sherwood Anderson, Henry Mencken, and all the other subversive philosophers and artists whom women were consulting everywhere..." (p. 263).

One night she talks to her friend Vida Sherwin about the dullness, the rigidity, and the sterility of the village. Vida, a "realist," suggests measured steps toward reform. But Carol, for all her new reading and thought, replies that she wants "startling, exotic things": "Strindberg plays, and classic dancers—exquisite legs beneath tulle—and (I can see him so clearly!) a thick, black-bearded cynical Frenchman who would sit about and drink and sing opera and tell bawdy stories and laugh at our properties and quote Rabelais and not be ashamed to kiss my hand!" (p. 270). This is a moment of considerable psychological importance. Whatever the booklist of "American sociologists, French realists, Russian horrorists" may have brought her, Carol's quixotic nature defeats her efforts at new understanding. Her transforming imagination turns Gopher Prairie back into fantasy land.

Romantic love, the motif that particularly directs the yearnings of the female quixote, enters *Main Street* about three-fourths of the way towards its end. When Erik Valborg appears in Gopher Prairie, he is less a substantial character than a projection of what Carol fancies him to be. Much of the confusion surrounding her platonic escapade with Erik occurs because she wavers between at least two images of him. At times she recognizes that he is a commonplace, uneducated, shallow young man; at other times she believes him to be a poet—a Keats or Shelley or (as Lewis plays with Carol's values) an Arthur Upson. Carol is insistent: "He's Keats—sensitive to silken things. . . . Keats, here! A bewildered spirit fallen on Main Street. And Main Street laughs. . ." (p. 339). Thinking of him later, however, she asks herself, "Was he anything but a small-town youth bred on an illiberal farm and in cheap tailor shops?" (p. 345). Valborg himself, like Pollock, brings to his relationship with Carol his own quixotism. It is reported that he reads a great deal, but his taste tends toward "Suppressed Desire" and "The Black Mask." He recalls that, when he lived in Minneapolis, he used to "tramp clear around Lake Harriet, or hike out to the Gates house and imagine it was a château in Italy and I lived in it. I was a marquis and collected tapestries—that was after I was wounded in Padua" (p. 391).

Valborg continues to stimulate and confuse Carol's romantic imagination. While she is doing household tasks, she pictures "herself and a young artist—an Apollo nameless and evasive—building a house in the Berkshires or in Virginia; exuberantly buying a chair with his first check; reading poetry together. . ." (p. 352). She wishes him to be a "playmate," not a lover. She is always dissatisfied, however. In moments of self-awareness, she calls her love affair "pitiful and tawdry. . . . A self-deceived little woman whispering in corners with a pretentious little man" (p. 363). Then she makes a sudden quixotic shift: "No, he is not. He is fine. Aspiring." She is in a turmoil of distraction. She wishes Erik were "a fighter, an artist with bearded surly lips." But "they're only in books." Her mind is spinning, but not toward suicide, like Emma's; Carol knows all too well that the tragedy of her life is "that I never shall know tragedy; never find anything but blustery complications that turn out to be a farce" (p. 374). One moment she is convinced she loves Erik; the next she cannot love him because his wrists are too large, his nose is too snub. She knows that the poem he writes her ("Little and tender and merry and wise / With eyes that meet my eyes" [p. 392]) is bad. After Carol and Erik have wandered, talked, and daydreamed for some time, Kennicott confronts her. He is certain he knows what has poisoned her mind: "These fool stories about wives that don't know when they're well off" (p. 363). Her affair ends when Will chases Erik out of town.

About forty pages remain in the novel. Now the problem is whether Carol will retain her illusions or face whatever reality Gopher Prairie presents. She might somehow find a balance of dream and fact that would result in growth. Levin suggests that the quixotic experience need not end negatively. "Rather," he says, "it is a register of development, an index of maturation. Its incidental mishaps can be looked back on as milestones on the way to self-awareness."[11] But when Carol breaks from Gopher Prairie and settles in Washington, she seems not much different from the person she was before, though she believes herself to be changing. For instance, the "Washington" she finds (or, one suspects, creates) is a city of "leafy parks, spacious avenues, twisty alleys" (pp. 425–26), of "Negro shanties turned into studios, with orange curtains and pots of mignonette," of marble houses and butlers and limousines, and "men who looked like fictional explorers and aviators" (p. 426). After a year, her husband comes to woo her back. His gesture is exactly the one he had made when he first courted her about ten years earlier, and her response is just what we expect and fear. "He tossed over to her thirty prints of Gopher Prairie and the country about. . . . She remembered that he had lured her with photographs in courtship days; she made a note of his sameness, his satisfaction with the tactics which had proved good before; but she forgot it in the familiar places" (p. 435). She has built no defense against this well-intuited appeal to her illusions, though she thinks that she has developed what she calls "personal solidarity." Back in Gopher Prairie she wears her eyeglasses on the street (perhaps because she wishes to see more clearly now). The townsmen say of her that "she knows a good deal about books —or fiction anyway," and of her affair with Valborg that it was "just talking books and all that junk" (pp. 446–47). She believes that, though she may not have "fought the good fight" (p. 451), she has kept faith with her ideals.

By seeing Carol Kennicott as a quixote, we come to realize that Lewis satirized both his heroine and the village. Lewis attempted, in his flamboyant, crude, and often careless way, to anatomize a woman torn among illusions and realities. For Carol, Lewis drew up an archetype, so that Carol touched familiar responses in readers in America, where quixotism has long existed but has not been fully recognized as an important aspect of the national character. In the sub-literature and popular culture of the late nineteenth and early twentieth centuries, romance flourished. There were cults associated with the Orient, the exotic, the adventurous, the Kiplingesque, poesy, and vagabondia. These formed a state of mind which attracted and repelled several generations of writers. Mark Twain, who understood much of what made and moved America, portrayed quixotism in *Tom Sawyer, Huck Finn, Life on the Mississippi,* and *A Connecticut Yankee.* A towering figure like Mark Twain gathers ideas from the past and opens up potentialities for future writers. His indications of the presence of quixotism in American life are significant; Lewis also sensed such a presence and the conflict that attends it.

Quixotism induces an ambivalent and confusing response, for it embodies both foolishness and idealism. Recognizing that *Main Street* is uneven and in some way inconclusive, we can speculate that the quixotic elements in Lewis's nature disallowed the kind of transcendence that Cervantes and Flaubert achieved. Lewis came to *Main Street* after writing five apprentice novels, among them *The Trail of the Hawk* and *Free Air,* in which young Americans travel the roads in pursuit of adventure and golden ladies. Perhaps he called *Main Street* "the real beginning" of his career because he believed that he was freeing himself from the shackles of romance by satirizing a literary idea of the village that maddens its readers and that had misled him for too long.[12] Carol was his vehicle and victim. Now he was joining a realistic movement that was already well under way without him.

At any rate, I think that we are better informed about *Main Street* —and better able to assess it—if we see it as an account of a quixotic figure—idealistic, disillusioned, of limited vision yet a challenge to the community. Amidst the comedy, she is, if not tragic, at least worthy of our concern, because her idealism drives her into further suffering. She becomes aware that her vision is faulty, falsely inspired, and mistaken, but she continues to see as her aspirations demand. She is more honest and more deceived than anyone around her, and thereby both more trapped and more alive.

Notes

1. *The Gates of Horn: A Study of Five French Realists* (New York: Oxford University Press, 1963), p. 255.

2. Some reviewers saw *Main Street* as an American *Madame Bovary.* In an essay on Lewis, Stuart P. Sherman developed the contrast for a few pages, devoting much of his space to praising Lewis for portraying the "erotic passion" as less perturbing to Americans than to Frenchmen. "The Significance of Sinclair Lewis," *Points of View* (New York: Charles Scribner's Sons, 1924), pp. 204–09.

3. "Introduction," *Selected Short Stories of Sinclair Lewis* (Garden City, New York: The Literary Guild, 1935), p. x.

4. "Editor's Table," *Yale Literary Magazine,* 72 (December 1906); reprinted in

Harry E. Maule and Melville H. Cane, *The Man from Main Street: A Sinclair Lewis Reader; Selected Essays and Other Writings, 1904–1950* (New York: Random House, 1953), p. 58.

5. "My First Day in New York," in Harry E. Maule and Melville H. Cane, ed., *The Man from Main Street: A Sinclair Lewis Reader* (New York: Random House, 1953), p. 58.

6. See Grace Hegger Lewis, *With Love from Gracie: Sinclair Lewis, 1912–1935* (New York: Harcourt, Brace, 1935), pp. 7–14. "From the beginning [of the courtship] he chose for himself the roles of Jacques the Jester and Francois the Troubadour who sang to the Lady Grace . . ." pp. 8–9.

7. *The World of "Don Quixote"* (Cambridge: Harvard University Press, 1967), p. 53.

8. *The Gates of Horn*, p. 257.

9. *Main Street* (New York: Harcourt, Brace and Company, 1920), p. 29. Subsequent references will be included parenthetically.

10. Mark Schorer, *Sinclair Lewis: An American Life* (New York: McGraw-Hill, 1961), p. 102.

11. Levin, "The Quixotic Principle: Cervantes and Other Novelists," in Morton W. Bloomfield, ed., *The Interpretation of Narrative: Theory and Practice; Harvard English Studies* I (Cambridge: Harvard University Press, 1970), p. 65.

12. Lewis to Alfred Harcourt (8 February 1920) in Harrison Smith, ed., *From Main Street to Stockholm: Letters of Sinclair Lewis, 1919–1930* (New York: Harcourt, Brace and Company, 1925), p. 25.

Sinclair Lewis and the Implied America

James Lea*

That Sinclair Lewis recorded the social history of a major sector of the American population in the first third of the twentieth century is a generally accepted literary axiom. An ear for the rhythms of Midwestern speech and a descriptive power which E. M. Forster likened to that of photography[1] combined with intelligent curiosity to produce in him one of the country's most astute social critics. Especially during the decade of the Twenties, the mirror which his novels held up to the material crassness and spiritual befuddlement of middle-class Americans established Lewis as a forceful cultural commentator, a best-selling novelist and the darling even of those whom he damned.

But Sinclair Lewis wrote—or, we should say created—another sort of American history as well. In the work of most social satirists, criticism of the contemporary world derives in large part from the writer's assumption that there was, or is, or could be a better world. Lewis assumed

*Reprinted, with permission, from *Clio* 3 (October 1973):21–34.

that there *had been* a better world, or at least a better America, and that his twentieth century had betrayed the potential for freedom and productive happiness implicit in the people, life, and very land itself of eighteenth- and nineteenth-century America. Sheldon Grebstein has observed that "the theme of Lewis's serious books, beginning with *Main Street*, is disillusionment."[2] But disillusionment is more than a theme; it is the tonal foundation of Lewis's major works. Lewis's picture of a banal present is underpinned by his concept of a more meaningful past, a concept which is manifested both in implication by contrast and in detailed representation throughout his principal novels. The center-stage actions of Lewis's novels—the struggling of Carol Kennicott, the blustering of George Babbitt, the soul-searching of Neil Kingsblood—are always played against a back-drop depicting the America that has been, and that by extension could be, but is being perverted.

To aid the process of delineating the character of the American past which is continuously implied by Lewis, I have chosen to examine seven novels which present an interesting historical chronology through the periods in which they are set. *The God-Seeker*, although not published until 1949, is Lewis's only work that follows Sir Walter Scott's classic definition of the historical novel.[3] Its action is laid between 1830 and 1856. *Main Street* (1920) covers the years 1907 to 1920, *Babbitt* (1922) the years 1920 to 1922. *Arrowsmith* (1925) is set between 1897 and 1923, and *Elmer Gantry* (1927) between 1902 and 1926. *Dodsworth* (1929), called by some Lewis's last great novel, covers the years 1903 to 1928. *Kingsblood Royal* (1947), lying far beyond the limits of Lewis's "golden decade" with respect to quality as well as to publication date, treats the period 1944 to 1946. While Lewis calls upon his vision of the American past in other novels, these seven offer particularly illuminating examples of the methods by which he describes what may be called his Implied America.

When Sinclair Lewis was a boy, in the late years of the nineteenth century, Sauk Centre, Minnesota, was only two generations removed from the crude huts and the cavalry stockade of the early plains pioneers. It is quite probable that when he boarded the train for New Haven and the lifetime that lay beyond, he took with him at least a germinating sense of the land which earlier eyes had seen and earlier feet had walked. This imaginative perspective, reinforced by the sort of research which stood behind every Lewis novel, appears in the setting and characters of *The God-Seeker*. In this, the last Lewis novel published during the author's lifetime, Aaron Gadd traces in microcosm the trail of the Yankee missionaries and merchants who settled the northern plains in the mid-1800s. Physically, Aaron moves from his boyhood home in Clunford, Massachusetts (where his American lineage is firmly established in the person of his grandfather, a Revolutionary War veteran) to a missionary

post among the Sioux and Chippewa, and from there to the growing
frontier camp which becomes St. Paul, where he sets up shop as a hous-
ing contractor. In the course of his progress, Aaron is identified—either
directly or by association—with most of the forces which shaped the
character of the American frontier as Lewis sees it represented in pioneer Minnesota. Perhaps more idealistic than many of the early migrants,
Aaron departs Massachusetts "to go west! To bring order and civilization to the aborigines!"[4] Traveling by train, river boat, canoe, and horse-
back to his job at the Mission, he encounters the fur-traders, voyageurs,
gamblers, soldiers, preachers and barons of commerce who are writing
the history of the territory. His frontier mentors are Caesar Lanark, one
of the traders who "pioneered the way for a lot of scoundrels who want
to butcher the Indians at once, instead of gently pasturing them and
milking them over the years" (p. 178), Squire Harge, the missionary
whose mission is to impose his own Christianity upon a people with a
centuries-old cultural identity of their own, and the St. Paul carpenter
Seth Buckbee, whose social posture in the free, new land is supported
by his belief that "the Irish and the Scandinavians were as shiftless as
the Injuns" (p. 356). Among them and the proud but desperate Indians,
and on the face of the Minnesota wilderness, Aaron finds his place alongside other frontiersmen, "men with stars in their heads and solid boots
on their feet, men with a sense of elevated piety and of slick politics and
land-options, in their violent and everwestering lives" (p. 18).

If Aaron Gadd's physical travels and his contact with the western
up-and-comers seem to reflect the movements of the Yankee pioneers,
his spiritual progress represents the development of Lewis's ideal of
the nation-builder. Beginning in a youthful innocence shaped by his
father's New England Puritanism, Aaron is seized by a religious conviction and a missionary fervor which are perhaps similar to the fever for
free land and a free life which drove more than one mid-nineteenth
century easterner westward. His service at the Mission loosens his resolution and implants in his mind grave doubts about the superiority of
his creed and his white race. His escape to St. Paul and his success as
a carpenter in a town where building is as much a function of the heart
as of the hands mark his initiation into that class of men who neither
advertised nor traded but actually produced the flesh and bone of America. Aaron's representative spiritual completeness is not realized, however,
until he takes the ultimate democratic step and helps his own employees
organize a labor union. So Aaron Gadd—and, Lewis seems to say, all
those who helped shape "a just, orderly and enduring commonwealth"
(p. 368)—travels the circle from the innocence of externally ordered
youth to the dawning human awareness of autonomous manhood.

The God-Seeker must be judged one of Lewis's weaker novels. But
in the consideration of his formulation of an American past clearly in

contrast with his American present it holds an important place. In this novel Lewis establishes his idea that the crassness and pettiness of the twentieth century are both a perversion of the ideals of a time when "men cast longer shadows" (p. 368) and at the same time directly traceable to it. For as Aaron Gadd ascends to success on the Minnesota frontier, Lewis continues to remind us that "the future history of Minnesota, like that of every other state in the Union, would be the inept struggle of mechanics and farmers and shopkeepers to get back a little of what they never intended to give away in the first place" (p. 369). *The God-Seeker* probably should not be read as Lewis's "final statement," but rather as an indication of his late recognition of the need for a preliminary statement. The total impact of the body of Lewis's major work resides not only in its social character, but in its historical character as well; it is in *The God-Seeker* that Lewis gives substance to that age of promise against which his age of disillusionment is measured.

From this level of historical perspective, we read more than irony in the frontispiece note to *Main Street*: "Main Street is the climax of civilization. That this Ford car might stand in front of the Bon Ton Store, Hannibal invaded Rome and Erasmus wrote in Oxford cloisters. . . . Our railway station is the final aspiration of architecture."[5] For Lewis seems to consider it very important that we understand that the life and times of Gopher Prairie which he is about to present are of historical value in a double sense: they are a representation both of what we are and of what we have made out of what we could have been. Main Street does not exist as an independent construct, but as a point on the continuum of time, accountable to the past and to the future.

The Implied America makes briefer appearances in *Main Street* than in *The God-Seeker*, but it appears early. The novel opens with a description of Carol Milford (later to be Mrs. Will Kennicott) standing "on a hill by the Mississippi where Chippewas camped two generations ago" (p. 1). It is 1907, and the Chippewas Lewis refers to are the sons and grandsons of the Chippewas whose hunting grounds Aaron Gadd had walked. In those two generations, much has changed; the Indians and the frontiersmen are gone, although their presence remains woven into the fabric of the era: "She saw no Indians now . . . Nor was she thinking of squaws and portages, and the Yankee fur-traders whose shadows were all about her" (p. 1).

Main Street, of course, marked Lewis's turn, as Robert J. Griffin phrases it, from "the celebration of national potentialities to the castigation of national failings."[6] Lewis's five novels which preceded it were buoyant little books of apprenticeship, and, except for *The Job* (1917), they are rarely discussed today. In those early novels, Lewis treated the escape of the young innocent from the village into the outside world, a sort of idealized spiritual autobiography. By 1920, however, his vision seems to have panned down from the fresh leaves fluttering in the blue sky to the roots of life in America and the native soil in which they were sunk.

While Lewis's five apprenticeship novels dealt with the native Midwestern villager confronting the smug big city establishment, *Main Street* relates the confrontation between urban naivete and small-town smugness. Carol Kennicott was brought up in "Mankato, which is not a prairie town, but in its garden-sheltered streets and aisles of elms is white and green New England reborn" (p. 6). Her childhood is delightfully secure, her education—both at home and at Blodgett College—is entertaining and shallow. She steps out on the trail to Gopher Prairie garbed in Aaron Gadd's Yankee innocence and idealism, a cultural pioneer armed with the Good Book-and-broadaxe of her own Romantic self-assurance.

Though she finds the plains no longer menaced by outraged Indians; though "the days of pioneering, of lassies in sunbonnets, and bears killed with axes in piney clearings, are deader now than Camelot" (p. 1); still Carol encounters history in Gopher Prairie. There is the sense of the seemingly eternal land, into which she retreats in her most desperate moments. There are the Scandinavian farmers, belying the calendar by clawing the earth as their pioneer predecessors had done fifty years before: "a forest clearing: pathetic new furrows straggling among stumps, a clumsy log cabin chinked with mud and roofed with hay" (p. 18).

There are the last frontiersmen, the Champ Perrys, whom Carol sees as merely another possible means to her end, but whom Lewis suggests are the remnants of an age degraded by "the era of aeroplanes and syndicalism" (p. 152). And there are the records of the Minnesota Territorial Pioneers. Carol muses for a moment over the years when Gopher Prairie consisted of four cabins and a stockade, when men and women lived with difficulty and vigor and a certain buoyancy, now lost. For Carol, stranded in an America which is "neither the heroic old nor the sophisticated new" (p. 151), the past is a panacea which she frivolously schemes to reclaim.

For Sinclair Lewis, the past is yesterday's reality. Miles Bjornstam is its only vitally extant embodiment in the novel. His socialism is the modern echo of the dead frontier equalitarianism. In a sense, he is a tragic anachronism, caught, as Mark Schorer would say, between "the individual impulse for freedom and the social impulse to restrict it."[7] Bjornstam no sooner abandons his freedom of foot and spirit for an attempted accommodation with twentieth-century domesticity than he is crushed. When he leaves Gopher Prairie to find a new starting place, his directions are northward to Alberta and backward to the frontier

past. Bjornstam's judgment upon the town, Lewis suggests, is the judgment of American history upon the Main Street of the American present.

For all its high towers of commerce and sprawling circumference
of modern economic splendor, the city of Zenith, as Lewis depicts it
in *Babbitt*, is built over a pit. Located in Lewis's mythical Midwestern
state of Winnemac, Zenith was "an ancient settlement in 1897, one hundred and five years old, with two hundred thousand population."[8] By
1920, it is a city on the make, rudely displacing its nineteenth-century
buildings with "clean towers . . . thrusting them from the business center"
(p. 1), re-surfacing its land—formerly "a wilderness of rank second-
growth elms and oaks and maples"—with the "bright roofs and immaculate turf and amazing comfort" (p. 28) of Floral Heights. If in 1856,
Aaron Gadd's St. Paul was on its way to becoming "the most mammoth,
gorgeous and powerful metropolis on this globe,"[9] Zenith is Lewis's
unpleasant representation of what the realization of such a goal can
produce.

Turning from his examination of the mid-American village to a
study of the mid-American city, Lewis finds a social phenomenon inflated
to the bursting point with the hot air of its own gusto. Zenith has long
since lost touch with its agricultural beginnings; that aspect of its history
is no longer even relevant. For generations its citizens have occupied
themselves with the manufacturing of products, the buying and selling
of property, the lending of money and other vocations which contribute
to the collection of masses of people into easily manipulable units. In
the process, they have all but eradicated the city's link with the land
and their own link with their forebears. For their own purposes, they
have no history: in Zenith in 1920, Lewis writes, "an old house is one
which was built before 1880" (p. 213).

The result of Zenith's exorcism of its past to make room for a booming present and a "promising" future is reflected in the befuddlement
which creeps into the soul of George Babbitt. Outwardly brash and
blustering, Babbitt inwardly represents a population in limbo, at a
point in history when, as Walter Lippmann has written, "they have lost
the civilized traditions their ancestors brought from Europe and are
groping to find new ways of life."[10] Cut off from a vital past, they have
lost the vitality to pursue their personal dreams: Babbitt is a real estate
salesman who has dreamed of being a lawyer: Paul Riesling is a roofing
salesman who has dreamed of playing the violin; even Chum Frink,
author of versified pap and "Ads That Add," has once dreamed of being
a poet.

It seems that Zenith's pioneer past is all the more conspicuous because of its absence in the present. Modernity's hollowness and shallowness go unrelieved, except when Babbitt discovers the restorative effects
of a vacation in the Maine woods with Paul Riesling. It is a return to the

frontier for Babbitt, a chance to touch "something sort of eternal" (p. 149) that has eluded him in the city. The woods invite Babbitt's dreams of what is strangely like an idealized frontier life: "If he could but take up a backwoods claim with a man like Joe, work hard with his hands, be free and noisy in a flannel shirt, and never come back to this dull decency!" The plague of city life disappears as Babbitt imagines "Moccasins—six-gun—frontier town—gamblers—" (p. 295).

But in the end it is too late for Babbitt. The frontier is too far past. He can't draw from it sufficient courage to face down the forces of materialism that Zenith can marshall at the first sign of individual diversity. At the end of the novel, there is a quiet note of hope as Babbitt encourages his son to "Tell 'em to go to the devil!" (p. 401). But Babbitt disappears again into the crowd of faces—mindless behind their smiles—of Americans who have severed themselves from history.

In April, 1926, Sinclair Lewis was awarded the Pulitzer Prize for his ninth novel, _Arrowsmith_. With considerable malice aforethought, he rejected the award on the grounds that he would not be bought off by an agency of the tasteless American literary establishment. Given the probability that after the Pulitzer debacle of 1920 Lewis would have welcomed any opportunity to snub the Columbia University trustees, it is nonetheless interesting that _Arrowsmith_ gave him that opportunity. For Martin Arrowsmith is also a man who will not be bought off by the establishment, and this is only one of the traits which mark him as Lewis's most nearly autobiographical character.

With this novel, Lewis undertook a series of studies of the professional person that developed from Arrowsmith the doctor through Gantry the preacher to Dodsworth the retired manufacturer and others. Each of these different characters moves in a milieu in which the historical past, Lewis's Implied America, plays a significant role. In _Arrowsmith_, the role is dual, incorporating history both as personal lineage and as a standard for the measurement of modern contrasts.

The story of Martin Arrowsmith opens sometime in the early nineteenth century, with a brief vignette in which a fourteen year-old girl is driving a wagon westward. Despite the pleadings of her fevered father and her responsibility for a horde of younger brothers and sisters, she presses on: "There's a whole lot of new things I aim to be seeing!"[11] The girl turns out to be Martin Arrowsmith's great-grandmother, and thus Lewis establishes an historical referent for Arrowsmith's character, linking him personally to the past.

Because he has a new story to tell, Lewis revolves his artistic gels a few turns and sheds a new light on Winnemac and Zenith. As he describes it, the character of Zenith's contemporary population has not changed noticeably since Babbitt, but Lewis works to re-establish the area's historical groundings. Prior to taking a satiric crack at the University of Winnemac, Lewis explains that the state's tradition goes back to the Revolutionary War. Zenith, as we learned earlier, was founded in 1792—the year Kentucky joined the Union—but outlying counties were not settled until 1860. (Of Elk Mills, Martin's hometown, we learn nothing directly.) Then, having established that Winnemac is to a notable degree rooted in history and that Martin Arrowsmith is very much rooted in it, Lewis seems to drop the matter. His chief interest in this novel is the development of a contemporary pioneer stalking the frontier of science.

Hazard offers an interpretive construct of American history as representing three stages of pioneering: the regional stage, in which man attempts to control nature; the industrial stage, in which man attempts to control the labors of his fellow men; and the spiritual stage, in which man attempts to control himself.[12] She suggests that *Arrowsmith* contains elements of all three stages, that Martin's ancestors were the regional pioneers, that his contemporaries are the industrial pioneers and that he becomes a spiritual pioneer in the manner of the Transcendentalists when, at the end of the novel, he resigns wealth and celebrity in New York and goes off to the Vermont woods to pursue pure science (pp. 283–5). Hazard's speculation should be extended somewhat, for from his first practice in the plains village of Wheatsylvania, Martin is seeking first of all to serve his fellow man. There is, therefore, a strain of the spiritual pioneer running in him throughout.

But Lewis is treating modern science in much the same way he treated the physical wilderness in *The God-Seeker* and the cultural wilderness in *Main Street*—that is, as an untracked space in which man could leave prints as deep and as permanent as he could make them. Martin Arrowsmith remains the regional pioneer in this open domain, much as Miles Bjornstam remains one in the broad lands beyond the short horizons of Gopher Prairie. Both of them occasionally pass through the clutches of their industrial contemporaries, sometimes with tragic consequences. But in the end each succeeds because each is free. For Martin this freedom is the fruit of the dogged determination inherited from his pioneer great-grandmother. Arrowsmith is characterized as Lewis may have characterized himself: a solitary and beleagured spiritual survivor of the frontier past.

Although *Elmer Gantry* is set between the years 1902 and 1926, the voice of the narrator obviously speaks from the late years of that span. In the chapters dealing with Elmer's days as a student at Terwillinger College and as a rising young cleric, the voice is almost reflective in tone: "His Mother was able to give Elmer the three hundred dollars a year which, with his summer earnings in harvest field and lumber-yard, was enough to support him—in Terwillinger, in 1902."[13] Speaking not in the past tense but in a sort of past-imperfect, Lewis writes of Gritzmacher Springs, the home of Terwillinger College: "The springs have dried up and the Gritzmachers have gone to Los Angeles, to sell bungalows and delicatessen" (p. 9). On the day of Elmer's ordination ceremony, "It was 1905; there was as yet no Ford nearer than Fort Scott" (p. 81). The author's sense of historical distance becomes clearer when he writes: "In the virginal days of 1905 section gangs went out to work on the railway line not by gasoline power but on a hand-car, a platform with two horizontal bars worked up and down like pump handles" (p. 101). This impression of a distance in time and place between the narrative voice and the action of the novel is one which Lewis manages to achieve in several pieces of his fiction. One effect of this device is to raise the reader above the plane of the story, to give him a share in the author's omniscience, to allow him to view plot and characters in the temporal context in which the author has placed them. Rather than weaving historical dates and events into the narrative, Lewis alludes to their presence outside the narrative. By this means, the action of the novel is historically anchored, and, at the same time, the reader is aware that the action is distinct from, but contiguous to, other events of its time.

The clarification of this distinction is particularly important to the reading of *Elmer Gantry*, for in this novel Lewis has created his least sympathetic character. Elmer is a universal type, rather than a character representative of some national epidemic of the heart. He is the operator immemorial, egocentric and ruthless. He is Squire Harge with no core of sincere religious zeal, he is Juanita Haydock with no limit to his perfidy; he is Babbitt with no suspicion of his fallibility. Elmer Gantry's prototype is the ahistorical Ananias.

But Elmer does not move independently of history. There are around him the identifiable characters of the Twenties: Billy Sunday, Amiee Semple McPherson, and others. And there is the suggestion that historical perspective itself can be manipulated, as when Katie Jonas, of Utica, New York, acquires enough money to be able to put on the aristocratic home, lineage, and name of Sister Sharon Falconer.

So while *Elmer Gantry* is set before Lewis's ubiquitous backdrop of history, the relationship between the present and the past is somewhat different in this novel from that in those novels we have previously examined. Lewis is describing here not so much a society brought to its present state by its betrayal of its own past, as a phenomenon—Elmer —emerging in a society that is as historically ready for him as its early nineteenth-century counterpart was ready for the revivalists of that time.

Maxwell Geismar has offered the idea that the plots of Lewis's early apprenticeship novels turn on the confrontation between the aristocratic Easterner (or his tradition) and the Western democratic hero, and that the novels' complications arise from this conflict of cultural values.[14] By comparison, *Dodsworth* turns largely upon the confrontation between a johnny-come-lately American and an historically imposing Europe. By the time *Dodsworth* was published in 1929, Sinclair Lewis's fame and increasing fortune had allowed him to make several trips to Europe and to get glimpses both of Europeans at home and of Americans away from home. The sense of contrast which such glimpses aroused in him, and the notion that between the American and his European heritage was a gulf even wider than the one which separated the American from his own national past, were manifested in Lewis's thirteenth novel.

Dodsworth is another admirable frontiersman who has outlived his time. The Champ Perrys of *Main Street* were of this sort, lost in an age when their courage and determination no longer had the focus provided by torturing elements and belligerent Indians. In the industrial twentieth century, Dodsworth has pioneered new designs and techniques in the building of automobiles. He has outfought the industrial reactionaries and the financial bamboozlers, and he has lasted long enough to see the Revelation, the product of his own work and bearing the stamp of his own imagination, become a world-famous motorcar. By 1925, he has become the victim of advancing civilization; his outpost on the leading edge of the industrial frontier has been overrun from behind by a more efficient—albeit less refined—technology. Dodsworth at age fifty is an analogical national soul who has experienced the rigors of regional and industrial pioneering and now—like America in the 1920's —stands at the threshold of a new spiritual frontier and a new self-perception.

Dodsworth's European experience is Lewis's idealization of a post-pioneer America learning to live comfortably and unobtrusively with itself. From a posture of boom-time smugness rooted in the mood of *Main Street*—"Three guests had come in these new-fangled automobiles, for it was now 1903, the climax of civilization"[15]—Sam evolves through self-doubt to an ultimate new sense of his place in the commonality of human experience. Europe is a testing ground on which his personal character—and, by implication, America's national character—is tried. His first considered reaction to Europe is historically framed. Though he is enchanted by the atmosphere of England and disgusted by the superficiality of the Continental salons, he—like Irving's Geoffrey Crayon a century earlier—is unequivocally impressed by the air of solid permanence which he senses in old Europe. He finds Paris "stately, aloof, gray with history, eternally quiet at heart for all its superficial clamor" (p. 116). This captain of American industry responds to Europe with the shrinking awe of a small child: "Gee ... this town has been here a long time, I guess.... This town knows a lot.... I wish I did!" (pp. 116–7). He reflects on the lost bliss of his egocentric American ignorance. "Life was a lot simpler then. We knew we were It. We knew that Europe was unbathed and broke, and that America was the world's only bulwark against Bolshevism and famine" (p. 126).

Dodsworth becomes first defensive, then contemplative in response to Europeanism's challenge to Americanism. In defense, he calls not upon America's "steel-and-glass skyscrapers and miraculous cement-and-glass factories and tiled kitchens and wireless antennae and popular magazines" (p. 360), but upon the tradition of his national past: "the tradition of pioneers pushing to the westward across the Alleghenies, through the forests of Kentucky and Tennessee, on to the bleeding plains of Kansas, on to Oregon and California, a religious procession, sleeping always in danger, never resting, and opening a new home for a hundred million people" (p. 352).

After the disintegration of his marriage, and under the subtle tutelage of Edith Cortwright, Sam achieves a stability of perspective which suggests a new Lewis vision of the place of America in the history of the world. Sam is no longer unsure of himself as "the rich American . . . uncouth and untraditional" (p. 363) in comparison to the European cultural heritage. Fully aware of his failings, he learns to revel in being "a most American American." After despair and self-denunciation, Sam can gloat "I am real!" (p. 361).

Dodsworth, in the chronology of Lewis's Implied America, marks a shift in setting and characterization from the Midwest of the Kennicotts and the Babbitts and an expansion in the scope of Lewis's historical perspective. No longer does a ponderous American history loom behind a frantic modern Zenith, reducing its loftiest self-serving ambitions to sheerest banality. In this novel, Lewis's vision of the entire American character, past and present, is re-adjusted through a thoughtful comparison with European civilization. Dodsworth himself is "not a Babbitt, not a Rotarian, not an Elk, not a deacon" (p. 11). He is as sound and sympathetic an American character as Lewis created before 1930. When, at the conclusion of the novel, Sam establishes something of a hold on happiness, he becomes complete as Lewis's post-pioneer American, still endowed with his natural awkwardness, perhaps, but possessed of a new historical and societal equilibrium. *Kingsblood Royal* was a highly topical novel when it was published in 1947, since it deals with racial tension in a small Midwestern city of Grand Republic. It also provides a chronologically and thematically satisfactory culmination to this study of Lewis's use of an implied American past. In the central plot device in the novel—Neil Kingsblood's discovery of his own past and that discovery's effect upon him and those around him—Lewis seems to have found a feasible working model of his own sense of history and the individual's relationship to it.

In 1944, Neil Kingsblood has "always wanted to be a frontiers-man, an Astor Company trader of 1820 on the Minnesota border,"[16] but his life is a world and a couple of World Wars away from the frontier. It is his father's unlikely theory that the family line may carry the blood of Henry VIII which puts Neil on the trail of the genealogy of his mother's ancestors. He is excited enough to press his research when he learns that this great-great-great-grandfather was one Xavier Pic, "a voyageur for the Hudson's Bay Company," a man belonging "not to evening and mist and gossiping cowbells but to alert mornings on the glittering rapids of unknown rivers" (p. 47). Neil's investigation gives form to the desire of a more mature post-war America to ally itself with a national past which, two decades before, it had been happy to ignore.

The startling discovery that Xavier Pic was a full-blooded Negro—thereby making Neil a Negro by legal definition—opens the door to another exercise in spiritual pioneering, and also lays the foundation for Lewis's explication of his own hypothesis on the relationship of the past to the present. As Neil determines to testify to his racial status, regardless of the cost, the confluence of forces which time brings to bear upon the equilibrium of any given moment becomes apparent. The mixture of blood lines in Neil's ancestry is like the mixture of social, political and economic forces which, along with the whims of countless individuals, accounts for the character of an age. The inevitable conclusion to the story, with Neil waging a valiant but futile fight for his rights as a human being, rounds out not only Lewis's condemnation of racism in America, but also his implication that a nation must be willing to recognize and act upon the obligations imposed by its own past.

The chronological domain of these seven Sinclair Lewis novels spans more than a century of American history. During that century, America changed more radically in structure and character than any other nation had ever changed in an equal amount of time. The Upper Midwest passed from a state of wilderness to a state of prosperous modernity, and Lewis took it as one of his artistic tasks to chronicle that passage. As an observer of American life, he planted himself squarely in the twentieth century, but his vision ranged backward to the beginning and forward to the unknown but hopeful future. In *The God-Seeker*, he attempted to capture the flavor of optimism and expectancy and the nearly equal potentialities for glory and for ruin which pervaded the nineteenth-century frontier. He warned his readers to look carefully upon those pioneers, for what they did and saw and said would count for something in the development of the quality of the years which followed theirs. *Main Street, Babbitt, Arrowsmith, Elmer Gantry* and *Dodsworth*, written amidst the fury of the decade in which they were set, described the harvest which the twentieth century was reaping from its own reckless tending of the national garden. *Kingsblood Royal* suggested the degree of courage which is necessary for a people to ride successfully the crest of their own history.

It would be presumptuous, even silly, to suggest that the body of Sinclair Lewis's novels constitutes a grand epic of the American Midwest. But the evidence of his attention not only to documentary accuracy but also to historical perspective in the recording of his era's manners and meanness clearly implies that Lewis was generally and artistically conscious of the prominent role which history plays in the affairs of his most memorable characters.

Notes

1. E. M. Forster, *Abinger Harvest* (New York, 1964), pp. 129–130.

2. Sheldon Grebstein, *Sinclair Lewis* (New York, 1962), p. 64.

3. See the individual Introductions and the revised General Introduction to the *Waverley* novels. Later readers, rather than Scott himself, are responsible for the formulation of strict definition from these introductory comments.

4. Sinclair Lewis, *The God-Seeker* (New York: Random House, 1947), p. 57; subsequent references to all novels follow the original citation by page numbers in parentheses in text.

5. Sinclair Lewis, *Main Street* (New York, 1920), frontispiece.

6. Robert J. Griffin, "Introduction," *20th-Century Interpretations of Arrowsmith,* ed. R. J. Griffin (Englewood Cliffs, N. J., 1962), p. 7.

7. Mark Schorer, *Sinclair Lewis: An American Life* (New York, 1961), p. 811.

8. Sinclair Lewis, *Babbitt* (New York, 1922), p. 89.

9. *The God-Seeker,* p. 107.

10. Walter Lippmann, *Men of Destiny* (New York, 1927), p. 83.

11. Sinclair Lewis, *Arrowsmith* (New York, 1925), p. 1.

12. Lucy L. Hazard, *The Frontier in American Literature* (New York, 1927), p. xviii.

13. Sinclair Lewis, *Elmer Gantry* (New York, 1927), p. 33.

14. Maxwell Geismar, *The Last of the Provincials: The American Novel, 1915–1925* (Boston, 1943), pp. 83–84.

15. Sinclair Lewis, *Dodsworth* (New York, 1929), p. 1.

16. Sinclair Lewis, *Kingsblood Royal* (New York, 1947), p. 11.

Popular Artists and Elite Standards:
The Case of Sinclair Lewis   Stephen S. Conroy*

The confusion with which elite critics view the work of truly popular artists who happen to be gifted is the same as the confusion with
which white critics often view Black literature. That the confusion is
similar is only natural; they are the same critics, white and elite, and
their standards, whether Aristotelian, New Critical, or what have you,
are classbound as well as racebound. Classbound standards prove to be
of limited usefulness in evaluating the careers of writers such as Mark
Twain and Sinclair Lewis who were more than (or less than) serious
writers of fiction.

Even before more useful standards can be devised for judging popular artists an attempt must be made to identify them, especially those
writers of great worth who do not happen to meet the exacting standards
of the critical aristocracy. There is little difficulty in discriminating among
worthwhile popular artists and "lumpenwriters" with their tasteless
pandering to what they conceive to be the low level of mass taste. What
is needed in the beginning is a way to distinguish between an elite artist
such as Henry James and a popular artist such as Sinclair Lewis. High
culture criticism tends to make a dichotomy out of what surely is a spectrum. Its Calvinistic division of the world of art into a small group of
the saved and a large mass of the damned not only arrogantly dismisses
much of true worth, it also results in confusing arguments about writers
along the borderline. Sinclair Lewis was not Henry James, yet he was
a writer of real distinction. There are a considerable number of authors
of comparable stature. Perhaps an examination of some seldom noted
facts about the writing career of Sinclair Lewis will lead to meaningful conclusions about the nature of the popular artist and will give some
clues to the ways in which he differs from the elite artist.

Sinclair Lewis is a particularly dramatic example of a marginal
writer, one whose acceptance by the public has been high but whose
reception by the critics has been mixed. He was, first of all, an incredibly
popular writer; his novels,the primary source of his fame and also of his
decidedly uneven reputation, were widely distributed. Main Street, his
first best-seller, sold more than 800,000 copies by 1929 and has been
called, "the most sensational event in twentieth century American publishing history."[1] Babbitt was even more sensational; it was "one of the
greatest international successes in all publishing history," selling a
quarter of a million copies more than Main Street.[2] Huge publication
figures continued throughout Lewis's career: 700,000 for Arrowsmith,

*Reprinted, with permission of the author and the publisher, from Forum (Houston)
12 (Spring 1974):28–32.

600,000 for *Elmer Gantry*, 1,500,000 for *Kingsblood Royal*, and so on.³
Many of his novels are in print today and continue to sell well. Obviously
Lewis had the knack of catching the interest of the reading public. His
uncanny success stemmed no doubt from his own nature, from his
essential oneness with George F. Babbitt and what he stood for; and
this in turn is the reason why the high culture critics were confused by
him and never knew whether to praise or damn him—with the result that
they did both. H. L. Mencken greeted each new Lewis novel enthusiastically but Joseph Wood Krutch assigned him to oblivion.⁴

    Those critics who were displeased with Lewis's writing accused him
of lowering his true talent with crudities and vulgarities. They mis-
understood Lewis, for he was not a writer from the high culture who
lamentably slipped in taste too often; he was instead a popular artist who
was so expert a craftsman that on occasion he transcended himself. He
was what an elite critic would call a "hack," but one who happened to
be blessed with genius. He always sought for and spoke to the mass
audience, usually with great success. As early as 1906 he published in
Woman's Home Companion and forty-five years later the same mass
circulation magazine serialized his last novel. Sandwiched in between
are literally hundreds of appearances in *The Saturday Evening Post*,
Redbook, *The American Magazine*, *Cosmopolitan* and similar slick
periodicals. Lewis also became a columnist for *Newsweek*, went on the
lecture circuit, appeared on radio programs, and tried his hand at acting.
A popular writer works hard for his audience, and eagerly seeks the
widest possible one, even if it means performing in person before the
public, as Mark Twain, Robert Benchley, Sinclair Lewis and others did.

    A popular culture artist will also search for a large audience even
if it means attempting genres other than the one he has mastered. Sinclair
Lewis's genre was the novel, although he also felt at home in the short
story form. But in his search for audience he also wrote works for the
motion pictures and for the stage. Early in his career, even before his
extraordinary success as a novelist, he sold an original script to Universal Studios which was released as "The Unpainted Woman." And often
during his long career Lewis was involved in numerous projects planned
originally for the screen which did not pan out for one reason or another,
including one script, an anti-fascist allegory masquerading as a Western
entitled "Storm in the West," which he co-authored with Dore Schary.
Lewis was also interested in the stage, and throughout his career he
worked on theatrical pieces, many of which never reached the boards.
For example, he started to write a play about anti-Semitism in medical
schools and hospitals, to be called either "Undiscovered Country" or
"For Us the Living," but it was never finished. Later he worked without
success on a play about labor to be called "The Responsible Man," and

on another based on his married life with the famed columnist Dorothy Thompson to be called either "The Talking Woman" or "Felicia Speaking." But as an original playwright, sometimes with help from collaborators, he had more success. As early as 1917 Lewis worked on a play entitled *Hobohemia* with young Daniel Reed, who was knowledgeable about the stage. Even then the pecuniary attitude common to popular artists revealed itself. Reed later confessed, "I have since thought we were more enamoured of the title for commercial purposes than we were of the material itself."[5] "*Hobohemia*" had only a modest success in New York, yet for a time it was considered as the book for a projected musical. Years later, in 1935, Lewis wrote an original drama with the critic Lloyd Lewis entitled *The Jayhawker*. It was a weak play, so weak that even the drawing power of the famous father-daughter acting team of Fred and Paula Stone could not keep it from an early Broadway closing. Lewis also wrote, directed, invested in and toured with *Angela Is Twenty Two*, but never reached New York with it.

Sinclair Lewis as a popular artist often sought a wider audience by abandoning work in the novel, the genre in which he was most comfortable, and trying his hand at plays and screenplays. He was not tremendously successful at this. Yet he was always aware of the great appeal of the cinema and stage, so much so that he was willing to abandon control of his work to others to be prepared for these media. As they were published, he sold the complete film rights to many of his novels, including *Main Street* (screened as "*I Married a Doctor*"), *Babbitt*, *Arrowsmith*, *Elmer Gantry*, *Dodsworth*, *Cass Timberlane*, *Mantrap*, *It Can't Happen Here*, and *Bethel Merriday*. Not all of them were produced; *Bethel Merriday*, planned for Laurence Olivier and Vivien Leigh, was quietly scrapped, and *It Can't Happen Here* ran afoul of MGM's fear of losing the German and Italian markets. In addition to these novels, Lewis also sold *Angela Is Twenty Two* to the movies. It later was filmed under the title *This Is The Life*.

Since his novels sold so well, Lewis was able to secure lucrative contracts for his repeated involvements with the motion picture industry; he was paid handsomely even when his material was not used ($50,000 for *Bethel Merriday*, for instance). Lewis was not disturbed by the crass commercialism of Hollywood; he could often match it with ease. He even defended the industry against the validity of such attacks in a lengthy piece published in *Motion Picture Magazine* in 1942. Nor did Lewis suffer in the manner of Fitzgerald, Hemingway and others over the debasement of his "art" by the movies. Clearly he felt no debasement and honestly saw little or no conflict between the demands of art on the one hand and the demands of commerce on the other. "Rembrandt," he asserted, "was one of the most commercial bastards that ever lived."[6] This blindness or honesty, depending on your point of view, is no doubt one of the attitudes which distinguishes an artist of the popular culture from one of the high culture.

Lewis was attracted even more to the stage than he was to motion pictures, perhaps because of the immediacy of audience reaction. As has been noted, he had only middling success as a writer or collaborator working directly for the stage. But he also was very interested in letting playwrights of some ability take over his novels and rewrite them for the stage. *Main Street*, dramatized by Harriet Ford and Harvey O'Higgins, had a successful run in New York. Soon after, Lewis tried to interest Marc Connelly and George F. Kaufmann in dramatizing *Babbitt*, but they would not. *"Elmer Gantry"* was rewritten for the stage twice but the version produced by Patrick Kearny managed to remain on the stage only from August 9 to September 15, 1928. With *Dodsworth*, dramatized by the first-rate playwright Sidney Howard and starring the fine actor Walter Huston, Sinclair Lewis in 1935 had a genuine hit. One final time, late in his life, Lewis released one of his novels to a dramatist in the hope of reaching a wider audience. He hired H. S. Kraft and paid him nearly seven thousand dollars to rewrite *Kingsblood Royal*, but the result never reached the stage.

Popular artists are commercial minded; the glee Lewis took in the sales of his novels, in the success of *Dodsworth* on the stage, even his joy at receiving the Nobel Prize was partly pecuniary. Yet the production of the dramatic version of *It Can't Happen Here* by the Federal Theatre Project proves that he was more concerned with reaching an audience than he was with making money, and perhaps this is a key distinction between a popular artist and an exploiter of mass taste. The movie rights of the novel had been sold to Metro-Goldwyn-Mayer and when they decided not to produce it a furor arose, enflamed by Lewis himself. He charged that Will Hays, the czar of moviedom, had ordered its production quashed because he feared offending Hitler and Mussolini. Both Mayer and Goldwyn denied Lewis's accusation, although their stories of the "real" reason for its cancellation did not correspond with one another. Mayer said the film had been abandoned because it would cost too much to produce, but Goldwyn said it was withdrawn because of casting difficulties.[7] As always Lewis had been well paid for the movie rights and had no further financial interest in the motion picture. His complaint was based not on greed but on his unhappiness over losing an audience.

This unhappiness was partially relieved later in 1936 when the Federal Theatre agreed to produce *It Can't Happen Here*. The event proved to be a high point in Sinclair Lewis's career as a popular artist in direct contact with an audience. *It Can't Happen Here* was planned to open simultaneously in twenty theatres in seventeen states on October

27, 1936 as a celebration of the first anniversary of the Federal Theatre Project of the Works Progress Administration. As the deadline approached, Lewis and his collaborator J. C. Moffitt frantically rewrote scenes which were frantically mailed out all over the country. Complaints, demands and queries poured in from all sides. Newspapers gave the play reams of publicity and conservative politicians vented their outrage at it. Hallie Flanagan, the miniature dynamo who was the national director of the Federal Theatre, gave up striving for uniformity and decided to let the local directors put on differing versions of the play, in addition to the versions in Yiddish and Spanish which had already been planned. As a result, Denver had the dictatorship taking over a small Colorado mining town and Detroit set the scene in a factory district. Los Angeles' effort included a prelude in pantomime, and Seattle had a double company—one black and one white. Miami gave its audience an early version of a mixed-media presentation, using elements of radio and motion pictures in its production.[8] Audience reaction ranged from mildly favorable to enthusiastic. Burns Mantle, surveying the phenomenon of the simultaneous openings for the Chicago *Tribune*, wrote:

> Denver, though the audience was small, liked it. Boston was quite excited by it, 1,000 being present and 300 turned away. Cleveland's capacity audience shuddered a bit, but recovered and gave the actors nine curtain calls. Tacoma accepted the production as an "important and significant event." Omaha reports a capacity crowd and a lot of excitement. Seattle, with 1,500 present, gave the play a "tremendous ovation." Miami liked the play in English, and Tampa was strong for a Spanish translation. Birmingham approved. Newark cheered, Bridgeport was a little stunned, San Francisco divided. Los Angeles found it pretty bald as a drama and not very interesting as propaganda. Detroit thought it dignified and worthwhile and Chicago, we hear, took it in their critical stride, but reported audience reaction as being definitely and noisily in the play's favor.[9]

The New York opening at the Adelphi Theatre was the major one and was attended by Hallie Flanagan, high WPA officials, theatre celebrities, drama critics, and Sinclair Lewis, among others. The audience received this production with enthusiasm and the cast took repeated curtain calls.

Sinclair Lewis had worked exceptionally hard on the Adelphi production of *It Can't Happen Here*, casting the play and rehearsing the actors. He certainly realized by the end of the play that it was a success, and later he must have been gratified by its nationwide reception: the Boston company toured Pittsfield, Holyoke, North Hempstead, Worcester, Fitchburg, Brockton, Springfield and Lowell; the Detroit production travelled to Ann Arbor, Flint, Lansing, Saginaw, Kalamazoo and Grand Rapids. Companies from Los Angeles, Miami and Tacoma also toured. In four months the travelling companies played to a quarter of a million people, not counting the audiences of the Suitcase Theatre which was designed from the beginning to tour Long Island and played to nearly a quarter of a million itself. The parent Adelphi Company gave ninety-five performances to 110,000 people. All in all, *It Can't Happen Here* was given the equivalent of a run of 260 weeks, almost five years![10]

On opening night at the Adelphi the insistent call for the author was raised. As Lewis approached the footlights he began to receive the plaudits of the crowd. Six years earlier, awkward and fearful of stumbling, he had made his way down the red carpeted stairs in the Concert House in Stockholm to receive from King Gustav of Sweden a gold medal and a portfolio containing a certificate and a check for $48,000. Then it was the Nobel Prize for Literature, now it was the applause of an American audience, applause that would continue for a long time in many cities across the country. We may wonder as to which accolade gave Lewis greater pleasure. Lewis strove for the respect of the literary elite, partially and temporarily achieved it with the Nobel Prize, but found it ashes. Always more basically he sought for the adulation of the mass audience, but certainly not just for the celebrity and wealth it brought him. For *It Can't Happen Here* he received half of the token fifty-dollar-a-week fee allowed for author's royalty by the Federal Theatre, a grand total of $6,500.[11]

For the student of popular culture the career of Sinclair Lewis is an enlightening one. What it seems to reveal is the importance of the "set" from which the writer views his own work. For the popular artist it seems to be the drive for an audience which impels him, while the elite author, although not unaware of a potential audience, is more wrapped up in the creative act itself. In terms of craft, the popular artist seems to have no loyal adherence to forms and genres. Often the structure is weak: there has been almost as much criticism of the plot weakness of *Babbitt* as there has been of *Huckleberry Finn*. Both Lewis and Twain have been accused of putting incidents into their novels in no particular order, like beads on a string. At any rate we may assume that intricate, highly developed plots are often not the strong point of the popular artist, though baroque plotting is often the mark of the exploiter. The popular artist is also more than willing to try other genres and even other media. Sinclair Lewis wrote novels, short stories, essays, speeches, criticism, movie scripts, plays, and poems. It should be admitted that writers of all kinds, even the most elitist, try their hands at other genres. Henry James, for instance, shared Lewis's enthusiasm for the stage, and wrote plays which like most of Lewis's were not particularly successful. And William Faulkner, Lewis's fellow Nobel laureate, wrote many screenplays for the movie factories. Faulkner, somewhat like Graham Greene, seems to have been able to adopt two personae. Like Greene, Faulkner could switch from serious artist to writer of "entertainments" with seeming ease. The popular writer, *always* interested in the audience, has no such schizophrenic defense; Sinclair Lewis was always the same and always put the same amount of energy and interest into the project at hand. But Lewis's sense of proprietorship in what he had written, like that of most popular writers, was weak. The popular artist tries his skill at other genres and media but he is also happy to let others translate his work from its original genre into another, and is not usually over-critical of the result, for he is more interested in audience than in anything else. The popular artist also seems to get involved in other facets of the communication process: he seems almost to need the direct stimulation of the audience, unlike the explorer who is stimulated only by the cash register. Sinclair Lewis acted in *It Can't Happen Here* and in other plays, and even wrote and preached sermons. Contemporary popular artists appear frequently on television talk shows, just as Lewis earlier had often been on the radio. And finally, popular artists are usually fully aware of the commercial possibilities of what they do and feel no shame over large incomes. This is one attribute they share with the exploiters. Sinclair Lewis gloried in the wealth his activities brought him; he neither hid from his success nor agonized over it.

The popular artist, it may be said in summary, shows little adherence to genres, and little loyalty to his own writings. He experiments with other genres trying to widen his audience, and lets others transform his work into other genres and other media. He is honestly interested in financial success but is even more interested in the size of his audience. He reaches out to the people; he does not callously try to exploit them. The problem of identifying this popular artist is the basic one, and the single criterion of sales success is not solely applicable. Sales figures will reveal the sub-literary set—Robbins, Wallace, *et al.* But other and worthier figures have had books on the best seller lists. Perhaps the criteria derived from a study of the career of Sinclair Lewis can help us appreciate Gore Vidal, Truman Capote, and similar marginal figures.

Notes

1. Mark Schorer, *Sinclair Lewis: An American Life* (New York, 1961), p. 68. This massive biography is the source of all factual statements in this paper not otherwise credited; any writer on Lewis must present Mr. Schorer a bouquet of *Ibids*.

2. Mark Schorer, "Afterword" in the Signet Classic Edition of Sinclair Lewis, *Babbitt* (New York, 1961), p. 324.

3. The figures for *Main Street* are from A. B. Maurice, "Sinclair Lewis," *Bookman* LXIX (March, 1929), p. 52. The sale figure for *Babbitt* is from Schorer's "Afterword" to the Signet Classic Edition of that work. The totals for *Arrowsmith*

and *Elmer Gantry* are from Schorer's *Sinclair Lewis*, p. 474 and those for *Kingsblood Royal* from p. 759.

4. H. L. Mencken, *The American Mercury, passim.* Joseph Wood Krutch, "Sinclair Lewis," *Nation* CLXXII (February 24, 1951), 179–180.

5. Schorer, *Sinclair Lewis*, p. 249.

6. *Ibid.*, p. 753.

7. *New York Times*, February 23, 1936, Section LV, p. 1.

8. *New York Times*, October 28, 1936, p. 30.

9. Burns Mantle, "Lewis Drama in Eighteen U. S. Theatres," *Chicago Sunday Tribune*, November 8, 1936, Section 7, p. 13, quoted in Jane DeHart Mathews, *The Federal Theatre, 1935–1939: Plays, Relief, and Politics* (Princeton, New Jersey, 1967), pp. 99–100. See also Hallie Flanagan, *Arena* (New York, 1940) for a lively account of the production of Lewis's play.

10. Mathews, pp. 100–101.

11. *New York Times*, October 28, 1936, p. 30.

Baedekers, Babbittry, and Baudelaire
David G. Pugh*

If T. S. Eliot published a Baedeker's Guide to the landmarks of a spiritual wasteland in 1922, then the same year Sinclair Lewis constructed a sociologist's Ideal-Type to analyze a cultural wasteland, both on Main Street in smalltown Gopher Prairie and in Zip City, George F. Babbitt's Zenith, Winnemac, U.S.A. The first one-fourth of the novel closely follows Babbitt's daily routines and rituals, as the individual's symbolic behavior surfaces in his use of artifacts and in his social contacts, revealing the spirit and unspoken assumptions of an era. Often, one vivid image will encapsulate an entire spectrum of attitudes, as does the billboard of Dr. Eckleburg's eyeglasses over the valley of ash heaps at the dump outside New York City. Once visualized in the pages of F. Scott Fitzgerald's, *The Great Gatsby*, the eyes become a quick shorthand reference, a symbol of the wasteland for the reader to absorb, to recall, and along with Eliot, to have "shored against my ruins."

Is the image of George F. Babbitt, Realtor, still this encapsulated shorthand? Even though Lewis predicted accurately in a letter to his publisher (Dec. 17, 1920) that in two years the country would be talking of "Babbittry," is it still a *potent imagent*, (as is Don Quixote, tilting at windmills, impossible dream or not) or has it joined many others, once

*From *The Twenties: Fiction, Poetry, Drama*, ed. Warren French (Deland, Fla: Everett Edwards Press, 1975), 87–99. Reprinted by permission of the author and editor.

trippingly on the tongue,—a Pecksniff? a Malaprop?—now smelling of the academic lamp or attic dust? Lewis, in his 1930 Nobel Prize address, himself accused the American Literary Establishment of preferring its literature "clear and cold and pure and very dead," and offered Henry Wadsworth Longfellow as a horrible example, from fifty years before, of such embalmed, boring, genteel artistry. Should we now, another half-century later, insert Lewis' name in Longfellow's place? Is Babbittry dead? Geoffrey Moore, an Englishman, writing a few years after Lewis' death, asked if we had outgrown *Babbitt*—had it gone the way of the flivvers, Kitty Hawks, and the unfenced prairies; . . . yet hypocrisy, provincialism, prejudice, all forms of materialism, have only changed their clothes, (and not just in America). Babbitt: alive, readable? . . . or cold, boring, and very dead?

Recently, attempts to interest new readers in Lewis have emphasized his "sociological imagination," his documentation, his early use of concepts and reportorial devices since popularized by David Riesman, C. Wright Mills, and Erving Goffman, among others, such descriptions of behavior as Inner- and Outer-directed, as alienated, or as gamesmanship. Ever since the Lynds, analyzing Muncie, Indiana as *Middletown* (1927, 1936), social scientists have fashioned their prose techniques after ones Lewis had already used, so that now he reads (more so than in 1922) "just like a sociology book." Sophistication about peer-group pressures is much more likely these days, when sociograms of who prefers whom for "best friend" can be charted and interpreted for fifth graders. There are still signs around us today revealing a wasteland of boredom and conformity, and we may be even more willing than readers in 1922 to look for symbolic significance in ordinary behavior, to "read meaning into" surface details of a small incident in daily life.

Do the surface incidents in *Babbitt* (or *Main Street*, 1920) provide enough cues and contexts to relate them to our habitual daily behavior? Are the images in Eliot's *Waste Land* also discernible in Lewis' prose reporting life in the "Unreal City," *Zenith*? Will observing George F. Babbitt serve as an objective correlative, a tangible image for a feeling, a state of emotion, as Eliot theorized? As readers, are we able to recognize part of ourselves in Babbitt's behavior? Can we simultaneously discern the "state of feeling" Lewis furnished us? A reader can obtain an image of daily life from a Sears Roebuck or Monkey Ward catalog, although the esthetic goal of also deriving a state of feeling from any image may require noticing rhetorical forms of presentation which are somewhat different from those found in most sociology books.

One way of getting at the "state of feeling" evoked by Babbitt is to compare the original impact with the retrospective interpretations after his death. *Babbitt* was read in 1922 partly by young rebels fleeing the bourgeois middle class backgrounds in which they had grown up, venerating H. L. Mencken, who having coined a label, the *Booboisie*, quite understandably felt in his review of the novel that *Babbitt* was a "social document of a high order." May Sinclair, acknowledging the realistic effects, predicted, however, that "though nobody will recognize himself . . . everybody will recognize somebody else." One small phrase in her review is suggestive of our reactions to the book so many years later. "You can smell the ash heaps behind every house." This minor image can evoke a not so minor feeling in anyone who has removed large clinkers and either powdery or wet ash from a coal-fired grate furnace; it evokes a multi-sensual kinesthetic effect—but most of us now have experience only with oil or gas heat.

Lewis may be ". . . cold, and very dead" for readers today, unless they can enter the social world the novelist very clearly created at the time he wrote. This holds true for any non-contemporary work. If Thackeray mentions a young woman wearing lavender gloves and a yellow scarf with a purple and wine-red shot silk dress or notes that there were fires (fireplaces) in the bedrooms of a house, some awareness of the significance, of the *variation from the norm*, is helpful. Heated bedrooms are not likely to seem luxurious to a reader today. Babbitt's clearglass bathroom towel-racks set in nickel wall brackets have to be compared to porcelain or wood-dowel racks, (the 1922 norm) to feel their "uptodateness."

Literature is not so much a mirror which *reflects* life realistically as it is a prism or lens which *refracts* selected, condensed aspects of thought and feeling. This refraction exaggerates, as does a convex mirror such as a shiny chrome hubcap, and one frequent justification for scholarly labor is the need to give a reader in a later time some sense of the actual knowledge of the world possessed by the readers at the time of original composition or publication—knowing that it is, indeed, an impossible dream to evoke 100% of it. Any work which has staying power transcends these limitations and offers enough internal clues of tone and context to remain intelligible without recourse to guide books or prefatory essays or "bogus" footnotes like Eliot's to *The Waste Land*. But isn't a Baedeker for a foreign city similar to footnotes and explanations? Should one read it before a trip, or carry it along and stop at every street corner, or read it afterwards?

Mark Schorer, summing up his massive 867 page biography of Lewis, emphasizes Lewis' *documentation*, his creation of Babbitt, showing the "standardization of business culture and the stultification of morals under middle class convention," concluding that as Americans, even today, we can hardly imagine ourselves without drawing upon Lewis' writings as a background. As recently as April 1968, in a CBS TV documentary filmed in Duluth, Minnesota, a Lions Club heard Pat Hingle deliver a speech spoken by Babbitt to a Booster Club in the 1922 novel and reacted favorably to its sentiments. His values live on. D. J. Dooley, on the other hand, feels that it is not documentation, but satiric exaggeration, the shaping by genre and formal technique, by literary convention, which enables the book to affect us, by *intensifying* and *ordering* our experiences, pointing out to us, Baedeker-fashion, what we then perceive. If art historian Ernst Gombrich is right that in viewing a painting "the innocent eye sees nothing," because it is both naive and untutored in what to look for, the same conclusion seems doubly applicable to the reader of such a genre as satire. How do you tell photographic realism from the satirical warping of the shiny hubcap?

Lewis, especially in later life, when he went camping with some Duluth real estate men, gave evidence of liking much of George F. Babbitt as an individual. Some of his readers, in 1922 and later, selected only the details they wished to dislike; and many times over the past several decades, particularly during the booming enrollments of the 1960's, academics in English departments have snorted at poor Babbitt playing with his new toy, an automobile dashboard cigar lighter, while themselves fingering the latest cassette or photocopy gadget and measuring the zip in their department in quantified terms. (They are more likely to recognize Babbittry and Boosterism in an administrator's request for the total number of student credit hours produced in their classes, however.)

Any cluster of literary or cultural conventions can trip up "the innocent eye"; conventions, by their nature, are often common, unobtrusive, accepted as a matter of course, as unspoken agreements by writer and reader, speaker and hearer, agreements "to act as if X were really so," even though both know that it is not true.

When Lewis mentions the German immigrant farm women in Gopher Prairie waiting patiently for their men while sitting in the wagons hitched outside the saloon on Main Street, we can, fifty years later, recognize some shift in the cultural "convention." (Don't kid yourself, though, that all the wives would now be in the bar, too.) Lewis was capable, even as late as 1949, failing in health, two years before his death, of recording significant small changes in the details of daily life, changes in fashion and cultural conventions. On returning from a year in Italy, he noticed that men's clothing was more colorful, that moccasins were worn in public *even* by elderly men, and that TV was becoming common in bars. In an introduction to David L. Cohn's *The Good Old Days* (1939), a collection of materials from old Sears, Roebuck catalogs, Lewis himself judges the value of reporting "things," the social and material surface of life. He put it this way: "Mankind is always more interested in living than in Lives. . . . By your eyebrow pencils, your encyclopedias, and your alarm clocks shall ye be known."

There are, in addition to cultural conventions, cues for the reader in the conventions and techniques of humor: dialect, exaggeration, juxtaposition, all embodied in this sample by Finley Peter Dunne, creating the comments of Mr. Dooley, an Irishman in a tavern on Archey Road back of the stockyards in Chicago at the turn of the century—the cultural tradition for Mayor Daley, if you please. Discoursing to the bartender and all the others, Mr. Dooley packs into one sentence many of the shifts of tone which let us know that satire, even with a straight face, is not the same as a tape recorder set next to the draft beer spigot. The subject is the benefits of progress and inventions during the reign of Queen Victoria: "An' th' invintions—th' steam-injine, an' th' printin'-press an' th' cotton-gin an' th' gin sour, an' th' bicycle an' th' flyin' machine an' th' nickel-in-th'-slot machine an' th' Croker machine an' th' sody-fountain an'—crownin' wur-ruk iv our civilization—th' cash ray-gisther." Readers can leap the seventy year barrier here by noting the contrasts and the build-ups: locomotives to one-person wheels, the pun on gin, the latest (airplane experiments) to the less lofty items, including the New York City political machine of Boss Croker, from the productive to the consumptive—sody fountains—and finally to the basis of it all, money. This is not too far a cry from the satirical accumulations of detail in both *Main Street* and *Babbitt*.

Some critics, even in the twenties, perceived Lewis as sharing one traditional frame with Eliot, feeling that both men evoked comparison with Dante's *Inferno*. Such a suggestion for reading a work "places" it, offering a perspective for the innocent eye. Alfred Kazin has suggested that the "sheer terror immanent in the commonplace" makes Lewis' picture of Babbitt's unsuccessful rebellion and return to the values of conformity and boredom more terrifying than some of Faulkner. Lewis was reacting against a romanticizing taste which was either interested only in the distant (long ago or far away) or could treat the commonplace only by glamourizing, falsifying, sentimentalizing or prettifying it. This "literary" tone contrasts with the clichés Babbitt and his cronies use, or with Eliot's colloquial description of Lil in the pub or of Madame Sosostris with her *wicked* pack of cards, drawing ironically on both the older use by non-card playing Methodists and the more contemporary use as a term of approval. Today, furnishing a Baedeker for Babbitt's desert (placing it in the tradition of the dark night of the soul would be a bit much) and sharpening the reader's reactions to the details in texture and surface, the effects of language, may be the most effective helpful guides.

"JUG, JUG" TO DIRTY EARS

One major problem in reading a Lewis novel after fifty years have passed concerns its accessibility. Eliot, for instance, footnoted *The Waste*

Land in 1922 to make it a thicker book, and in doing so mentions much which he assumed was out-of-the-way reference: Jessie Weston's *From Ritual to Romance*, Tarot, Fisher-Kings, and allusions to Elizabethan drama. He did *not* footnote (although college undergraduate texts now wisely do so) references to the City of London banking district, paintings, St. Augustine, Hamlet-Ophelia, *the Tempest*, the Bible, or the meaning of the nightingale's cry, "Jug, Jug." Lewis, also, does not explain allusions, mimicry or traditional references that he assumed would be clear. For the reader today, these sounds may well fall on dirty ears, which miss the tone, just as the innocent eye fails to perceive the structure and symbolic shorthand behind the surface "things" in a painting. Isn't a stock response to "Jug, Jug" likely to link it to moonshine whiskey, hillbillies, or maybe a crock? Or, for those more genteel, not in associations to L'il Abner or Daisy Mae in the comics, but possibly to a link with a loaf of bread and a Thou under a tree somewhere?

In *The Waste Land*, a brief sample of the multi-leveled problem is the reference, which Eliot notes only to an Australian Ballad, for "O the moon shone bright / on Mrs. Porter / and on her daughter / They wash their *feet* in soda water." A Romantic American Indian Maiden often sung about in Eliot's youth in St. Louis, Mo. was Pretty Red Wing, and the lyrics of the refrain indicated that the moon shines bright on pretty Red Wing, with a lot of sighing and crying and some dying thrown in. The opening lines, however, use a fairy-tale convention which was soon turned obscenely into an infantry marching song. There once was an Indian maid, who said she wasn't afraid . . . the military version (known to American Legionnaires and high school students between the wars) continued "to lie on the grass . . ." etc., etc. Old Wives' Tales and such Southern folklorists as William Faulkner have also sensitized readers nowadays to the effects of lying out under the naked moon, like Eula Varner and others in Yoknapatawpha County. Such echoes of old popular songs may fall on deaf or innocent ears now, just as the title of Faulkner's short story "That Evening Sun Go Down" (which includes a reference to St. Louis in the text) may escape any linkage with "St. Louis Blues." Lurking even further under the surface of Eliot's supposed Australian ballad is the question of tone which shows up in the reference to "feet" as a euphemism and to the soda water as a possible douche or VD prophylaxis. Mrs. Porter can be a conventional reference for brothel-keeper. A reader who picks up the ballad associations only, classifying it as a song of former love, may have enough to move through Eliot's mind-set here, but some of the "Jug, Jug," is falling on dirty ears.

When George F. Babbitt, dressing for work in the first few pages of the novel, puts in his pocket a loose leaf address notebook containing many items, including a curious inscription: DSSDMYPDF (an item

Lewis uses the whole paragraph to build up to and leaves unexplained), the function of the detail, like the function of the ballad for Eliot, is clear enough from the context without a footnote—it is a motto or a reminder to himself. Does it gain from a gloss? Lewis wrote to his publisher (Dec. 28, 1920) that Babbitt would be a GAN about a TBM, and we have not lost the facility for using abbreviations over the intervening decades. It is psychologically fitting that Babbitt himself do such things and that in this Great American Novel the Tired Business Man may be telling himself "Don't Say Something Dumb-Mouthed You Poor Damn Fool."

Lewis indicated in an interview later published in the *University of Kansas City Review* (1958) by Allen Austin that he had deliberately had Carol Kennicott in *Main Street*, decorate a room in bad taste to show that while she was bright, she was not *that* bright. The old golden oak table, brocaded chairs, and family photographs were replaced with a japanese obi hung on the maize wall, sapphire velvet pillows with gold bands, and in keeping with the yellow and blue color scheme, a squat blue jar placed on a square cabinet, between yellow candles. Since Lewis arranged the list in this order, ending climactically with the jar, a reader today might have some contextual cues for the "bad taste" in her decorating.

When Chum Frink (the "poet") tells his fellow Booster Club members that they ought to Capitalize Culture (supporting the symphony orchestra for instance), is the pun for capital as $ and capital as emphasis—big letter C—sufficiently clear? Babbitt's son, Ted, was named for the President in office at his birth, Teddy Roosevelt, a good liberal reform Republican. Even this small detail gives some insight into George F's penchant for conforming to current fashions, for admiring the powerful, and for respecting the Great Institutions of American Life.

Lewis could be blatant in his choice of names or his characteronyms. The evangelist, Billy Sunday, turned ever so slightly into Mike Monday preaching at a revival meeting. Babbitt was first tentatively named George Pumphrey, then Fitch, but whether Lewis intended to evoke all the associations since discovered in the sound of his final name, Babbitt, is unanswerable. Does the name currently suggest any of the following— B. T. Babbitt Household Cleaner (and who remembers Bab-O and Sapolio?); a frictionless metal used in machine tool work (the Realtor in the gears of Commerce); *babble*, as the talk in the novel goes on and on; or *babyish*, as his details of dreaming at the beginning are added to later in the novel? As with reading a Baedeker *afterward*, these can be fitted into the experience of reading the novel on recalling it, but do they jump out crying "Jug, Jug" on first reading?

When Genevieve Taggard, commenting upon a machine age exhibition of artists in New York, quoted one artist, Louis Lozowick, approvingly from the viewpoint of the *New Masses*, the Marxist magazine she was writing for (July 1927), she used the word "plastic" in a different sense than it is likely to have for many readers now: "The artist must objectify the dominant experience of our epoch in plastic terms that possess value for more than this epoch alone." (Printed in F. J. Hoffman, *The Twenties*, p. 291.) Here "plastic" seems to have favorable connotations of shapable and adaptable, without the negative, imitative, unnatural, unfeeling associations more likely today. Does Lewis, conveying the tedium of the porch swing and the mosquitoes on a hot summer night in Gopher Prairie, or the boredom and ennui of George Babbitt as he moves daily through his "plastic" life—in the recent sense—objectify the emotional experience for the reader so that it now possesses value for us? Just such shifts in the tonal resonance for common words can impede our access to an earlier work, Eliot's, Lewis' or that of any other author.

Lewis' most widely recognized technique, however, is the catalog, probably epitomized in the two views of Dyer's drug store in *Main Street*, when both Carol and Bea Sorenson (a Swedish farm girl just coming into town who becomes the Kennicott hired girl or maid) see greatly different details for the soda fountain. Carol's "electric lamp with the red and green and curdled yellow shade over the greasy marble fountain," becomes Bea's "huge fountain of lovely marble with the biggest shade you ever saw—all different kinds of colored glass stuck together; and the soda spouts they were silver, and they came right out of the bottom of the lamp shade!" In *Babbitt*, this device was augmented by the description of daily rituals, dressing, starting the car, filling the gas tank on the drive downtown, each with its own style of ceremonial behavior and speech. These devices offered readers in the 1920's a fresh way of looking at the routines of life around them, but they were not likely to accept that view as factually accurate, since they could discount exaggeration on the basis of their own experiences. While they might find Veblen's notions of conspicuous consumption should lead them to the conclusions, as Anthony Hilfer puts it, that Babbitt, like his dashboard cigar lighter, was decorative but non-productive, and that many of the real estate subdivisions really were the way Lewis described them, they knew life around them and how people actually spoke. They could recognize the half-truths and mimicry on a different plane of experiential evidence than we do fifty years later, when we must pay more attention to stylistic devices and stock responses in order to recognize Babbitt as a real toad, maybe, but in an imaginary garden. Some readers and critics in the past have reversed this order; Lewis reported parts of a real garden, but created a cardboard toad. In contrast to this, there are still some students, after finishing their reading, who will sigh, "but he sounds just like my father."

The ultimate question, then, for investing time and energy in reading *Babbitt* or about a woman's life in a small town before the automobile changed things, as in *Main Street,* is whether or not the plastic terms, the technique and surface texture of the novels, clear in their own epoch, can transmit to a later time a feeling about values, ennui, a wasteland or a wasted life. Do the details we notice in reading *order* and *intensify* our own experience(s)? Do we experience, and not just cognitively recognize, the stultification, the boredom, the desire for escape, and gain insight into what Lewis (at age 46) writing to his publisher (Dec. 28, 1920) called Babbitt's life of compromises: "He is all of us Americans at 46, prosperous but worried . . . wanting—passionately—to seize something more than motorcars and a house *before it's too late."*

The opening paragraphs of the novel show Babbitt dreaming of a faery child before the alarm goes off in the morning. In the last sentences of the novel, Babbitt, dreaming now while wide awake, tells his son to live life however he wishes, "Go ahead . . . The world is yours." The myth that youth will be better off dies hard in this country. But his own motto, in the small loose-leaf notebook in his pocket is not the Rabelaisian motto over the abbey of Theleme (masterfully ironic satiric statement about Calvinistic predestination in itself)—*fais ce que voudras* (Do what you will). The notebook page, impermanently recorded, loose-leaf, as Babbitt's magic motto, his talisman to ward off evil, his rabbit's foot, is DSSDMYPDF. And this is the way the world ends, not with a bang, but a whimper. (Which quotes another tag line that, like Dr. Eckleburg's view of the ashheaps, we often use as a fragment to shore against our ruins.)

It is a whimper of and for the main character and the society in the novel, not necessarily for a great part of the psyche of the reader. What *Babbitt,* as a good read, can become for us now is a fragment shored against the ruins, against our own psychological memories, our own potential half-forgotten dreams, our own responses to the Sears' and Ward's ads in the Sunday paper. To make this possible requires revivifying, recreating some of the era of 1910–1922 and of attitudes toward spiritual wastelands and backyard ashheaps then, and also requires paralleling those ash heaps from our own experiences.

As Eliot's old man epitomizes it in "Gerontion," "Whatever is kept must be adulterated." We cannot help but adulterate what a reader of 1922 might have responded to, and we cannot help but add, with an uninnocent eye, not only our own experiences (plastic and otherwise), but also those conventions, literary frames, traditional references, ("Jug, Jug!"), which enable us to sense the boredom, as well as the pleasures of George F. Babbitt's day in the life.

Some travelers may require a Baedeker before the trip, rather than afterward. Even knowing what to look for may not completely suppress the potential for inattentive boredom. The motivation of nostalgia, particularly for an era prior to one's birth, is a very tricky bit of magic. How does Lewis show us How We Live Today? The best advice before picking up the book is that which Eliot uses to close the first section of *The Waste Land*: Baudelaire's Preface (about ennui) to *Fleurs du Mal*:

> You know him, [boredom], hypocrite lecteur, mon semblable, mon frere. [My hypocritical reader, my double (or shadow), my brother.]

Kingsblood Royal and the Black "Passing" Novel
Robert E. Fleming*

After winning the Nobel Prize in 1930, Sinclair Lewis's career turned sharply downward. Between 1930 and 1947 only the anti-Fascist novel *It Can't Happen Here* (1935) attracted the sort of popular and critical attention accorded the five major novels of the 1920s. Clearly, when he began to write *Kingsblood Royal* (1947), Lewis needed a success and thus returned to a formula that had served him well in the past. All of his best novels, with the possible exception of *Dodsworth* (1929), focused on a significant stratum of American society or an American institution—the small town, the businessman, the scientist, religion—and all dealt with subject matter that had previously been treated by other authors. That Lewis was never so much an innovator as he was a skillful modifier of themes that had been used before is exemplified by *Main Street* (1920), whose roots extend to E. W. Howe's *The Story of a Country Town* (1883) and Joseph Kirkland's *Zury: The Meanest Man in Spring County* (1887). Similarly, Lewis was somewhat indebted to Henry James and William Dean Howells in writing *Babbitt* (1922) and *Dodsworth* (1929) and to Harold Frederic's *The Damnation of Theron Ware* (1896) in writing *Elmer Gantry* (1927). For *Kingsblood Royal*, Lewis turned to James Weldon Johnson's *The Autobiography of an Ex-Coloured Man* (1912) and, to a lesser extent, other novels dealing with the same theme of a black person passing for white.

By the late 1940s interest in Afro-American authors and their themes was strong. Richard Wright had opened the door by becoming the first black writer recommended to members of Book of the Month Club; both *Native Son* (1940) and *Black Boy* (1945) became best sellers. Lewis chose for his own "Negro novel" the theme of passing for white, a favorite concern of Afro-American authors since William Wells Brown's *Clotel*,

---

*This essay was written specifically for this volume and appears here by permission of the author.

or the President's Daughter (1853). Two prominent white authors had also employed the theme: William Dean Howells's *An Imperative Duty* (1892) focuses on the problems of a woman with a trace of Negro blood who is passing for white, and Mark Twain's *Pudd'nhead Wilson* (1894) hinges on the substitution of a baby with some Negro blood for his master's son and heir. The Harlem Renaissance of the 1920s saw a group of novels about passing: Walter White's *Flight* (1926), James Weldon Johnson's *Autobiography of an Ex-Coloured Man* (first published in 1912, but republished in 1927 by Knopf), Jessie Fauset's *Plum Bun* (1928), and Nella Larsen's *Passing* (1929).

Because of his interest in liberal causes, Lewis had known two of these black authors personally since both James Weldon Johnson and Walter White were executives of the National Association for the Advancement of Colored People. Lewis met Johnson in New York City during the twenties and corresponded with him occasionally.[1] However, with Walter White, Lewis formed a warm friendship. Lewis wrote a favorable comment for the dust jacket of White's first novel, *The Fire in the Flint* (1924), but later told White that he preferred *Flight*, which introduced him to the passing novel. Charles F. Cooney, in an article tracing the literary friendship between Lewis and White, has speculated on whether Neil Kingsblood might "to a limited extent, . . . have been based on Walter White, who once was referred to by Lewis as a 'voluntary' Negro."[2] In addition to serving as a possible model for Kingsblood, White helped Lewis by introducing him to prominent black intellectuals and supplying material from the files of the NAACP while Lewis was working on *Kingsblood Royal*.

While the novel of passing has had a long history, we need go back no further than Charles W. Chesnutt's *The House Behind the Cedars* (1900) to see both the strengths and the weaknesses of the type. The difficulties experienced by characters in the passing novel may be roughly divided into two categories, the practical and the psychological. Practical difficulties include the fear of recognition by someone from one's past, the danger of being unmasked if one maintains contact with friends or relatives who are known to be black, the chance that one will be recognized because of traits which folklore attributes to the black race, and the possibility of a "throwback" among one's offspring—a black baby born to parents who appear white. Psychological traumata include the guilt and sense of loss brought on by the abandonment of friends and relatives, the feeling that valuable parts of one's cultural heritage have been left behind, the loss of self-esteem inherent in denying a part of oneself, and finally, the feeling that one has sold out or deserted under fire, leaving other members of the race to wage the war against prejudice and oppression. Chesnutt's Rena Walden, who has passed for white, is preparing to marry a wealthy white southerner when she is

trapped by practical and psychological obstacles: she must choose between visiting her seriously ill mother or ignoring her mother's need.
When she visits her mother, the plot becomes melodramatic: her fiancé
discovers that she is black and rejects her; Rena is approached by a
second suitor, a mulatto who objectifies her own view of herself as a
turncoat; and she dies after wandering in a swamp, which represents
the morass of psychological problems that have trapped her. Rena exemplifies the tragic mulatto caught between two cultures and ultimately
unable to belong to either, but Chesnutt emphasizes the practical nature
of her difficulties.

The next passing novel, the best work of its type and one with
which Lewis was almost certainly familiar, was James Weldon Johnson's
The Autobiography of an Ex-Coloured Man, written from the point of
view of a character who successfully passes for white. The real drama
of *The Autobiography* is internal, as Johnson's significantly nameless
protagonist is repeatedly forced to choose between identifying with the
race of his beloved Negro mother or his white father. He abandons his
boyhood ambition to distinguish himself as a "great coloured man" by
becoming a composer of racial music, but he is ultimately dissatisfied
with his life as "an ordinarily successful white man who has made a
little money" and fears that he has "sold [his] birthright for a mess of
pottage."[3] Other novelists of the 1920s, White, Fauset, and Larsen,
followed Johnson's lead, breaking no new ground. Their novels affirm,
as Robert A. Bone has noted, that "the invariable outcome, in fiction if
not in fact, is disillusionment with life on the other side of the line, a
new appreciation of racial values, and an irresistible longing to return to
the Negro community."[4] Bone classifies their novels as productions of
"the rear guard" and suggests that none of the three is worthy of comparison with Johnson's book.

Lewis breathed life back into the passing novel by reversing the
dramatic situation that provided the plot for the earlier works. Where
Walter White's Mimi Daquin and Nella Larsen's Clare Kendry move
from the black world into the white, there to live with a constant fear
of exposure, Neil Kingsblood moves from the white world into the
black. In effect, Lewis's novel asks what happens to the descendants of
those light-skinned Negroes who decided to pass for white during an
earlier stage of American history. Since Neil is only briefly in the
position of being an undiscovered Negro in a white world, the emphasis
of *Kingsblood Royal*, like that of *The Autobiography of an Ex-Coloured
Man*, is on psychological reactions rather than practical difficulties. Lewis
probes Neil's mind as he hesitates, poised between the white world and
the black, and the result is a thorough updating of an important theme
in American literature.

Although Walter White was a personal friend of Lewis, *Flight* does not approach the artistry of Johnson's *Autobiography of an Ex-Coloured Man,* and evidence in *Kingsblood Royal* suggests that Lewis used *The Autobiography* as a significant source. Both novels begin in the North, where there is theoretically less prejudice than in the South. Both protagonists trace their black genes through their mothers, early display dislike and contempt toward black people, and are crushed when classified with the race they have helped to degrade. Both novels employ as counterpoint a black contemporary, an intellectual acquaintance whose worth is recognized only after the protagonist discovers his own black heritage. Such parallels continue through the two novels. Lewis was too much the skilled professional author to simply reverse the earlier passing novel of Johnson, and he made *Kingsblood Royal* uniquely his own, but Johnson's influence is pervasive.

The Autobiography begins in a small unnamed Connecticut town to which the protagonist's father has moved his light-skinned mistress and his son away from the racism of Georgia, where the boy was born. *Kingsblood Royal* takes place in Grand Republic, Minnesota, another northern town which prides itself on being far more liberal than the South in its racial attitudes. In spite of the supposed open-mindedness of their communities, a great deal of racial bigotry exists, and both the nameless main character of *The Autobiography* and Neil Kingsblood grow up with distinct prejudices against Negroes. As a boy, the ex-colored man called his black classmates "niggers" and on one occasion participated in a physical attack on a group of black children. Neil, even as an adult, has definite prejudices against his black maid Befreda, the black men who date her, and the black soldiers he has seen in the army.

Both characters find themselves tied to this despised race by their mothers. The ex-colored man had always realized that his mother's skin was darker than his and that her hair was not so fine, but he had failed to recognize that these were racial characteristics. Neil realizes after he unravels the secret of his ancestry that his own mother has always been quiet and withdrawn, as if she had some dread secret and that his maternal grandmother, who he has always thought displayed "gypsy" characteristics, has signs of her Negro ancestry. "Mummy, Mrs. Staubermeyer says I'm a nigger. . . . Am I a nigger?"[5] asks Neil's daughter Biddy, when she confronts the racism of neighbors, echoing the ex-colored man, who as a boy asks, "Mother, mother, tell me, am I a nigger?" (17).

Before being unmasked, the ex-colored man has regarded the most intelligent of his classmates with a sort of good-humored contempt because of his race and has given him the nickname "Shiny," which Johnson ironically creates from the racial slur, "shine." After he realizes that he too is black, the protagonist regards "Shiny" as a sort of double, who later achieves the greatness as a black man that his lighter friend only dreams of. Neil has a similar acquaintance in his background, Emerson

Woolcape, who admired Neil in school even though Neil had nearly ignored Woolcape. After learning that he has Negro blood, Neil rediscovers Woolcape, who has become a sort of double for Neil in that he has achieved the same rank of captain during the war. But Woolcape is better educated than Neil and is practicting dentistry in Grand Republic. Like Neil, Woolcape looks white, but unlike him, Woolcape has always acknowledged his race. Like the ex-colored man, Neil has to admit that his Negro friend is his intellectual and moral superior. Both "Shiny" and Emerson Woolcape display sympathy and understanding for their friends who have recently discovered their racial backgrounds and attempt to make their lives as Negroes easier for them.

Johnson's novel is structured around the narrator's fruitless search for identity, as symbolized by the fact that he never tells the reader his name. By the end of the novel, a logical conclusion is that the narrator in fact does not know who he is, for he has changed his name and his way of life, taking on the protective coloration of his environment.[6] Neil's symbolic search for identity coincides with his literal research into his family origins, spurred on by his father, who asserts that "According to my dad's theory ... 'Kingsblood' was originally a kind of nickname for our forebears, indicating that they had the blood of kings— as you and I have!" (38–39). Neil's genealogical search for his royal origins leads to nothing, but when he follows his mother's family tree, he discovers a pioneer named Xavier Pic. His attempts to find out more about Pic lead to what might be called the revelation scene of *Kingsblood Royal*.

The revelation scene is a staple of the Afro-American novel. Even when the black protagonist is intellectually aware that he or she is black, such a scene brings home to the character just what it means to be black in America. The scene may feature violence as in the episode of Ralph Ellison's *Invisible Man* (1952), where the main character arrives at a meeting of prominent businessmen to deliver a speech and instead finds himself thrown into a prize fight with a group of tough black youngsters. It may be quiet and undramatic as when the heroine of Zora Neale Hurston's *Their Eyes Were Watching God* (1937) looks at a picture of herself with some playmates and is shocked to see that hers is the only black face. In *The Autobiography* the ex-colored man is unmasked when the principal of his school divides his class into white and "colored" and publicly rebukes the main character for joining the white group. Neil's revelation scene comes when he visits the Minnesota Historical Society for information about Xavier Pic, supposedly seeking information for a soldier who served under him during the war. Dr. Werweiss, a historian, tells him that Xavier Pic was "a full-blooded Negro" and that "in most Southern states and a few Northern ones, a 'Negro' is defined, by statute, as a person having even 'one drop of

Negro blood,' and according to that barbaric psychology, your soldier friend and any children he may have, no matter how white they look, are legally one-hundred-percent Negroes" (64–65). The revelation scene is a major trauma for Neil, as it is for most characters in Afro-American novels.

Since *Kingsblood Royal* is also a passing novel, the revelation scene is followed by what might be called a transformation scene. In passing novels, the main character must obviously have a light enough complexion so that he can pass for white. Frequently, like Neil and Walter White himself, the character may also have blue eyes and red or blond hair, so that nothing suggests he is not a pure Caucasian. Once the secret is known, however, the passing character finds his features being transformed, either in his own eyes or in the eyes of beholders, and he turns into an obvious Negro. The ex-colored man undergoes transformation after he has told the girl he loves about his racial background: "I felt her hand grow cold, and when I looked up, she was gazing at me with a wild, fixed stare as though I was some object she had never seen. Under the strange light in her eyes I felt that I was growing black and thick-featured and crimp-haired" (204). Neil's transformation takes place after he leaves the historical society and continues through several scenes. First he notices that a man is looking at him strangely on a streetcar and wonders if the man is about to denounce him as a Negro. In his hotel lobby he fears being unmasked if anyone notices the color of the half moons of his fingernails. Finally, in a fancy barber shop, he mistakes a barber's innocuous remarks about his curly hair for a racial taunt and notes with horror how, under the bright lights of the shop, the half moons of his fingernails have indeed taken on the telltale bluish color that folklore attributes to people with any African blood.

Once Neil has come to accept his split racial identity, he notes the same racial dualism that Johnson notes in *The Autobiography*. Thinking of himself as a black man, Neil can still be an eavesdropper on racial discussions just as Johnson's protagonist can. The ex-colored man, while sitting in the smoking car of a train traveling through the South, overhears a discussion between four men: two timid liberals, a fiery Civil War veteran, and a loud-mouthed bigot. Neil, before declaring his Negro blood, sits in on similar scenes, such as the luncheon at which Wilbur Feathering and Lucian Firelock, recent emigrants from Mississippi and Georgia, discuss the "Negro problem." Feathering is an outright racist, though he protests that "I don't hate the shines. . . . They're such sly, thievish monkeys, and they all dance good . . ." (200). Firelock, on the other hand, is what Feathering calls "one of those New Southern Liberals that claim it's okay to have niggers right at your house for dinner!" (200). Neil notes, as Johnson's ex-colored man did in the similar scene, that the racist has more courage and determination in his plans to stir up trouble for the Negroes than the liberal Firelock has in preaching moderation. It is on a similar occasion, the stag dinner of Grand Republic's most prominent men's club, that Neil finally decides to make his ancestry public.

Before the whites of Grand Republic, even the members of his own family, have been told about Neil's discovery, he confesses his Negro background to several black members of the community because he experiences a need to be introduced to what Johnson would call the "freemasonry of the race." Like Johnson's protagonist, Neil knows nothing about how to be a Negro, and as he moves about Grand Republic's black district, he is alternately attracted and repelled by the two sides of black character that he sees. On one side are Ash Davis, a chemist with a doctorate, Evan Brewster, pastor of the black church and holder of a Ph.D., and Sophie Concord, an attractive black nurse; these characters, like a Washington doctor who befriends the ex-colored man, have been successfully assimilated into white society. Yet Neil, like the ex-colored man, also feels that unassimilated black people, while they make him uncomfortable, live life more fully than more inhibited whites. One of Neil's boyhood memories is of seeing the Woolcapes on a picnic and feeling "that they were having more fun than his family ever had" (101). When he grows close to the Woolcapes, he finds that they are disappointingly like his own family. Yet characters like his former maid Belfreda or her tough boyfriend, a bootlegger and nightclub owner, remain exotic primitive figures that recall the spirit of the Harlem Renaissance. Neil's desultory forays into Grand Republic's Five Points area are less systematic than the ex-colored man's folkmusic collecting expedition to the South, but both activities serve the same purpose of allowing the two men to try to find their identities.

Finally, as in Johnson's *Autobiography* and most other passing novels, Neil Kingsblood cannot make his decision as to whether to remain in the white world in a vacuum. He must think not only of himself but of his wife Vestal and his daughter Biddy. Johnson's protagonist confessed his racial background to his wife before they became engaged; Neil, of course, confesses to Vestal after his research uncovers his roots. Neither woman is pleased with the news: the ex-colored man's future wife first flees from him to think things over before she returns to marry him, while Vestal alternately supports Neil and attacks him for embracing what she sees as a quixotic struggle against racism. In each book the family is isolated from both black and white society. Like the ex-colored man, who vows never to tell his secret because of what it would do to his children, Neil hesitates for a long time before announcing his discovery because he cannot condemn his daughter to the sort of discrimination that he is ready to face.

Lewis's book differs most sharply from Johnson's in the direction of the plot and in the ending. The ex-colored man has turned his back on his black identity and regretfully assumed a spurious white identity. Neil renounces the white world to confront the often painful reality of his black identity. Lewis creates a situation in which Neil, surrounded by a group of black friends and an assortment of white liberals, fights off the mob that has come to eject him and his family from their home in Sylvan Park. Thus, Lewis contends that times have changed since the 1920s, that one's race is no longer something that has to be hidden, that black people will defend their rights if necessary, and that well-meaning whites will join their Negro neighbors in a just cause.

Though a number of the first reviews were positive, *Kingsblood Royal* failed to revive Lewis's literary reputation completely. While he had put a great deal of effort into research for the book and had based it on a timely theme, Lewis had simply spent too little time on the actual writing—only five weeks for the rough draft, according to Mark Schorer.[7] Although he reworked his first draft extensively, *Kingsblood Royal* is not as carefully finished as Lewis's great novels of the 1920s. However, the intellectual concepts on which the book is based show that Lewis retained his basic ability as a satirist into the 1940s, and the novel continued to interest critics of the 1960s and 1970s.[8] Lewis's rare ability to trouble the conscience of the nation and thus capture the attention of the reading public is as manifest in *Kingsblood Royal* as it had been in works such as *Babbitt* or *Elmer Gantry*.

Notes

1. One letter from Lewis to Johnson, dated 21 May 1929, has been preserved in the James Weldon Johnson Collection in the Beinecke Library, Yale University. See Correspondence, Series I, Folder 291.

2. Charles F. Cooney, "Walter White and Sinclair Lewis: The History of a Literary Friendship," *Prospects: An Annual Journal of American Cultural Studies,* 1 (1975):71.

3. James Weldon Johnson, *The Autobiography of an Ex-Coloured Man* (New York: Knopf, 1927), 211. All future references to this novel are inserted parenthetically.

4. Robert A. Bone, *The Negro Novel in America* (New Haven and London: Yale University Press, 1965), 98.

5. Sinclair Lewis, *Kingsblood Royal* (New York: Random House, 1947), 330. All future references to this novel are inserted parenthetically.

6. In his own autobiography Johnson recalls that his brother nearly convinced him to use the title "The Chameleon," and he wondered if that title might have made his point more clearly. *Along This Way: The Autobiography of James Weldon Johnson* (New York: Viking, 1933), 238.

7. Mark Schorer, *Sinclair Lewis: An American Life* (New York, Toronto, London: McGraw-Hill, 1961), 748.

8. See, for example, Harry E. Hand, "The Rise of a Modern American Hero,"

Laurel Review 6 (Spring 1966):14–20; Edwin H. Cady, *The Light of Common Day: Realism in American Fiction* (Bloomington: Indiana University Press, 1971), 147–48; Sarah J. McCullough, "*Kingsblood Royal*: A Revaluation," *Sinclair Lewis Newsletter* 4 (Spring 1972):10–12; and Robert L. Coard, "Sinclair Lewis's *Kingsblood Royal*: A Thesis Novel for the Forties," *Sinclair Lewis Newsletter* 7–8 (1975–76):10–17.

The Sauk Centre Sinclair Lewis Didn't Write About

James Lundquist*

Every summer over a hundred thousand people pull off Interstate 94 at the Sauk Centre exit to visit the Sinclair Lewis Interpretive Center and to drive along the Original Main Street to Sinclair Lewis Avenue, where a left turn will bring them to the Sinclair Lewis Boyhood Home, now a National Historic Site. Some of these visitors may even want to inspect the restored Palmer House Hotel, where Lewis worked briefly (and superbly ineptly) as a night clerk. A mile or so east of town is Greenwood Cemetery and the Lewis family plot, where one tombstone reads:

SINCLAIR LEWIS

1885–1951

AUTHOR OF

"MAIN STREET"

On most afternoons during June, July, and August, two or three cars or trucks with out-of-state license plates can be found parked beside the cemetery gates. Tour guides at the Interpretive Center and the Boyhood Home soon become used to questions of a particular sort: Are any of Lewis's "characters" still living in the town? Is Sauk Centre still the grimly hypocritical prairie village that Lewis shows us through the eyes of Carol Kennicott in *Main Street*? And just how was Red Lewis turned into an alien cynic by the home town that rejected him when he was a boy and supposedly wanted to lynch him when he achieved his first great literary success as a man?

All of this attention is surprising considering that Sinclair Lewis has generally been regarded by his critics and biographers as one of the least autobiographical of American writers. And Lewis himself took great pains to emphasize that he was not writing directly about himself

*This essay was written specifically for this volume and appears here by permission of the author.

in any of his books and that even in *Main Street* he is not actually writing about Sauk Centre, claiming in his famous preface to the novel that "The story would be the same in Ohio or Montana, in Kansas or Kentucky or Illinois, and not very differently would it be told Up New York State or in the Carolina hills." Nonetheless, Lewis is profoundly associated with Sauk Centre in the popular imagination, and one could argue that he, more so than any of his contemporaries, is primarily remembered because of what he had to say about a particular place, a town that, as unlikely as it must once have seemed, has now become something of a literary shrine, a roadside attraction set in the rolling prairie, broken by extensive woodlots, that makes up much of Stearns County. Not Friendship Village exactly, and not all that pretty, but nice enough to make one wonder just what it was that set young Harry Lewis off and made his life a continual and ultimately futile flight from his native ground.

Mark Schorer faces this question at the outset in his biography of Lewis, *Sinclair Lewis: An American Life*, and asks "could a 'totally normal boyhood' have produced such a wild man, at once so mad and so unhappy?"[1] Schorer later documents the madness and the unhappiness, the compulsive drunkenness that again and again took Lewis to death's door (and apparently eventually killed him at age sixty-five), the pathetically failed marriages, the broken friendships, the cruel jokes, all the instances of deliberately bad manners that so often hurt Lewis's long-suffering friends. But what seems most disturbing is that despite his tortured life, Lewis never seemed to confront himself in the one way that could have helped—that is, through the very process of fiction, which just might have offered the kind of therapy that he most certainly needed. Schorer stresses that Lewis "was almost never to write subjective autobiography," and suggests by way of explanation that Lewis "was expelled from rather than repelled from his environment, ejected rather than rejecting. In him we have the doubly pathetic sight of a youth who is driven into an inner world even more bleak and barren than the exterior world that expelled him, who would gladly have chosen that world."[2] Schorer goes on to emphasize such early influences on the young Lewis as the cold, demanding father, the cruelty in the pranks played on the poor misfit of a boy by the other kids in town, and the general unwillingness of Lewis to fit in—all of this reasonably enough presented as a way of explaining what Lewis turned out to be.

But Schorer, despite providing a good physical description of the Sauk Centre Lewis knew, does not actually invite the reader to confront the "bleak and barren" world that was Sauk Centre and the larger environs of Stearns County during the last fifteen years of the nineteenth century when Lewis was living there. In failing to do so, Schorer as Lewis's major biographer overlooks the bizarre brutality of the world

Lewis knew, a world revealed through the local newspapers of the time as being grotesque, overwhelmed by "American nervousness," and obsessed with macabre events. This was an environment full of repulsion as far as Sinclair Lewis was concerned, and understanding its very nature, its very hideousness, is at least one way of coming to terms with Lewis's often disturbing lack of subjectivity and his ambivalent, often contradictory, relationship with Sauk Centre and rural Stearns County.

For Lewis, the town and the county in which it is located came to represent an odd force that pulled him this way and that throughout his life and work, a force that he perhaps unintentionally acknowledged in the title of the sincerely sentimental essay he wrote in 1931 for the fiftieth-anniversary issue of his high-school annual, "The Long Arm of the Small Town." This essay is in part a deliberate attempt by Lewis to answer those critics (mostly local) who charged that he had represented only one side of small-town life and that his main problem was that he never had any of the "normal fun" that boys were supposed to have during the time when he was growing up. And in response, Lewis said of himself, "I am quite certain that I could have been born and reared in no place in the world where I could have had more friendliness."[3] This statement, along with the accompanying description of a bucolic childhood involving picnics, the old swimming hole, and long fall rambles with a shotgun, is often taken at face value as an explanation of the "real way" Lewis felt toward his Minnesota origins—and there is no reason to doubt the seriousness of his intentions as he wrote the piece. But set against the facts of Lewis's youth and the testimony of *Main Street*, the idea of friendliness rings a little hollow and the metaphor of the "Long Arm" becomes downright sinister.

The Sauk Centre into which Sinclair Lewis was born on 7 February 1885 was a place fully as ugly and threatening as the early photographs make it out to be. It was a raw prairie town, with a combined population in the village and township of 2,807, and had only been incorporated since 1876. It of course had its Bryant Public Library, its hotel, its opera house, and a public school, but the town already had something of a bleached-out look. The streets were muddy in the spring, dusty in the summer, and gauntly rutted during much of the winter. The sidewalks were wooden, tobacco juice was splattered everywhere, and Main Street had only a few blocks of business buildings, all with false fronts. It was indeed just as Lewis describes it in *Main Street* when Carol and her husband Will arrive at the town after their honeymoon: "Now the train was passing the elevator, the grim storage-tanks for oil, a creamery, a lumber-yard, a stock-yard muddy and trampled and stinking. Now they were stopping at a squat red frame station, the platform crowded with unshaven farmers and with loafers—unadventurous people with dead eyes. She was here. She could not go on. It was the end—the end of the world."[4] It is, of course, 1912 when Carol is introduced to Gopher Prairie, but the negative descriptions of the town derive from Lewis's childhood recollections, a point Schorer underscores in writing that "Lewis's experience in Sauk Centre is poured into his novel: his [step]-mother's club, the Gradatim, become now the Thanatopsis, and its efforts at uplift; the famous rest room and the anti-fly campaign; his father's country practice and the little professional rivalries; the Bryant library; the amateur theatricals and the traveling performers, the summer cottages and the church affairs—it is a whole scrapbook of his youth."[5]

But *Main Street* is a strange kind of scrapbook, one that is disturbing as much for what it omits as for what it includes. Schorer briefly touches on this problem when he acknowledges in his discussion of the novel that much of Lewis's experience of small-town life is omitted. "The curious omission has not been observed," Schorer writes; "in Gopher Prairie there is apparently no childhood at all, no boyhood or youth except for a single, revolting boor."[6] How can one explain this? How can it be that the greatest of American documentary novelists fails to document his own most formative experiences and chooses instead to show us the town he knew so intimately and so painfully only indirectly and only then through the eyes of a newlywed exlibrarian from St. Paul? What was there that so bothered him in the Sauk Centre he chose not to write about?

A possible starting point in answering this question is that Sauk Centre was first of all a place of loneliness for Lewis in his youngest years, and very soon a place of death. His mother, Emma Kermott Lewis, had suffered for years with tuberculosis and, like so many other women at the time, was labeled "consumptive." Although there is no evidence that she purposely neglected her youngest son, her weakened condition and the time she spent in New Mexico and California seeking a cure necessitated that he be left under the admittedly cold supervision of his father. And then in May 1891, Mrs. Lewis returned to Sauk Centre; one month later she was dead. Lewis was six years old; the event must have been traumatic given the custom of prolonged review of the body, the cloying morbidity of the Congregational service, and the long, slow procession to the graveyard. Mrs. Lewis's early death was, of course, not regarded as anything unusual. A casual walk through Greenwood Cemetery quickly shows that many other wives in Sauk Centre had life spans no greater than hers, yet it is remarkable that Lewis never mentions much at all in his subsequent writing about his mother and how her death might have affected him.

A point worth noting here, however, is that the only moments of true pathos in Lewis's novels involve the early deaths or near deaths of young women—Bea in *Main Street*, Leora in *Arrowsmith*, and Jinny in *Cass Timberlane*. By all accounts, Lewis was treated well by his step-mother, Isabel Warner, whom his father married a little over a year after his mother's death, but there is something disturbingly pathetic in Lewis's description of Bea's funeral in *Main Street*. Bea, who has been Carol's maid and cook before marrying Miles Bjornstam, the village handyman, tramp, and atheist, had died of typhoid fever a few hours after her son Olaf had succumbed to the same acutely infectious disease, both deaths the consequence of bad water in Swede Hollow where the Bjornstams lived. Carol, who had been up for nights nursing Bea, is too exhausted to attend the funeral, but she catches a glimpse of the procession through her bedroom window: "There was no music, no carriages. There was only Miles Bjornstam, in his black wedding-suit, walking quite alone, head down, behind the shabby hearse that bore the bodies of his wife and baby."[7] This sounds very much like an echo of the feelings a bereaved six-year-old Lewis might have had—alone in his grief, perhaps wishing that he too were dead, his body in the hearse with his mother's just as little Olaf's lay beside the wasted form of Bea. If this seems a bit too much to lay upon one of our least introspective writers, the significance of one of the few genuinely moving moments in all of Lewis's work cannot be overlooked. Could he have written about the funeral of Bea and Olaf and not thought about his mother's funeral and his own reaction to it? It seems unlikely.

But it was not only his mother's death that apparently had an influence on Lewis's probable childhood anxieties and phobias. As Warren I. Susman writes in his preface to Michael Lesy's *Wisconsin Death Trip*, "Many historians have become convinced that there was a major crisis in American life during the 1890s; some have gone so far as to call it a 'psychic crisis' and have attempted to explain its existence or, even more commonly, to use the presumed existence of such a crisis as an explanation for a wide series of developments in American domestic and international political life."[8] Whether this crisis can be explained through reference to the great depression that swept the United States during the decade or through a general feeling of defeat or ennui caused by the so-called disappearance of the last frontier and the end of westward expansion, the newspapers of the time—and particularly the *Sauk Centre Herald*—document an era that was most certainly characterized by an obsession with death and destruction. Lewis would hardly have had to read the papers to be aware of this as a boy. His father was, after all, a physician, and Lewis most likely was treated to daily accounts, perhaps even at the dinner table, of who had been injured or who had died that day and from what. It was a time when life was brutally hard, particularly on women and children, and just a few hours spent reviewing old newspaper files will reveal a sense of the hideousness young Sinclair Lewis had to deal with from the start.

In the year of his birth, for example, readers of the *Herald* could scan such headlines as "The Whole School Dead" concerning the deaths in a blizzard of a teacher and sixteen pupils stranded in a country school-house, or "Seven Cremated" concerning a fire in a boarding house. On 8 March subscribers could read the kind of story that appeared with relentless frequency over the next fifteen years:

> ATTEMPTED SUICIDE—Peter J. Schops, proprietor of the Albany flour mill in this county, attempted suicide by cutting his throat. On Fri. last he was at the depot in Albany, looking over mill machinery which had been received. He was dissatisfied for some reason, and suddenly pulled out a razor and slashed it into his throat. Men who were near him sprang towards him and took the implement from him, as he was about to make the second cut. The wound inflicted is close under the chin, and into the fleshy part of his neck, to which fact may be attributed his failure to inflict a fatal cut. He is a good citizen and highly respected. Medical aid was summoned from this village.

The "medical aid" could well have been Dr. E. J. Lewis, who was "summoned" again and again to deal with the other suicides as well as with murders, drownings, scaldings, railroad accidents, and other mishaps of the sort that can only be termed strange. Perhaps he tried to do what he could for "Little Maggie Botz," the three-year-old daughter of Jacob Botz, who died in May "from the effect of poisoning by wild parsnips. The little one got hold of the poisonous weed on Saturday and suffered terribly with convulsions until death came to her relief" the following Thursday. Or he could have read the same month that "Two ladies at Sauk Rapids were made seriously ill by drinking water from a well which, upon cleaning, was found to contain a half dozen dead rats. They thought the peculiar taste was due to mineral impregnations and drank the more freely in consequence." And one wonders what Dr. Lewis might have made of this item from 19 July: "A Mr. Meyer of St. Cloud last Saturday evening suddenly became ill and complained of pain in the stomach. Shortly after he vomited violently and threw up a lizard eight inches long. The doctors believe he had drank [sic] it in the water when it was quite small, and Meyer must have had it in his stomach for several months. He feels relieved and no fatal results are anticipated." These accounts are followed by dozens of others involving mad dogs, robberies, the "tramp nuisance," babies abandoned on door-steps, bodies of strangers found lying alongside muddy roads, and even obscene letters, as evidenced by this entry from 18 April 1889: "A dastardly wretch has written an insulting letter to a young woman in this town, and but for the publicity he would be arrested and dealt with according to law. But a repetition of the offense will bring its punishment with it."

So common and striking were events of this sort that William Bell Mitchell in his two-volume *History of Stearns County*, published in

1915, includes an entire chapter of newspaper clippings from both the *Herald* and the *St. Cloud Daily Times*, with this heading as preface: "TRAGIC EVENTS: Unhappy Incidents in the Life of Stearns County—Murder and Suicides—Accidents Which Have Resulted in Deaths—Rivers and Lakes Prove Fatal to Many Youths—Railroads and Unruly Horses Claim Their Share of Victims—The Tragedies of Nearly Six Decades."[9] Events of this sort seem to have reached their peak occurrence in the 1890's just at the time, of course, that Sinclair Lewis himself became a reader of newspapers, and some categories of these incidents do have their parallels in *Main Street* and, in one instance, directly involved Sinclair Lewis himself.

The first thing one notices in reading through Mitchell's collection of clippings is the number of suicides. One of the first entries for the decade is among the most notable: "John Kopp, an old man living at Sauk Rapids, committed suicide Oct. 1 by shooting himself. The objections of his family to his marrying again were supposed to have been the cause of his taking himself off. A note on the table read, 'I will give you the satisfaction of carrying me out.' " Other men committed suicide by hanging themselves, taking morphine, or as in the 1891 case of Joseph Thielen, partner in a "pop manufactory" in St. Cloud, by drowning themselves. Mr. Thielen tied a large boulder around his waist and waded into the Mississippi River. But what is most striking is the incidence of female suicide. Some of these suicides involve single women, such as nineteen-year-old Eliza Marty whose body was found by the Tenth Street Bridge in St. Cloud on the morning of 6 September 1893: "A post mortem examination showed that she had committed suicide by taking an overdose of strychnine." Most of the female suicides, however, were wives. On 13 May 1893, "Mrs. Lizzie Kline, wife of H. D. Kline of Paynesville, died . . . from the effects of a gunshot wound." Another woman, Mrs. Gustave Opitz of Fair Haven, died 6 June 1895 "from the effects of a dose of rat poison." One cannot help thinking of Carol's remark near the start of *Main Street* as she and Will are observing their fellow travellers, particularly the women, on the train that is bringing them to Gopher Prairie: "Life seems so hard for them—these lonely farms and this gritty train."[10] And Will's response many pages later to Carol's housewifely question about what he did in his office on a certain day is particularly haunting given the "suicide epidemic" through which Sinclair Lewis and all of Stearns County lived: "Today? Oh, there wasn't much of anything: couple chumps with bellyaches, and a sprained wrist, and a fool woman that thinks she wants to kill herself because her husband doesn't like her and—Just routine work."[11]

In contrast to the number of suicides in the county, the number of murders committed during the 1890s seems comparatively slight. Most of them seem to have involved family disputes or arguments over property, although a few, such as this one from 1893, were particularly vicious: "The body of a young girl, Alice Leonard Hayes, was found in the road in the town of Lynden on the night of May 14, all indications pointing to a murder. The coroner's jury failed to find any clue to the person by whom the crime had been committed. A reward of $500 was offered by the county."

But by far the largest part of "TRAGIC EVENTS" is given to accidents, most of them involving farmers who are injured trying to stop runaway teams, gored to death by bulls, or crushed under wagon wheels, all of this vividly described, as in this item from 1897: "While on his way home from St. Cloud January 11, with a loaded sled, John Fischer, a well-known farmer of the town of St. Cloud, was thrown from his seat and falling before the runners was dragged a distance of half a mile. When the driverless team was discovered, his mangled body, from which life was extinct, was still in the position in which it had fallen." In detailing Will Kennicott's medical practice, Lewis mentions this side of rural life most directly when he writes:

> Familiar to the doctor's wife was the man with an injured leg, driven in from the country on a Sunday afternoon and brought to the house. He sat in a rocker in the back of a lumber-wagon, his face pale from the anguish of the jolting. His leg was thrust out before him, resting on a starch-box and covered with a leather-bound horse blanket. His drab courageous wife drove the wagon, and she helped Kennicott support him as he hobbled up the steps, into the house.[12]

Other farmers were not so lucky in real life, and Lewis must have heard of or read about dozens of such ax injuries as this one from 1892: "While chopping wood near Richmond, March 11, a young man named Henry Behman met his death. A falling limb knocked him to the ground, and as his ax which he dropped was held blade upward, he struck it with his head which was literally split in twain."

Trains were another source of danger, and hardly a week went by in the county during the decade when some unfortunate person did not suffer the fate of Thomas Haefner in 1890: "Haefner, living in the town of St. Wendel, while walking the railroad track near Collegeville, July 7, was struck by a passing train and instantly killed." In 1895, Mrs. Nancy W. Kilgore, of Paynesville, "fell between the cars of the train on which she had been riding, August 31, and was almost instantly killed. The deceased was 68 years of age." And in 1897, "A wash-out on the railroad near St. Joseph caused the wreck of an extra freight train on the evening of July 6, resulting in the death of Charles Washburn, son of F. H. Washburn, Great Northern yardmaster at St. Cloud, who was crushed between the cars." All of this did not escape Lewis's attention, and when

the Thanatopsis Club coldly and self-righteously rejects Carol's suggestion that they "ought to help the poor of the town," Carol thinks of
poor "Mrs. Vopni, who husband had been killed by a train," and who
was left with ten children to raise.[13] Although no more is mentioned of
Mrs. Vopni and her husband's death receives no elaboration in the book,
an inevitable question arises concerning just how many victims of the
speeding freights and passenger trains were actually suicides.

Another distressing category of accidents in Mitchell's *History* involves children. In 1893, for example, this news story appeared in the
St. Cloud Daily Times: "Mabel, the two-year-old daughter of J. D.
Sullivan, of St. Cloud, in falling from a chair April 2, thrust a button-
hook into her neck, the inflammation which resulted causing her death
on the seventh." Later in the same year, "The two-year-old daughter of
A. H. Luther, of St. Cloud, was fatally scalded Dec. 1 by falling into a
large pan of boiling water." Many of the childhood tragedies were the
result of fires. "While a little son of Casper Fiedler, of St. Cloud, was
asleep in a small barn, August 21," begins an 1892 story, "the hay was
set on fire by some older boys who were smoking, they running away
forgetting their little companion, who was burned to a crisp." Some of
the deaths were simply pathetically gruesome, such as this one, which
Lewis was certain to have heard about: "Anton, the three-year-old son
of Jacob Botz, of Sauk Centre, drank the water from a saucer in which
arsenic fly paper had been soaked June 14 [1895] and died in a few
hours afterwards." A different kind of tragedy Lewis also had to have
known of in the same year was one of several involving firearms: "Another 'didn't-know-it-was-loaded' tragedy occurred June 29 at Sauk
Centre when George Carver, a lad of ten years of age, got possession of
a gun and in play snapped at his brother Marvin, aged thirteen, who was
sitting on the floor reading, the charge tearing a fearful hole through
his body, causing instant death."

Death by water also is a factor in these accounts of life during the
1890s, and children most often were the victims, although hunters and
fishermen figure prominently, such as sixteen-year-old Henry Weber who,
while hunting near Richmond, 29 March 1898, "went on the treacherous
ice on Sauk River, which gave way and he was drowned in seven feet
of water." A particularly significant story as far as Lewis himself is
concerned appeared in 1898:

> Struggling in an endeavor to save his younger brother's life, Fred
> Neimeier went to a watery grave in McGowan's Lake, near Albany,
> Oct. 23. The two brothers were in a boat which capsized, and five
> times Fred, who was an excellent swimmer, succeeded in placing his
> brother on the flat bottom of the upturned boat, but each time the
> boy, who was 13 years of age, slipped off. The elder brother was

urged by men on the shore, who could render no assistance, to save himself, but he replied that he would save both or neither, and both went to the bottom.

In reading this story, Lewis would have been forced to painfully recall a similar (although ultimately happier) account that appeared on 1 August 1895 in the short-lived *Sauk Centre Avalanche*:

> What might have been a fatal accident to Master Harry Lewis last Friday was narrowly averted by the prompt action of his brother Claude. It was while they were swimming with several other boys. . . . The bottom shelves off very suddenly at this place and Harry had been warned not to venture beyond his depth, as he could not swim, but he accidently slipped off into deep water and went down. His disappearance was not at once observed by the boys, but Mr. Al Pendergast, who was watching the bathers, noticed that he did not come to the surface after going down, and, convinced that something was wrong, he spoke to the other boys. Claude was on a springboard and with one quick plunge succeeded in finding the lad and bringing him to the surface, still conscious but dazed and gasping for breath. Harry was a pretty thoroughly scared lad, but as he was otherwise none the worse for the accident it is perhaps not to be much regretted as it taught him a lesson he will not soon forget.

The last sentence unintentionally underscores the general lesson in Stearns County life that Lewis could not have helped learning. He was a near victim of drowning, but he was an actual victim of the distressingly threatening emotional climate in which he lived. First the death of his mother, then a daily litany of suicides, murders, terrible accidents, drownings, and finally his own helpless confrontation with disaster—all of this contributed to a lifelong revulsion that years of travel, two marriages, and dozens of attempts to settle down somewhere else could not overcome.

As early as the age of thirteen, Lewis's reaction to his experiences apparently became one of horror, and he sought escape as soon as he could. In the *Herald* for 28 April 1898, we can find the first evidence of this reaction: "Harry Lewis, the thirteen year old son of the doctor, felt that the United States needs his services in the present Spanish unpleasantness. On Tuesday evening he left a note stating that he had gone to enlist as a drummer boy. He walked down to Melrose and was awaiting an eastward train when his father walked in and dampened his patriotic zeal. . . . The lad had about fifty cents with which to reach the seat of the war." Years later Lewis presented his recollections of the episode in an article entitled "This Golden Half-Century, 1885–1935,"[14] and as is typical of his reminiscences of his boyhood, he is inaccurate in his details and attempts to be too jocular about what surely must have been more than a matter of mere "patriotic zeal" on the part of an ignorant and idealistic youth. The facts are that Harry Lewis ran away from Sauk Centre, and the train he intended to board was eastbound. It was not to be the last time he would want to board that train, and once he went east to Oberlin College and then to Yale, he was, in a sense, gone for good. But in another sense, he never could be.

One of the ideas about Sauk Centre and Stearns County that Lewis might have found disturbingly amusing if he did indeed know about it (and there is the possibility that he did) is something that every new resident to the county sooner or later has to encounter—the so-called "Stearns County Syndrome." This phenomenon is never precisely defined and no one is quite certain about the origin of the term. One rumor is that a professor at St. John's University in Collegeville, twenty-five miles east of Sauk Centre, came up with it as something of a joke on his students. Whatever the source, the concept, by now a part of local folklore, involves the notion that because of the way the county was settled, because of the heavy and persistent ethnic influence, the large, often in-bred families, and the cultural isolation that still is a problem in some parts of the county (it is the largest county in the southern half of Minnesota), a peculiar oppressiveness has developed, resulting in hostility toward strangers, high rates of alcoholism, and a disturbing number of suicides, murders, and sex crimes (incest being one of the leaders here).

If the Stearns County Syndrome is a valid theory, it can, of course, be valid only in the most impressionistic sense. But the actual basis for the Syndrome, I suspect, goes back beyond the first use of the term, back to conditions in the county during the time Sinclair Lewis was growing up. A syndrome is, after all, a number of symptoms occurring together and characterizing a specific disease or condition. As we have seen, Lewis as a boy lived in what by any standard has to be defined as a brutal, cruelly repressed culture in which he was exposed almost every day to the symptoms of suicide, tragedy, and madness. He apparently could never bring himself to write about these things directly, and even though he allows brief glimpses into the dark side of his young life in Sauk Centre and Stearns County in *Main Street*, he ultimately ends by repressing his experience. And Anthony Channell Hilfer in his book *The Revolt from the Village* is certainly correct in writing that "Although his life was, in a sense, a continual flight from Sauk Centre, he was never able to transcend the limiting dichotomies bequeathed him by his background."[15] What Lewis went through as he grew up did indeed provide him with dichotomies, paradoxes, and sadder yet, psychic dead ends. If there indeed is a Stearns County Syndrome, perhaps Sinclair Lewis is the best place to go to understand it.

But did Lewis ever fully understand the symptoms that lie behind such a concept himself? There is not a great deal of evidence in *Main*

Street (undoubtedly his best, most lasting book) that he did. His primary attack in the novel is, after all, on the complacency of the typical small town. But this is a complacency made all the more horrendous by what Lewis actually experienced in his own small town as he grew up there. Behind this book, as the newspaper accounts from 1885–1902 reveal, is a generally unacknowledged background of horror that explains much about Lewis's personality and why he wrote the way he did. "That Main Street is the climax of civilization" had to have a bitterly personal irony in it for a man who had survived a childhood in a place beset with stories of incest, wife-beating, wells full of dead rats, accidental poisonings, obscene letters, babies abandoned on doorsteps or boiling to death in wash-water, people vomiting up lizards, and desperate men and women making suicide in various bizarre forms the most imaginative act in town.

The extent to which this dark background remained with Lewis can be seen, however, in something of a more self-conscious way in his last novel, *World So Wide*, published after his death in 1951. Hayden Chart, Lewis's central character, believes that to gain the kind of self-knowledge he has wandered the world to find, he must be willing "to burn his own house, destroy his own city, so that he might in fiery freedom see all of this world so wide."[16] But Hayden Chart, like Lewis, cannot quite bring it off; the childhood house is still there, and so is Sauk Centre itself. It is sad, pathetic, and touching that Lewis chooses as his last hero an architect who would "build that prairie village which was to have been all housed in one skyscraper: the first solution in history of rural isolation and loneliness."[17] For Sinclair Lewis, from Sauk Centre, Stearns County, there was never to be such a solution. But at least, at the end, he seems to have understood the problem.

Notes

1. Mark Schorer, *Sinclair Lewis: An American Life* (New York: McGraw-Hill, 1961), 3.

2. Ibid., 4.

3. Reprinted in *The Man from Main Street*, eds. Harry E. Maule and Melville H. Cane (New York: Random House, 1953), 272.

4. Sinclair Lewis, *Main Street* (New York: New American Library, 1961), 31.

5. Schorer, *An American Life*, 273.

6. Ibid.

7. Lewis, *Main Street*, 311.

8. Warren I. Susman, Introduction to Michael Lesy, *Wisconsin Death Trip* (New York: Random House, 1973), n.p.

9. William Bell Mitchell, *History of Stearns County* (Chicago: H. C. Cooper, 1915), 554 ff. Unless otherwise noted, subsequent newspaper quotations are from this chapter.

10. Lewis, *Main Street*, 26.

11. Ibid., 94.

12. Ibid., 175.

13. Ibid., 141.

14. Reprinted in *The Man from Main Street*, 260–61.

15. Anthony Channell Hilfer, *The Revolt from the Village* (Chapel Hill: University of North Carolina Press, 1969), 175.

16. Sinclair Lewis, *World So Wide* (New York: Pyramid, 1961), 26.

17. Ibid., 12.

INDEX